THE SYSTEMATIC THEOLOGY OF PAUL TILLICH

A Review and Analysis

ALEXANDER J. McKELWAY

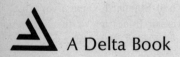 A Delta Book

A Delta Book
Published by Dell Publishing Co., Inc.
750 Third Avenue, New York, N.Y. 10017
Copyright © M. E. Bratcher 1964
Delta ® TM 755118, Dell Publishing Co., Inc.
Reprinted by arrangement with John Knox Press, Richmond, Va.
All rights reserved
Library of Congress Catalog Card Number: 64-13969
First Delta printing—March, 1966
Manufactured in the United States of America

COVER DESIGN BY JOHN MURELLO

Scripture quotations are from the Revised Standard Version copyright
1952 and 1946 by the Division of Christian Education of the National
Council of the Churches of Christ in the United States of America.

Grateful acknowledgment is made to The University of Chicago Press
for permission to quote from Paul Tillich's SYSTEMATIC THEOL-
OGY: Volume I copyright 1951 by The University of Chicago; Volume
II copyright 1957 by The University of Chicago; Volume III copyright
by The University of Chicago.

CONTENTS

5

Acknowledgments

This study of the complete *Systematic Theology* would not have been possible without the generosity and trust of Paul Tillich who allowed the author a copy of his working manuscript of the third volume in the summer of 1961. Professor Tillich's helpfulness in this way, as well as his willingness to send other materials which were needed from time to time, is appreciated more than can be expressed. The author feels a special indebtedness to Karl Barth, who, by his encouragement and helpful suggestions, is largely responsible for whatever merit this work may have. Thanks are also due to the Reverend Horace T. Allen, who was of great assistance in preparing the proofs, and to the Reverend Joseph Burgess, who worked through the manuscript with the author, making many helpful suggestions as to organization and style. Gratitude must also be expressed to my wife, who prepared the manuscript beautifully and helped in the proofreading and correcting.

An Introductory Report by Karl Barth

This book, begun by the author in Vienna and continued in Basel, is the result of several years' intensive study of the theology of Paul Tillich. Mr. McKelway took part in a seminar I once held on the first volume of Tillich's *Systematic Theology*. It was my greatest concern from the very beginning to restrain the students from any immature or superficial critique of Tillich, and to require of them a careful examination of his underlying intention—possibly even with an earnest attempt at an *interpretatio in optimam partem*. I strongly urged Mr. McKelway also to work in this direction and, in my opinion, he has done so in a most exemplary way.

Throughout this book it is evident that while the author reacts to the thought of Tillich with reservations and objections, he never simply rejects him. What reservations he has are discernible only in the form of questions found occasionally at the end of the individual chapters and summarized at the end of the whole presentation. The author's purpose is to make Tillich understandable by tracing the various lines of his thought, presenting them in their internal and external relations in Tillich's own words and according to his own meaning. Moreover, the author neglects no opportunity to give eloquent expression to his agreement with Tillich's presentation. Indeed, often enough he expresses his appreciation for Tillich's execution as such, for the breadth of his knowledge and interests, for the unfailing consistency of his thought, and for his great artistry which unfolds on every page. Tillich is not affirmed in this book, to be sure, but neither is he placed in some shadow; rather, he is brought to light as one who is in his own way a great theologian. I can conceive that Tillich himself will receive this analysis of his work with interest, and acknowledge it, if not exactly with delight, nevertheless as one undertaken and carried through in openness and fairness.

"Systematic Theology" is the title of Tillich's comprehensive
work, of which at this writing only the first two volumes have
been published. However, the author, having received from
Tillich permission to photocopy the manuscript of the third
volume as far as it was finished, and a summary of its conclusion,
has been able to make the literary basis of this book practically
complete. Moreover, for elucidation throughout his report, the
author has drawn from the entire early and later writings of
Tillich, and from the literature on Tillich, which, strikingly
enough, is not yet very extensive. Such a complete presentation
has been lacking until now. Thus this book fills a gap and may
for a good while present a useful, and perhaps in its way indis-
pensable, means of orientation for all future debate with Tillich,
in that in this abbreviated form it places within easy access of the
reader the whole breadth of his thought.

Tillich does not use the concept of "systematic theology"
merely for the sake of convention; indeed, he would consider such
a use incongruous. Furthermore, "systematic" means for Tillich
only secondarily the order and coherence of the material thought-
complex treated here in Chapters II-VII, in which, with effort, one
can recognize the traditional theme-row: prolegomena, the doctrine of creation, the doctrine of reconciliation, the doctrine of the
Holy Spirit, and eschatology. Rather, the word "systematic" for
Tillich designates a science given to a conceptual (semantic),
logical, and methodological rationality which deals with man's
ultimate concern (his being). This science is "systematic philosophy" in that being-itself as such is predominant, and it is
"systematic theology" in that the meaning of being-itself for us
is inclined to be predominant. Or, from another point of view,
it is "systematic theology" in that it introduces with philosophy
only the immanent *questions* of human existence, but introduces
the *answers* through the Christian message—even if it does this
philosophically. Tillich's methodology, already revealed in the
title and concept of the system, proceeds in such a way that both
successively and simultaneously the philosophical concepts of
reason, being, existence, life, and history are set in correlation

with the theological concepts of revelation, God, Christ, Spirit, and the Kingdom of God.

The problematic nature of this undertaking is obvious. Since Tillich's theological answers are not only taken from the Bible, but with equal emphasis from church history, the history of culture generally, and the history of religion—and above all, since their meaning and placement is dependent upon their relation to philosophical questions—could not these answers be taken as philosophy just as well as (or better than?) they could be taken as theology? Will these theological answers allow themselves to be pressed into this scheme without suffering harm to what in any case is their biblical content? Is man with his philosophical questions, for Tillich, not more than simply the beginning point of the development of this whole method of correlation? Is he not, in that he himself knows which questions to ask, anticipating their correctness, and therefore already in possession of the answers and their consequences? Should not the theological answers be considered as more fundamental than the philosophical questions and as essentially superior to them? If they were so considered, then the question and answer would proceed, not from a philosophically understood subject to a "divine" object, but rather from a theologically understood object (as the true Subject) to the human subject, and thus from Spirit to life, and from the Kingdom of God to history. Such a procedure would not actually destroy the concept of correlation, but would probably apply to it the biblical sense of "covenant." This application, however, is unknown in Tillich.

These questions indicate the direction of Mr. McKelway's reflections on Tillich's project. Occasionally he directly states the form of the corrections implied in his questions. For instance, he calls attention to partly conscious and remotely perceptible contradictions and dislocations in Tillich's thought which seem subtly to manifest the possibility of a corrective methodological change in the understanding of each correlation (although it must be admitted that the priority and superiority of the objective over against the subjective is basically nowhere obscured). Mr. McKelway wishes especially to grant to Tillich the centrality

of his Christology (Chapter V), for although its propositions
give rise to the gravest suspicions, it has yet become unmistakably
the middle point of his thought. I am glad that in this sense he
has read Tillich so hopefully (or rather not without hope) and
that this has allowed him to judge many important details of
Tillich's statements as worthy of consideration—indeed, good in
themselves. And I am glad that in viewing the whole of Tillich's
undertaking he has ultimately and finally remembered Philippians 1:18! It is to be hoped that some experts of Tillich and
also some readers of this book may learn to think as cautiously
in this matter as has the writer. And I would like to know what
Tillich himself will say after reading this book with its *in optimam* (in any case *meliorem*) *partem* assessment of his work.
For even if the author had failed in this kind of assessment, I
would still have preferred and considered it as more correct that
he let his suggestions and evaluations serve simply as pointers,
than had he censured Tillich on the inarguable dubiousness of
his enterprise and with the legendary pitilessness of a genuine
Basler Doctorandus separated the sheep from the goats!

A detailed historical placement of Tillich in European and
American theology would have overstepped the framework and
style of this book. Yet it is hoped that in the future we may have:
(a) an evaluation of the amazing fact that just in the twenty
years following Germany's first political collapse there could
have appeared not only the much-praised Luther and Kierkegaard renaissance, but also, in the context of a renewed interest
in the best traditions of the early nineteenth century, such a
speculative structure as that which Tillich announced from the
very beginning; or (b) an explanation of the enthusiastic response which this (one wants to think completely German)
thinker has found in the quite different intellectual climate of the
United States, and of the astonishing adjustability which, from
his own side, Tillich has demonstrated; or (c) a consideration of
the fact that over and above highly successful and quite different
movements, such as "dialectical theology," "existentialism,"
and "confessionalism," which occurred in the meantime, Tillich
has been afforded such an interest in the Germany of the second

postwar period as to constitute for him something like a "second spring" (or should one call it an "Indian summer"?).

However, these questions of historical connections are so complex that they necessitate special research and exposition. Perhaps the day will come when another, stimulated by that which this book offers, will take up these questions and the special work here indicated.

Basel
January, 1963

THE SYSTEMATIC
THEOLOGY OF
PAUL TILLICH

I

A SHORT INTRODUCTION
TO THE THEOLOGY OF PAUL TILLICH

Before beginning our review and analysis of Paul Tillich's *Systematic Theology*, it may be helpful to give some orientation concerning both the man and his thought. To do this we must mention some of the more important aspects of Tillich's career and attempt a brief survey of his place in modern theology by way of a typological comparison with other modern theologians.[1]

Paul Tillich was born in 1886 in Starzeddel, Germany, the son of a pastor and later superintendent of the Lutheran church. He studied in several universities, and received in 1911 the degree of Doctor of Philosophy from the University of Breslau, having written his dissertation on Schelling's positive philosophy. He served as an army chaplain during the First World War. After the war he began his teaching career at the University of Berlin, and later was Professor of Theology at Marburg, Dresden, and Leipzig. Finally in 1929 he became Professor of Philosophy at the University of Frankfurt. During this period Tillich wrote and spoke on a wide variety of philosophical, theological, and political subjects, in which the basic concepts found later in his *Systematic Theology* may be seen in their formative stages. At least half of his astonishing productivity in this decade was devoted to the Religious-Socialist movement. This activity together with his open antagonism toward National Socialism[2] brought about Tillich's dismissal from his university chair and forced him to leave Germany.

---

[1] More detailed biographical and autobiographical sketches may be found in: *The Theology of Paul Tillich*, eds. Charles W. Kegley and Robert W. Bretall (New York: The Macmillan Company, 1952); Paul Tillich, *The Protestant Era* (Chicago: The University of Chicago Press, 1948); and George H. Tavard, *Paul Tillich and the Christian Message* (New York: Charles Scribner's Sons, 1962).
[2] Cf. Tillich's "Zehn Thesen" in *Die Kirche und das Dritte Reich* (Gotha: Klotz, 1932), pp. 126-128.

Soon after his departure from Germany in 1933 Tillich accepted the invitation of Union Theological Seminary in New York to become Professor of Philosophical Theology and remained in that position until 1955. Thus at the age of forty-seven Tillich learned and mastered English to such an extent that he could write and speak it creatively in the highly abstract idioms of philosophy and theology! During these years of adjustment and transition in which he continued to address himself to cultural and political questions, Tillich's *Systematic Theology* began to take shape, the first volume appearing in 1951. Through both his prolific writings and many public addresses, Tillich, now a citizen, came to be acknowledged as the foremost American theologian. Since the end of World War II he has returned often to Germany to lecture, and has received there the highest honors, among them being the *Grosse Verdienstkreuz* and recently the German Publishers Peace Prize. In America Tillich has received more than ten honorary degrees. After his retirement from Union Theological Seminary in 1955, he was given the coveted position of University Professor at Harvard, and in 1962 a special chair was created for him at the University of Chicago.

Tillich has written literally hundreds of articles and well over a score of books. The most important of these are of course the three volumes of his *Systematic Theology*. His *Protestant Era* and *The Courage to Be* stand out among the most popular and widely read of his works, and with these must be mentioned two small volumes of his sermons, *The Shaking of the Foundations* and *The New Being*, which have perhaps done most to popularize his thought and win for him an enthusiastic following.

There is no doubt that the depth and breadth of Tillich's thought, together with the clarity and reasonableness of his presentation, have been decisive in the positive reception which, by and large, his theology has enjoyed. And yet there seem to be two additional factors which have contributed to his great popularity in America. The first may be what has been called the "activism" of the American churches. The fact that Tillich has addressed himself to almost every area of life, and that he has interpreted the role of the church in various aspects of secular culture, has given him a hearing in the American churches which has perhaps been denied him on the Continent. The second factor is more problematic but nevertheless suggestive. The great tradition of liberalism which swept European theology in the nineteenth century affected the American church only in isolated cases. Whatever its significance and whatever its cause, it is a fact that in America instead of a Schleiermacher there was a Finney, instead of a Ritschl there was a Dabney, and instead of a Herrmann there was a Machen. The religious situation into which Tillich came in 1933 was one in which the bankruptcy of fundamentalism was becoming apparent, and yet one in which liberal theology had received no wide support. Nor had the American churches experienced those calamities which had convinced many European theologians of the inadequacy of the optimism and humanism inherent in the liberal tradition. It would be a gross oversimplification to label Tillich as a "liberal" theologian without recognizing important differences. And yet his system is certainly much closer to that tradition than other contemporary alternatives. In any case it cannot be denied that his apologetic theology has been interpreted and received in a way not unlike Schleiermacher's famous *Religion, Speeches to its Cultured Despisers*. Whether it has been his intention or not, it is obvious that Tillich has answered a demand for liberal theology in the reaction against fundamentalism. Of course the lines are not nearly so clear as we have drawn them—other movements and other forces have been at work. But no doubt the situation in which Tillich built his astounding systematic structure, built with all the skill and creativity of his own genius, could hardly have been more propitious. In 1923 Karl Ludwig Schmidt wrote that "the discussion and commutation of systematic theology in our time will be in great measure determined on the one side by Barth and Gogarten, and on the other side by Tillich."[3] These words have proven prophetic, for certainly today Paul Tillich represents one of the two or three most distinct and important directions of contemporary theology.

[3] See "Kritisches und positives Paradox," *Theologische Blätter*, Vol. III (Dec., 1923), p. 299.

To say that Tillich represents a liberal approach to theology is not to say that he can be unambiguously identified with that tradition. This becomes apparent if we examine his relation to nineteenth-century liberalism. Especially in Tillich's relation to the theology of Friedrich Schleiermacher we can find the kind of partial acceptance and partial rejection which distinguishes his attitude toward liberal theology generally. Tillich's criterion of theological statements, i.e., "ultimate concern," finds a close parallel in Schleiermacher's use of "feeling of absolute dependence." And, as Tillich's "concern" and Schleiermacher's "feeling" both include man's self-interpretation, we can say that for both men anthropology is the proper starting place for theology. But here an important distinction must be noted: Schleiermacher in his *Christian Faith* had finally to say that theological statements can never allude to anything other than man's own feelings. Thus a confusion of man's finitude with infinity was inevitable. But Tillich's view of the unity of all being enables him to break through this noetic circle. His concept of the symbolic power of language, which follows from that unity, allows him to say that finite theological statements may nonetheless have a real relation to their infinite object.

Tillich himself acknowledges the similarity of his view of Christ as the New Being to Schleiermacher's view of Jesus as the *"Urbild"* (original image) of man's essentiality. Both men reject the traditional description of Jesus Christ as the hypostatic union of two natures, divine and human. Both prefer to speak of a general divine-human relationship which simply becomes most apparent in Christ. Schleiermacher speaks of the "God-consciousness" of Jesus, and Tillich speaks of Jesus' "transparency" to the divine. But Schleiermacher's concept of Jesus "God-consciousness" does not go beyond the limitations of finite existence; it remains basically anthropological in character. On the other hand, Tillich's view of Christ as the New Being, the "essential unity between God and man," has an ontological character, and thus allows a real relation between the finitude of Jesus and the infinitude of God. Because the God-consciousness of Jesus in Schleiermacher's view is trapped within Jesus' finite existence, the essential image of man in Christ (*Urbild*) is excluded from that existence. Thus for Schleiermacher the humanity of Jesus must be an idealized, transcendent nature which neither participates in nor transforms man's existential situation. But for Tillich, the humanity of the New Being seen in Jesus as the Christ is not merely idealized essentiality, but realizes within existence the eternal unity of God and man; thus the New Being transforms man's existence and makes it really new.

Tillich has never denied his debt to the tradition of German idealism of which Schleiermacher is no doubt the greatest theological exponent. But, insofar as Schleiermacher proceeds from the premise of a necessary relation between thought and reality to the belief that the divinity we experience in the mind through feeling is really God, he parts company from Tillich. For Tillich takes the radical nature of sin quite seriously and maintains that the estrangement of man's existential being from God makes such an identification impossible. Because Schleiermacher does not see that the unity of man's thought about God with the reality of God is broken by the situation of man's existence, he does not attempt to to explain how fallen man is nonetheless able to know God. Tillich attempts such an explanation by saying that existential, fallen man nevertheless understands his participation in being, which knowledge constitutes a way in which he is able to apprehend the revelation of God as the ground and power of his being.

But in spite of all other differences, Tillich is in agreement with Schleiermacher's idealistic and anthropological approach to theology. This same affinity places Tillich in an amazing parallel with the quite different theology of Alois Emanuel Biedermann (1819-1885). What is interesting about Biedermann is that he constructed, in his *Christian Dogmatic*, a system of theology which, while substantially different at least in form and method, closely resembles Tillich's *Systematic Theology*. Like Tillich, Biedermann begins his theology with a philosophical analysis of man as a religious creature, and then proceeds, like Tillich, to a phenomenological description of traditional doctrine. And finally he criticizes, as does Tillich, the inadequacies of orthodox language and attempts to construct meaningful symbols to express for modern man the truth of the Christian faith. Of course, Tillich's critique of Hegelianism would apply also to Biedermann, and he would disagree with Biedermann's negative evaluation of symbols as unavoidable obscurants of truth. For Tillich, symbols are the only possible way to truth.

But if Tillich is in basic agreement with the idealism and anthropological approach of early liberalism represented by Schleiermacher and Hegelians such as Biedermann, he is for the same reason in basic disagreement with the liberalism of the late nineteenth century as it found expression in the Neo-Kantian theology of Albrecht Ritschl and his followers. It is strange that Tillich's attack on Ritschl should have caused some to identify him with the quite different critique of Barth and Gogarten in the second decade of this century. It is true that Tillich, together with Barth and others, rejected Ritschl's identification of the divine process with natural history, the law of God with human value, and the holiness of God with human love. But Tillich could not join these others in their wholehearted agreement with Ritschl's attack on natural theology or speculative metaphysics. However, the bourgeois moralistic interpretation of Jesus Christ which marks Ritschl's theology, as well as his basically intramundane interpretation of the Christian religion, is an aspect of Ritschl's thought which Tillich, along with most other contemporary theologians, has rejected. And although Tillich would agree with Ritschl's rejection of the "two nature" interpretation of the person of Christ, he would not agree with Ritschl's interpretation of the Christ as the highest human expression of "religious value," nor would he agree with his interpretation of Christ's work on the Cross as "exemplary." Furthermore, Tillich cannot follow Ritschl's view of sin, because sin for Tillich is an ontological state resulting from self-actualization, whereas for Ritschl sin is at base what man does *not* do: it is ignorance— perhaps compounded by laziness.

But it is the nominalism inherent in Ritschl's Neo-Kantian approach which, more than anything else, offends Tillich, and it may be just this that partially redeems Ritschl's theology for others. When Ritschl attacked the subjective-idealistic aspects of Schleiermacher's approach to the Christian religion and replaced them with the Christian experience of the gospel of Jesus Christ as the norm of theological statements, he indicated a way out of the sterility of early nineteenth-century theology which has had a profound effect upon the theological situation of today. But for Tillich, man's experience of the Christian revelation is intelligible only in the context of a higher principle and more universal truth apprehended through the unity of all being with being-itself. Thus, when Tillich speaks critically of nineteenth-century theology, it is usually the Ritschlian type of liberalism that he means. And so the work of Adolf von Harnack falls under the same sort of criticism in Tillich's writing as does Ritschl's work. Harnack's rejection of Greek idealism as a pernicious intellectual abstraction which obscured the meaning of Jesus for the early church is vigorously attacked by Tillich. Others have criticized Harnack for assuming that the *logos* idea in John's Gospel is an expression of Christian syncretism. Tillich admits this syncretism but denies Harnack's evaluation. Tillich argues that the Hellenic concept of *logos* is not incompatible with the Christian doctrine of Christ insofar as it is able to include not only the universal but also the concrete and particular modes of God's revelation. It is Harnack's blindness to the concrete-existential elements in Greek thought that Tillich constantly attacks. Tillich's attitude toward the tradition of biblical criticism which Harnack represents is ambiguous. On the one hand he accepts without question a critical method and scientific approach to the Scriptures, but on the other hand he strongly rejects any attempt to discover the "Jesus of history" behind the biblical narrative. For Tillich the New Being in Jesus as the Christ is transhistorical; its value and meaning does not lie in whatever historical picture New Testament scholarship may produce.

This partial acceptance and partial rejection of liberal criticism places Tillich close to Rudolf Bultmann's method of biblical interpretation, and yet this proximity can be deceptive. The fact that both Tillich and Bultmann have pointed to the symbolic and mythical character of the New Testament has led some to place them together.[4] This, however, is the very place where they are most to be distinguished. For Tillich, neither "symbol" nor "myth" means "untruth." Empirically, of course, a myth is untrue, but it nevertheless *has* the truth if it adequately expresses the revelatory event to which it points. Moreover, for Tillich there is no possible way, existential or otherwise, to speak of the divine other than in and through symbols and myths. "All mythological elements in the Bible . . . should be recognized as mythological, but they should be maintained in their symbolic form and not replaced by scientific substitution. For there is no substitute for the use of symbols and myths: They are the language of faith."[5] The myth must be "broken," that is, recognized as such, but it must not be abandoned. This means that for Tillich there is no possibility of *de*mythologizing the New Testament. Jesus is the Christ because he was received as the Christ, and this reception could only take place in terms of symbol and myth.[6]

For Bultmann, on the other hand, "symbol" and "myth" mean that which is not true—at least not true in any way applicable to modern consciousness. He everywhere speaks of the mythological element in the New Testament as a heteronomous influx of late Jewish apocalyptic and Greek Gnostic ideas, which, if inevitable for the era of the New Testament, can only obscure the saving work of God for the modern mind. It is the task of biblical scholarship, therefore, to strip away that alien covering

---

[4] Cf. R. Allen Killen, *The Ontological Theology of Paul Tillich* (Kampen: J. H. Kok N.V., 1956), p. 153.

[5] Paul Tillich, *Dynamics of Faith* (New York: Harper & Brothers Publishers, 1957), p. 51.

[6] Tillich's partial acceptance and partial rejection of Bultmann's program is easily seen in the following quotations. Concerning the mythological character of New Testament language itself, he writes: "Every literally understood myth is absurd, and therefore I stand completely on the side of the famous demythologizing program of my colleague and friend, Rudolf Bultmann" ("Das neue Sein als Zentralbegriff einer christlichen Theologie," *Eranos Jahrbuch*, Vol. XXIII; Zürich: Rein-Verlag, 1955, p. 263). But concerning the nature of that myth, Tillich writes: "Myth is more than a primitive world-view with which Bultmann wrongly equates it; it is the necessary and adequate expression of revelation. In this I agree with Barth, who for some questionable terminological reason calls it 'Sage' (Saga)" ("The Present Theological Situation in the Light of the Continental European Development," *Theology Today*, Vol. VI, Oct., 1949).

and expose the kernel of truth which is the saving event of God in the Cross of Christ. It is this kernel which constitutes the New Testament kerygma, and not its mythological shell. Far from being the only way of speaking of God, myth is an impossible way, because there is no possibility of an existential encounter between man and God if it takes place in the context of a story man cannot accept. Thus Bultmann and Tillich differ radically as to their evaluations of the New Testament canon. For Tillich it is all more or less acceptable as symbol and myth, but for Bultmann very little of it is, for that very reason. This makes Tillich appear almost conservative in contrast to the radical nature of Bultmann's criticism.

But in a deeper sense, Tillich's departure from traditional interpretation goes much further than Bultmann's. Bultmann at least keeps Jesus as a historical fact and event at the center of the Christian message. If all the myths were struck away, there would still remain a message and a man. But Tillich is not so sure that the man would remain. He can seriously consider the meaning of the Christian message apart from Jesus. It is the New Being, expressed in, but transcendent to, Jesus as the Christ, that is the subject of the saving act of God and which, therefore, is the *sine qua non* of the Christian faith. For Tillich the ultimate point of reference lies in his ontological interpretation of God's saving activity in the power of the New Being, which is transhistorical. For Bultmann God's saving event (*Heilsereignis*) always points to the actual historical figure of Jesus Christ.

But the above should not blind us to the similarities between Tillich and Bultmann. These can perhaps best be seen in the fact that in both their theologies Christology tends to become a subordinate part of soteriology. In Bultmann we find that instead of the message of salvation coming from and appearing in the Christ, Christ is to be found in and through the kerygma. He is to be interpreted in the light of the meaning of the Cross. This order can also be found implied in many statements of Tillich, perhaps most basically in his assertion that Jesus becomes the Christ when he is recognized and received as such. In other words, the concept of the New Being is applied to Jesus and he is called the ''Christ'' because he conforms to a prior principle of salvation represented by that title. This point becomes clear if we take as examples Tillich's and Bultmann's very similar treatments of the Cross and the Resurrection. In *Kerygma und Mythos* Bultmann writes of the Cross, ''Not because it is the Cross of Christ is it the event of salvation, rather, because it is the event of salvation, it is the Cross of Christ.''[7] If he means what he seems to mean, then there can be no doubt that for Bultmann, Christ is who he is because he takes the place he does in the salvation of men. In much the same way, Tillich sees the Cross as a symbol of the subjection to existence of the eternal principle of the New Being, so that we, experiencing the power of the New Being, or God's salvation through this subjection, are able to recognize Jesus as the Christ, the bearer of New Being. Similarly, for both Bultmann and Tillich, the Resurrection is the myth or symbol which points to the fact that the Cross is a sign of victory rather than defeat. The resurrected Christ must be interpreted in the light of the experience of salvation and faith in the church. To put it very simply, we do not know of God's salvation because Christ rose from the dead; rather, because we experience the sacrifice of the Cross as salvation, we may say that Christ rose from the dead. Thus in the thought of both, Christ is described in terms of either an event of salvation as in Bultmann, or a history of salvation as in Tillich's concept of the universal healing of the New Being. Bultmann interprets Christ in terms of a subjective and existential ''event'' of faith, while Tillich interprets him in terms of an objective and ontological ''principle'' of salvation.

The similarities and differences between Tillich and Bultmann are indicative of Tillich's relation to existentialism. Generally, Tillich may be called an existentialist insofar as his system of thought begins with the supposition that being can only be understood in the light of an analysis of man's existence. But Tillich must be distinguished from the mainstream of existential-

---

[7] Rudolf Bultmann in *Kerygma und Mythos*, ed. Hans Bartsch, Vol. I (Hamburg, 1951), p. 50.

ism, because he proceeds from an analysis of existence to essence, deriving a realm of essentiality from the universality of man's being. There is no doubt, however, that Tillich's thought is close to existentialism, especially the type of the early Heidegger. Methodologically they both find in man the proper beginning point for a knowledge of being generally, because in existential man there is a self-consciousness (Tillich) or understanding (Heidegger) of his relation to being. Moreover, both Tillich and Heidegger look to an experience within man's self-consciousness, which Heidegger describes as the experience of nothingness and Tillich as the threat of non-being. For both men it is this experience of negativity which poses for man the positive question of his being. These similarities of approach, however, should not obscure the more important differences which exist between their views of man and God. For Heidegger man is to be judged over against the potentialities of his own being, so that fallen man may be described as one who decides for the inauthentic existence of a mere "thing" instead of living in terms of the possibilities of the power of his own being. Tillich, on the other hand, argues that the fallen and estranged state of man is exactly the result of the realization of his potentialities, and that this is an inevitable outcome of the maturational process without which man could not be man, that is, an independent and free being. For Tillich, man is judged, not against his own potentialities, but against his essential nature from which he is estranged just because he realizes his potentiality. God for Tillich is being-itself which embraces man's essential being. Heidegger would agree that being-itself has the attributes of what he would call god, but he does not believe that this is the God of the Christian faith.

The influence of the German idealist tradition on Paul Tillich's theology is certainly one of the basic reasons for the differences which exist between his thought and that of many of his contemporaries. It is obvious, for instance, that where Tillich's thought is informed by idealism, Karl Barth's is influenced by the Kantian critique of that tradition. Barth no more than Tillich would deny that philosophical considerations contribute to the contradictions which exist between their theologies. Contrary to what seems to be a peculiarly American misunderstanding of Barth, he nowhere implies that the theologian can go about his business without using philosophy. At one place he can even say that "theology in fact, so surely as it avails itself of human speech, is also a philosophy or a conglomerate of all sorts of philosophy."[8]

But while the philosophical presuppositions of Tillich's thought are instructive, they are at the same time of limited value for understanding his relation to other contemporary theologies, especially his relation to Karl Barth. Here it is primarily theological considerations which control the issues between them. Tillich joined Barth in attacking Ritschlian theology in the first decade of this century. Both men objected to Ritschl's identification of human history with divine history, which could even mean an identification of the state with the church. Furthermore, there may be found in some of Tillich's early writings an emphasis on the transcendence of God reminiscent of Barth's *Epistle to the Romans*. Tillich then could say, "There is therefore no way from the self to God"[9]—rather, the way must be from God to the self.

But that such points of identity were, from the first, exceptions rather than the rule is just as clearly seen from the early debate between Barth and Tillich carried on in the journal *Theologische Blätter*, beginning with Tillich's article "Kritisches und positives Paradox" in December of 1923. In those articles the antithetical nature of their theologies was clearly exposed. It is, however, the mature works of Barth and Tillich which offer the most accurate picture of their relationship. Between the *Church Dogmatics* and *Systematic Theology* there exists a formal similarity in that they are among the few contemporary theologies to be written in the classical style, that is, with a prolegomena, followed by the doctrines of revelation, God, Christ, the Spirit, man, redemption, and the Kingdom of God. But in spite of this formal similarity, it

   [8] Karl Barth, *Church Dogmatics*, Vol. I, Part 1 (Edinburgh: T. & T. Clark, 1949), p. 188.
   [9] Paul Tillich, "Die Ueberwindung des Religionsbegriffs in der Religionsphilosophie," *Kantstudien*, Vol. XXVII (1922), p. 446.

would be difficult to imagine two more contradictory approaches.

In Tillich's prolegomena the apologetic task of systematic theology is established, while in Barth such a function is sharply rejected. The method by which Tillich correlates the questions of man's experience with theological answers is exactly reversed by Barth, who insists that theology must begin with God's revelatory answer which is the only basis upon which man can ask his questions. Tillich sees in man's reception of revelation the necessity for some natural ability to apprehend the divine, which ability he describes in terms of "the depth of reason." Barth rejects any such natural capacity, and bases man's ability to speak of God on God's grace and our faith rather than upon the universality of being, or the *analogia entis*. If man's ontological courage to be is that which leads him to ask for God in Tillich's system, in Barth's *Dogmatics* it is the fact that man is addressed by God through his Word. Both Tillich and Barth find difficulties in the traditional christological formulas. But where Tillich abandons the idea of incarnation for a view of Christ as a universal principle of salvation, and places Jesus in an adoptionist frame of reference, Barth holds all the more to incarnational theology, stating that Jesus Christ is "very God" and that he is not only human, but the only real and true man.

This difference in Christology is highly suggestive for the difference between the anthropologies of Tillich and Barth. Formally, Tillich's view of man might seem more positive and hopeful, insofar as he invests man with an apprehensible ontological relation to God that Barth denies, and insofar as he can view human culture as a positive medium of revelation. But Tillich finally analyzes man as one whose existence is estranged from God as an inevitable result of the actualization of his freedom. Thus man's destiny is tragic. Barth, on the other hand, while denying even the suggestion of a knowledge of God to natural man, is nonetheless saved from a pessimistic interpretation of man's existence, because he maintains that the natural ("old") man has in fact been overcome and replaced by the new man in Christ. This, for Barth, is the decisive thing about Christian anthropology. According to Barth existential man cannot be seen as fallen and estranged, as in Tillich's view, but as one called and chosen by God in Christ for salvation.[10]

And yet the sharp differences which exist materially between the theologies of Tillich and Barth must be kept in perspective. We have mentioned a certain formal similarity to their undertakings, and to this must be added the close personal friendship between the two men which has lasted for well over forty years. Barth has described their relationship as one of "menschliche nähe und theologische ferne." But this says more than is apparent, for the humanity of neither man can be divorced from his identity as a theologian. The fact is that they care about the same things, and have dedicated themselves to those common interests in an exhaustive way without parallel in our time.

No discussion of Paul Tillich's place in modern theology can be complete without reference to the thought of Reinhold Niebuhr. It does not seem too much to say that Tillich's early success in propounding a theology of culture in America was due in large measure to the fact that the ground had been prepared by Niebuhr. For Niebuhr, like Tillich, takes as the starting place for theology an analysis of human nature, and sees the function of theology as apologetic, as always turning toward the world and the problems of culture. But the way in which Niebuhr goes about his own correlation between the revelation of God and the questions of man is quite different from Tillich. "Broadly speaking, one may say that the categories of Niebuhr's thinking are biblical, personal, dramatic and historical, while Tillich's categories are those of philosophy and ontological structure."[11]

---

[10] It is interesting to note the contrast between Tillich's interpretation of the Judas-Jesus relationship, and that of Karl Barth, for it is highly symbolic of this difference between their views of man. Tillich's point and interest is the participation of Jesus in Judas' guilt, and with him in the whole tragedy of finite existence. Barth's point and interest is that Judas participates in God's gracious and saving act in Christ! For Judas, in spite of the negative and criminal way he goes about it, nevertheless is instrumental in "delivering" (*paradounai*) Jesus to the Gentiles. And this "handing over" accomplishes, in spite of everything Judas wishes to do and does, exactly the same grace as did Paul's "delivering" of Jesus to the Gentiles. (See *Church Dogmatics*, Vol. II, Part 2; Edinburgh: T. & T. Clark, 1957, pp. 458 ff.) Tillich sees Jesus as guilty because of Judas; Barth sees Judas as an instrument of grace because of Christ.

[11] John Macquarrie, *Twentieth Century Religious Thought* (New York: Harper and Row, 1963), p. 345.

The lack of systematic development in Niebuhr's thought makes consistent comparison difficult. However, he does seem to be in basic agreement with Tillich as to the nature of revelation. Niebuhr speaks of a private or general revelation in which the soul that reaches beyond the self encounters a reality which can only be called God. Except for the fact that Tillich would not be willing to name that reality, this view is not unlike his concept of the "depth of reason" in which the mind becomes sensitive to the divine *logos* structure of the universe. Furthermore, biblical revelation is seen by both Tillich and Niebuhr as offering not exclusive but normative knowledge of God. A radical difference, however, exists between Tillich and Niebuhr in the matter of anthropology. Niebuhr rejects Tillich's view of man's essentiality, and in this respect is the more consistent existentialist in that he holds that man is essentially what he is as a creature in existence. Where Tillich maintains that man becomes estranged from his essential nature by actualizing his freedom, Niebuhr argues that man's essential nature *is* his power of free self-determination. The wrong use of this causes him to contradict his essential nature, but he does not lose it. Thus there is a basic difference between the two in the interpretation of the fall of man into sin. Niebuhr claims that the unity of man and God in a relation of faith could and should be sufficient for man's life; therefore man does not necessarily sin and turn away from God, although he inevitably does so. Tillich would say that such a unity is not compatible with true humanity, for if man is to be really human, he must actualize his freedom and stand upon himself, and this means that he will stand away from God. Niebuhr has sharply criticized this position of Tillich as making sin a necessary part of being.

The nature of the person and work of Christ forms another area in which there is a mixture of agreement and disagreement between Tillich and Niebuhr. We have said above that Tillich rejects the traditional two-nature theory of the incarnation. Niebuhr, on the other hand, seems to accept it as a matter of course, and does not seem willing to be drawn into a debate over the problems involved. One feels that if he were, he might well have to adopt the same critique as Tillich. For Niebuhr too can speak of a "hidden" Christ operating in history, who is not the Christ "after the flesh," and who is responsible for "common" grace over against the "saving" grace of Jesus of Nazareth. This view is certainly not unlike Tillich's concept of the New Being which operates throughout history as a principle of salvation quite apart from its "final" manifestation in Jesus.

Finally we must say a word about Tillich and contemporary Catholic theology. It is clear that the Roman Catholic Church does not present a theological monolith. Quite apart from the conservative-liberal debate in evidence in the Second Vatican Council, one must consider the different approaches of, for instance, Jacques Maritain, who is perhaps the best representative of the Neo-Thomist-Aristotelian type of theology, and Erich Przywara, who brings to bear upon that tradition an Augustinian-Platonic line of thought. And certainly we must distinguish from a type of sterile interpretation of church dogma the theology of men like Karl Rahner, who brings to the traditional doctrines of the church insights from modern Protestant theology, and George Tavard, whose criticism of Tillich's Christology is much more informed by Barth's *The Humanity of God* than the theology of Aquinas. Catholic theology is certainly not without variation and contrast. And yet one may say that the "Neo-Thomist" movement represents the largest and best-defined development within the theological realm of Catholicism. This movement takes its origin from the encyclical of Pope Leo XIII, *Aeterni Patris*, in which the theology of Thomas Aquinas was commended to the church as the norm of Catholic teaching. It is especially this area of Roman Catholic thought which is most closely related to the theology of Paul Tillich.

"There is something Thomistic about this brilliant thinker," wrote the late Gustave Weigel, "not in the sense that he subscribes to the more characteristic Thomistic theses—he rejects many of them violently—but in the sense that he is moved by the same feeling for unity and completeness in his vision of the real."[12] As we shall see throughout our study, one of the con-

---

[12] Gustave Weigel, "Contemporaneous Protestantism and Paul Tillich," *Theological Studies*, Vol. XI (June, 1950), p. 185. The broad similarity here

stant themes of Tillich's theology is his sympathy with medieval "realism" (read "idealism") and his sharp critique of the nominalist tradition beginning with William of Ockham. It is this interest in ontology and a view of reality controlled by the concept of the universality of being in God which allies Tillich with Catholic and Thomistic thought against the nominalist critique.

It is of course Tillich's use of the *analogia entis* which forms his closest link with Catholic theology. For although he denies the possibility of a natural theology, Tillich's doctrine of revelation implies a natural, ontological, and noetic relation between man and the divine which differs from a developed natural theology only in degree. Tillich and the Neo-Thomists alike are concerned with the distinction between existence and essence, form and matter, substance and accidents, etc., and both attempt a synthesis between the functions of philosophy and theology. We can even find in Tillich an "existential" interpretation of classical ontology similar to that of Étienne Gilson in that they both hold that existential being as well as essential being is included within God who is being-itself.

And yet Tillich remains a Protestant theologian. He is constantly critical of Catholic theology's allegiance to what he calls the "heteronomous" imposition of church dogma and ecclesiastical authority upon the mind of man. When man's autonomy is threatened, his being is threatened. Tillich protests in the name of "the Protestant principle" against any finite authority which takes upon itself an infinite claim. He launches this protest against the Protestant tendency to identify its theology with ultimate truth as well as the Catholic identification of its own history with the history of revelation.

---

noted between Tillich and Aquinas should not obscure the differences between them. Weigel can also say that Tillich's ontology sounds "so familiar and yet so strange to Catholic theologians" (Gustave Weigel, "The Theological Significance of Paul Tillich," *Gregorianum*, Rome, 1956, p. 43). J. Heywood Thomas argues that because Tillich omits many ontological distinctions developed by Aquinas, he "is quite wrong when he says that he means by symbolic knowledge what St Thomas meant by analogy" (J. Heywood Thomas, *Paul Tillich: An Appraisal*, Philadelphia: The Westminster Press, 1963, p. 198).

Paul Tillich has described himself as being "on the boundary line" between religion and culture, theology and philosophy, and the various traditions within both theology and philosophy. Surely this is the picture that emerges from this brief sketch of his place in modern theology. Tillich is a philosophical idealist who works within a phenomenalistic framework and at the same time remains true to the existentialist approach to human life. In the theological realm, the same idealism which allies him with the liberalism of Schleiermacher brings him into conflict with that of Ritschl. And in terms of the contemporary reaction to liberalism, Tillich insists upon the transcendence of God and the impossibility of identifying the infinite with the finite, but at the same time defends the attempt of liberalism to establish some natural relation between God and man which enables man to receive revelation. In terms of the debate within New Testament scholarship, Tillich accepts the critical method and interprets much of the biblical narrative as myth. But he denies the possibility of discovering a "historical Jesus," considering it a naïve misinterpretation of the nature of the Christ. And, as we have seen, Tillich looks at both Catholicism and Protestantism from the boundary of the other, reminding Protestants of the value of the Catholic view of the holiness of being, and bringing to bear upon Catholic authoritarian structure the critique of the Protestant principle.

Tillich might be described as a mediating theologian. Certainly the task of synthesis was recommended to him by his early teacher, Martin Kähler. But if Tillich does seek some kind of synthesis by mediation, this is not to say that he does not bring to his task unique and original constructions. His place on the boundary is not to be defined by what lies on either side, but is the product of his own genius. Such is the erudition that he brings to his task and the virtuosity with which he accomplishes it, that his reader cannot but gain new insights into and understanding of the theological questions of our time.

The aim of this book is modest: to set out in as brief and yet clear and complete a way as possible the theology of Paul Tillich. And we are using his *Systematic Theology* as the primary source for our review, because it represents Tillich's basic position and the most mature and inclusive expression of his thought. Tillich's many articles and smaller books have been referred to throughout wherever necessary to clarify difficult passages or to show movement in his theological development. Our procedure will be to follow Tillich's own outline, giving special attention to the inner relations of its parts. Where we have occasionally changed the arrangement of subjects, this has been done only to make more clear Tillich's own meaning. In reviewing Tillich's *Systematic Theology* it has been necessary to confine ourselves to the more doctrinal aspects of the development, at the expense of other highly interesting areas such as comparative religion, religious art, and the psychology of religion. Thus, too, criticisms implied occasionally in the analysis can be no more than suggestive for the direction of possible corrections in the various parts of Tillich's system. They are not, nor are they intended to be, the last word. The questions raised in this report are considered extensions of friendly conversations with Professor Tillich at Harvard in the fall of 1960 and in Hamburg and Basel in the summer of 1961. The frank and cordial atmosphere of those discussions alone would oblige us to continue in the same way. Because our main concern is to understand Tillich, our approach cannot be polemical. We cannot begin with any a priori rejection of his use of philosophy, his interpretation of theology as apologetics, or even his method, which is the correlation of the human situation with the answer of revelation. We have only to ask what Tillich asks of himself, that is, whether the human situation has really been seen and interpreted and whether the answer of revelation has been heard and applied. As will be seen in the development itself, these questions reach a critical point in the doctrine of Christ, in whom, we maintain, both the human situation and the revelatory answer must be seen.

II

THE NATURE
AND METHOD OF THEOLOGY

*My purpose ... has been to present the method and structure
of a theological system written from an apologetic point of
view and carried through in a continuous correlation with
philosophy. The subject of all sections of this system is the
method of correlation ...* [vii][1] *[which] explains the contents of
the Christian faith through existential questions and theological answers in mutual interdependence.* [60]

THE NATURE OF THEOLOGY

We have said that for Paul Tillich, as for Schleiermacher,
anthropology is the proper starting place for theology. Before
speaking of God, he must speak of man. Of course, it could well
be argued that Tillich begins where every Christian theologian
must begin—with the revelation of God in Christ. But, while it
is certainly true that Tillich as a man, and as a preacher, finds
his orientation in God's revelation in Christ, we must say that
in his *Systematic Theology* Tillich does not begin there. This in
no way implies that his is not "Christian" theology, but the
revelation of Christ is not where he begins. It is not the first
stone laid for this astounding edifice he has built, although he
may well intend it to be the key.

Where does Tillich begin? One might more accurately say that
he begins with the proposition that man and the world, as
beings, are indissolubly bound in an ontological structure
(*Gestalt*) and to God as the ground of being.[2] This ontology is

---

[1] Numbers in parentheses in this chapter refer to page numbers in Paul
Tillich's *Systematic Theology*, Vol. I (Chicago: The University of Chicago
Press, 1951).
[2] This is the main thesis of David H. Hopper in his article, "Towards
Understanding the Thought of Paul Tillich," *The Princeton Seminary*

37

certainly the controlling concept of Tillich's system, and one which dictates the form of every theological statement made. But ontology requires abstraction, and as Tillich himself would be the first to point out, an abstraction may not logically precede that from which it is abstracted. It is *man* who abstracts from his own being his participation in universal being. "Man is the question he asks about himself, before any question has been formulated."[62] Thus the theology of Paul Tillich begins with man.[3] For it is man who, asking the question of his own being, discovers in God the ground of being; it is man's situation in existence which causes him to ask after the New Being in Jesus as the Christ. It is with man that Tillich begins, and it is this point of view, this interest, which controls his definition of the nature of theology and its method, and which regulates the form, if not the content, of his interpretation of the Christian message.

The Apologetic Nature of Theology

Our assertion that Tillich begins with man and his situation is corroborated by the fact that it is anthropology which establishes the nature of his theology. It is to the human situation that theology must speak. For Tillich the theological function must "satisfy two basic needs: the statement of the truth of the Christian message and the interpretation of this truth for every new generation."[3] This function he calls "apologetic." It has been the mistake of most theological systems that they have either sacrificed the truth or have failed to interpret it for the human situation. Tillich quite rightly sees this latter error in fundamentalism which elevates some past temporal expression of Christian truth to ultimate and absolute value. Perhaps less accurately Tillich sees this same mistake in what he calls "kerygmatic" theology, that is, theology which seeks simply to proclaim the message

---

Bulletin, Vol. LV, No. 3 (April, 1962), pp. 36-43. Hopper finds that "The major presupposition of Tillich's thought is the idea of the microcosm" (p. 42). This idea, of course, is directly dependent upon a developed ontology.

[3] Tillich means "man in relation." It is the self-world correlation with which Tillich begins, and that is what we mean when we say he begins with man (*The Theology of Paul Tillich, op. cit.*, p. 342).

(kerygma) of the New Testament that "Christ is Lord."
Kerygmatic theology, in the time of Luther and now with Karl
Barth, has "had prophetic, shaking, and transforming power.
Without such kerygmatic reactions theology would lose itself in
the relativities of the 'situation' . . ."[5] In such reactions
kerygmatic theology is right. But it is wrong, Tillich charges,
when it excludes the situation from theological statements. When
theology ceases to be apologetic it becomes irrelevant. But more
especially (and this is a point which we shall find made time and
time again) when kerygmatic theology speaks of placing its
message over against the human situation, when it is "thrown
like a stone," without involvement in the situation, it attempts
the impossible. For kerygmatic theology "cannot simply repeat
biblical passages. Even when it does, it cannot escape the conceptual situation of the different biblical writers."[7] Tillich
means that the theologian cannot escape language, and language
is the basic expression of man's situation. Kerygmatic theology
needs apologetic theology for its completion.

If in the development of our study we come to ask whether
or not Tillich himself has not fallen into a form of apologetics
which sacrifices the Christian message to the demands of the
human situation, it is not because he does not see the danger.
Apologetics, he says, must heed the warnings of kerygmatic
theology and make sure that the substance and criterion of its
formulations are based on the kerygma. But theology must be
apologetic. For the theologian, the situation of man is the
"given," the place where he must begin. This situation carries
with it social, political, cultural, linguistic, and religious problems, ambiguities, and questions with which the theologian must
deal if he is to speak to his time, if his message is to be heard.
Moreover, being a part of the human situation himself, the theologian cannot but speak from its context and in its terms.

Our Ultimate Concern

"Every understanding of spiritual things is circular."[9] It is
circular because all religious thought, whether philosophical or
theological, is rooted in an a priori, a mystical and intuitive

awareness of something ultimate, something which transcends the split between subject and object. Whether it is the "being-itself" of Scholasticism, or the "universe" of Schleiermacher, or the "absolute spirit" of Hegel, all religious thinkers, whether philosophers or theologians, have an awareness of the ultimate. "And if in the course of a 'scientific' procedure this a priori is discovered, its discovery is possible only because it was present from the very beginning."[9] Thus, all religious thought is circular.

Theology, however, differs from philosophy of religion in that the circle of the theologian is narrower than that of the philosopher. The philosopher as philosopher must necessarily remain detached from his subject and seek to abstract general and valid concepts of religion. The theologian, on the other hand, may not remain detached; he adds to a general awareness of the ultimate the special, unique, and concrete message of the church, and the acceptance of this message requires decision, commitment, and faith. The mark of theology, then, is that it operates within this smaller circle, and the test of whether a theologian *is* a theologian, whether he does operate within this circle, is whether or not he is committed to, and ultimately concerned with, its center, the Christian message. It could be said, of course, that it is a matter of whether or not he has faith. But no one *has* faith; the theologian, as every other Christian, is always in the situation of faith and doubt. Therefore, Tillich maintains that whether a man is a theologian only "depends on his being ultimately concerned with the Christian message even if he is sometimes inclined to attack and to reject it."[10] Tillich has thus given theology a very broad base, in spite of the fact that it may be narrower than that of philosophy of religion.

The first formal criterion for theology which distinguishes it from every other discipline then is this: "*The object of theology is what concerns us ultimately. Only those propositions are theological which deal with their object in so far as it can become a matter of ultimate concern for us.*"[12] What is this "ultimate concern"? Tillich calls it an "abstract translation" of the great commandment: "The Lord our God, the Lord is one; and you shall love the Lord your God with all your heart, and with all your soul, and with all your mind, and with all your strength.''[4] Ultimate concern is, therefore, distinguished from all preliminary concerns. It is a matter of surrender and passion. What is the *content* of our ultimate concern? What is that which is most important to man? Obviously, that without which he is not—his being. His ultimate concern is that which has the power to threaten or save his being. It is important to understand what Tillich means by ''being'' in this sense. He does not mean our ''existence,'' our life in time and space. Many things not of ultimate importance threaten or save our ''lives.'' The term ''being'' is larger than that; it indicates ''the whole of human reality, the structure, the meaning, and the aim of existence. All this is threatened; it can be lost or saved. . . . 'To be or not to be' in *this* sense is a matter of ultimate, unconditional, total, and infinite concern.''[14] The second formal criterion for theology therefore is: *''Our ultimate concern is that which determines our being or not-being. Only those statements are theological which deal with their object in so far as it can become a matter of being or not-being for us.''*[14] The first criterion sought to protect theology from the confusion of preliminary concerns with ultimate concerns. The second seeks to exclude from the object of theology things which have less than the power of being over us.

The object of theology is and must be a matter of ultimate concern. With this criterion Tillich establishes an apologetic relation between Christianity and other religions. ''Apologetic theology must show that trends which are immanent in all religions and cultures move toward the Christian answer.''[15] Theology may do this by showing that if the general and formal object of theology must be our ultimate concern, Christianity alone fulfills that requirement. For nothing can be ultimate for us which is not absolute and universal; and nothing can concern

4 Mark 12:29-30. In an excellent article contrasting the criteria of theology as stated by Tillich and Karl Barth, Edward Dowey calls our attention to the fact that Tillich has based his criterion for New Testament theology on Old Testament law! (Edward Dowey, ''Tillich, Barth, and the Criteria of Theology,'' *Theology Today*, Vol. XV, No. 1, April, 1958, p. 48).

us which is not existential and concrete. Mystical and meta-physical theologies can be very universal, but they lack concrete-ness. Priestly and prophetic theologies can be very concrete, but they lack universality. Only in the Christian doctrine that the Logos became flesh, that the divine manifestation has become manifest in the event "Jesus as the Christ," is there offered an absolutely universal and absolutely concrete theology which is an adequate object of our ultimate concern. This argument of course does not establish the fact that Jesus as the Christ is the Logos become flesh, but it does, Tillich maintains, prove that if it is true, Christian theology is *the* theology.

The Relation of Theology and Philosophy

The relation of theology to the special sciences (*Wissen-schaften*) has already been implied when we noted above that nothing can concern the theologian except what is of ultimate concern. Thus the theologian ought not to seek to influence scientific enquiry, and he need not fear it. It can be neither directly productive nor destructive to the theological task. The point of contact between theology and the sciences is the philosophical element in both.

The problem of describing the relation between philosophy and theology is that there is no universally accepted definition of philosophy. For Tillich, philosophy is "*that cognitive approach to reality in which reality as such is the object.*"[18] Reality as such, or reality as a whole, does not mean the whole of reality. Tillich means rather the structure which makes reality a whole, the categories and concepts which are presupposed in every cognitive encounter with reality. The search for the character of these structures which make experience possible is the basic prob-lem of philosophy. All philosophies must deal with this problem, and to deal with it they must begin with the common denominator of "being" in everything that is. This is one of the main tenets of Tillich's philosophy as it finds expression in his theological system—philosophy cannot and may not avoid the question of ontology, the study of being. Against the Neo-Kantian tendency to reduce philosophy to epistemology and ethics, Tillich maintains that "Since knowing is an act which participates in being or, more precisely, in an 'ontic relation,' every analysis of the act of knowing must refer to an interpretation of being (cf. Nicolai Hartmann)."[19] The schools of logical positivism and linguistic analysis attempt to do away with traditional philosophical problems and reduce philosophy to a kind of logical calculus. Tillich argues that in their research into semantics, they have overlooked the question of the relation of signs, symbols, and logical operations to reality. Any investigation of these relations involves the structure of being and is therefore ontological.

If philosophy cannot avoid the question of being, neither can theology. The object of theology, that which concerns us ultimately, must have reality, or else it could not concern us. And if it belongs to reality, it must have being. But it cannot be one being alongside of other beings, or else it could not concern us *ultimately*. Therefore that which concerns us ultimately, the object of theology, "must be the ground of our being, that which determines our being or not-being, the ultimate and unconditional power of being."[21] Theology cannot escape the question of being, the problem of ontology, for it is in being that the ground of being is manifest.

If they both must ask the question of being, what is the relation between the ontological question asked by the philosopher and the ontological question asked by the theologian? Their perspectives are different. "Philosophy deals with the structure of being in itself; theology deals with the meaning of being for us."[22] From this basic difference three others follow.

Attitude: The philosopher must seek to remain detached from the object of his study, and open for new insights and new truth, in much the same way as the scientist. But the theologian is not detached; he is passionately involved in his object. His attitude is not the *eros* of the philosopher for objective truth, but rather one of love which accepts saving, and therefore personal, truth. His approach is "existential," involving the totality of his existence.

Sources: The philosopher studies the whole of reality to discover the nature of its structure. He assumes that there is an analogy between his subjective reason and the rational structure of the universe. But the theologian looks to the place where that which is his ultimate concern is manifest. He does not examine being generally, but only the Logos of being become flesh.

Content: The content of the philosophical task is that of general knowledge: the categories of causality, time, and space, the problem of epistemology, the characteristics of life and spirit, the nature of history. The theologian on the other hand is not interested in general knowledge, but in saving knowledge. And if he uses general knowledge, he does so only as it relates to the object of his ultimate concern.

But the relation of philosophy and theology is not simply one of divergence. In the actualization of both disciplines there takes place a convergence. The philosopher becomes a theologian when, in spite of his desire to be universal, his existential situation and his ultimate concern shape his philosophy. Similarly, the theologian becomes a philosopher when in turning toward his ultimate concern, and in obedience to it, he seeks to demonstrate its universality. When he does this he must achieve a measure of detachment, he must become critical of every special expression of his ultimate concern. This, Tillich admits, may "destroy the necessary involvement of faith," but he adds, "This tension is the burden and the greatness of every theological work."(26)

This analysis of the relation between theology and philosophy means that there is no conflict and no synthesis possible between them. For a conflict there must be a common ground. The ground of theology is its ultimate concern and that of philosophy is the ontological analysis of the structure of being. If the discussion deals with this structure of being, then the theologian must take the analysis from the philosopher. If, on the other hand, the discussion concerns the ultimate meaning of being, then the philosopher must either take this meaning from the theologian or he must confess the hidden theologian within himself, the existentially conditioned elements in his own system. For as we saw at the beginning of this chapter, at the root of every significant philosophical effort there lies a hidden a priori which places the philosopher in as circular a movement as the theologian.

There is also no synthesis between theology and philosophy. Tillich objects to such an attempt as found in "Christian philosophy" on the grounds that any requirement placed upon philosophy by religion "mutilates" philosophy and denies it its legitimate function of the pursuit of the *logos* of being generally. In any case Christianity does not need "Christian philosophy."[5] The Christian claim is that the Logos who became concrete in Jesus as the Christ is at the same time the universal *logos*. Thus, "No philosophy which is obedient to the universal *logos* can contradict the concrete *logos*, the Logos 'who became flesh.' "[28]

We have seen that Tillich's formulation of the nature of theology arises from his concern with and conception of the human situation. Because the human situation is one in which man asks about the nature and ground of his being, theology may be delineated by a circle, the center of which is *man's* ultimate concern, the question of his being. Theology must be "answering theology," it consists of the questions implied in the human situation placed in a position of correlation with revelatory answers. At this point the nature and the method of systematic theology meet.

THE METHOD OF CORRELATION

The method of correlation is implied in Tillich's definition of theology. When he states that the nature of theology is apologetic, and its function is to answer the questions implied in the human situation, his method can only be to correlate those questions with that answer. "The method of correlation explains the contents of the Christian faith through existential questions and theological answers in mutual interdependence."[60] By "correlation" Tillich means a relationship in which both sides affect each other, and at the same time remain independent. The questions affect the answer, and in the light of the answer the questions are asked. But the method of correlation begins with the human

---

[5] This statement notwithstanding, Tillich does believe that what he calls the "ontological" type of philosophy of religion (Anselm) is useful, because it points beyond itself to the unity of being and thus "contributes to the reconciliation between religion and secular culture" (Paul Tillich, *Theology of Culture*; New York: Oxford University Press, 1959, p. 11).

question and proceeds in this way: first the human situation is analyzed in order to determine the existential questions which arise from it. Then the Christian message is presented in a way which demonstrates its answer to those questions. The questions are ''existential,'' meaning that they express man's deepest and ultimate concern. The analysis out of which the questions arise is also ''existential.'' By this use of ''existential'' Tillich means that man, trapped in his own selfhood, ''has become aware of the fact that he himself is the door to the deeper levels of reality, that in his own existence he has the only possible approach to existence itself.''[62] Then his analysis is existential. As examples of such analyses leading to the method of correlation, Tillich refers to Augustine, Böhme, Schelling, Heidegger, and, surprisingly enough, to John Calvin, who, he says, ''expresses the essence of the method of correlation.'' [63]6

The analysis of man's own situation yields the questions which theology must answer. This analysis is a philosophical task—even when it is performed by a theologian. Tillich goes so far as to say that if, in this analysis, the theologian ''sees something he did not expect to see in the light of his theological answer, he holds fast to what he has seen and reformulates the theological answer.''[64] Tillich risks such analysis and reformulation because he believes that they cannot change the *substance* of the answer because the substance of both analysis and answer is the same *logos* of being.

Existential analysis and the questions which arise from it are

6 The passage from Calvin which Tillich quotes is the following: ''The knowledge of ourselves is not only an incitement to seek after God, but likewise a considerable assistance towards finding him. On the other hand, it is plain that no man can arrive at the true knowledge of himself, without having first contemplated the divine character, and then descended to the consideration of his own.'' The citation is given incorrectly as: ''John Calvin, *Institutes*, I, 48.'' There is no such section. The quotation cited seems rather to be a very free translation of the *Institutes*, Book I, Chapter I, the last sentence of paragraph one and the first sentence of paragraph two. In any case we must respectfully object that neither Calvin's thought in general, nor this passage in particular, offers ''the essence of the method of correlation.'' That Calvin does indeed express a kind of correlation between our knowledge of ourselves and God is not to be denied. But that his is certainly not a Tillichian correlation is clearly seen from the second sentence of the quoted passage. His whole order is different: first God, and then man. He does not begin where Tillich begins.

one side of the correlation. The other side is the theological answer derived from revelation. We shall see below what the sources, the media, and the norm are which control this derivation. But now it is important to see what the relation is between existential question and theological answer in the method of correlation.

We said above that the relationship of "correlation" means for Tillich one in which both sides affect each other, but remain independent. They are "interdependent." "In respect to content the Christian answers are dependent on the revelatory events in which they appear; in respect to form they are dependent on the structure of the questions which they answer."[64] The method of correlation then depends upon a distinction and separation between form and content in the Christian faith about which we shall have more to say below. In any case, for Tillich the distinction is possible, and, for example, in the doctrine of God would operate in this way: "God" is the answer to the questions implied in man's finitude. But this answer cannot be derived from finitude. What can be derived from man's finitude is his participation in being, and the threat of non-being; man asks about the ground of his own being and a power which can overcome non-being. If these questions are correlated with the notion of "God" derived from revelation, then God must be called the ground of being and the infinite power of being which resists non-being. Thus for Tillich the content of revelation has remained the same, while the form of the revelatory answer has been conditioned by the question it answers. The question which we must later ask is whether or not, if treated in this way, the content of the revelatory answer actually does remain the same. Is the integrity of the Christian message maintained in the method of correlation when its form is dependent upon the questions of man? This is the crucial question concerning Paul Tillich's method of theology.

It is crucial because, as Tillich himself admits, it implies a relation of dependence on God's part toward man in revelation. "... although God in his abysmal nature is in no way dependent on man, God in his self-manifestation to man is dependent on the way man receives his manifestation.''[61] It is not simply that God is dependent upon man in that he must have an object for his revelation. No, it is the way in which man is this object, the way in which he receives revelation, upon which God is dependent. It is certainly not Tillich's intention to violate the freedom of God (in many passages of his theology he defends it passionately), but the question remains whether or not the method of correlation does not undermine this defense. For if one holds, for instance, that it is only God in his self-manifestation with which we have to do, or about whom we can know or speak, does not the above statement by Tillich lead to the conclusion that ''God'' as he is known by man is dependent upon man?

The first conclusion which we came to in this chapter is that Paul Tillich begins with man. Man determines the nature of theology as apologetics. In the same way we must say that Tillich begins with man in respect to theological method. It is man's questions which first must be heard before the revelatory answer may be given. Again, Tillich's intention is perhaps different. He makes the point again and again that the method of correlation is a movement; it is not static. It may not be isolated in such a way as to say, ''here it begins.'' He resists any order of precedence in the question-answer correlation. ''. . . God answers man's questions, and under the impact of God's answers man asks them.''[61] The method of correlation, insists Tillich, does not ''begin'' at any ''place''; it is a circular movement, the center and origin of which is a point where question and answer are united. This point is not in time, it belongs to man's essential being in which he is united with God. But we must again make the point that this essential nature of man is no more available to man than is the ''abysmal nature'' of God; in fact, according to Tillich's own ontology, they are the same ''point.'' Thus it is clear that at least in the very existential business of writing theology where question and answer are not united, the only possible starting place for the method of correlation is with the questions of man, and therefore with man as such, because ''man is the question he asks about himself, before any question has been formulated.''[62]

The Sources of Theology

The sources of theology are the Bible, church history, and the history of religion and culture.

"The Bible . . . is the basic source of systematic theology because it is the original document about the events on which the Christian church is founded." [35] However, the Bible is not the only source, for it could not have been either written or received without preparation in human religion and culture. God speaks to man also in religion and culture, therefore "Word of God" cannot be confined to the scriptural text. But the Bible is the basic document, for it contains original witness to the events upon which Christianity is based. The "inspiration" of these scriptural witnesses consists in their reception of Jesus as the Christ, and with him the New Being. And further, "Since there is no revelation unless there is someone who receives it as revelation, the act of reception is a part of the event itself. The Bible is both original event and original document; it witnesses to that of which it is a part." [35]

The problem of the use of the biblical material is this: it must be treated in a scientific, historical-critical way, and at the same time reflect the theologian's "spiritual" interpretation of, and devotion to, what he studies. Tillich notes as examples of these two sides of biblical study, respectively, the commentaries on Romans by C. H. Dodd and Karl Barth. In much the same way that he combines the philosophical and the theological tasks of the theologian, Tillich suggests that a focusing upon our ultimate concern makes a combination of both ways possible. For what concerns us ultimately does not impose upon the honest scientific study of the Bible and at the same time allows the devotional expression of the theologian to appear.

Church history is a source of systematic theology because the formulation of the biblical canon is an event which took place in church history. Tillich places himself between the two extreme positions of "radical biblicism" and the Roman Church. Against biblicism he insists that one cannot "jump over" two thousand years of church history and become contemporaneous

with the writers of the New Testament. The Reformers themselves used some parts of the Roman Church's tradition to combat
other parts, and even the radical biblicists themselves interpret
the Scriptures according to definite dogmatic developments in the
post-Reformation period. There is no escape from the use of
church history as a source.

On the other hand, Roman Catholic theology errs in subjecting
systematic theology to the decisions of councils and popes. They
assume a priori that those doctrines which have attained legal
(*de fide*) standing in the church are in agreement with the biblical message. Thus the theological task of Catholicism is reduced
to the rather sterile interpretation of its own dogmatic tradition.

Against both radical biblicism and Roman Catholicism, Tillich
places what he calls the "Protestant principle," which protests
"against the identification of our ultimate concern with any creation of the church, including the biblical writings in so far as
their witness to what is really ultimate concern is also a conditioned expression of their own spirituality."[37] Thus the
theologian is free to use and critically examine church history,
without being bound to it.

The third and by far the broadest source of systematic theology
is that presented by the history of religion and culture. Again,
it is unavoidable that the theologian use these materials, for the
language he uses, the culture in which he is educated, the social
and political climate in which his thought is based—all these
influence and give content to every theological formulation he
makes. Such use is unintentional and unavoidable, but the theologian must also use them intentionally. Culture and religion are
his means of expression; they confirm his statements and, above
all, they imply the existential questions "to which his theology
intends to be the answer."[38]

The problem with this broad source of systematic theology is
that just how it is made available to the theologian has yet to be
described. It was one of Tillich's first theological concerns to
suggest a method of dealing with the material presented by
religion and culture in his first published speech entitled "Über
die Idee einer Theologie der Kultur." Theology of culture "is

the attempt to analyze the theology behind all cultural expressions, to discover the ultimate concern in the ground of a philosophy, a political system, an artistic style, a set of ethical or social principles."[39] This third and broadest source of theology then is primarily the source of the *questions* which it is theology's task to answer. It is the source of the first part of theology's method—the method of correlation. As such, this analysis of all cultural expression is the subject matter of the first half of every part of the theological system. And it is important to note that although the history of religion and culture is placed last in this listing of the sources of theology, it is in fact treated first throughout the system. It is the source of the existential questions which the theologian must answer and, therefore, determines at least the form of every theological answer derived from the Bible and church history.

The Place of Experience in Theology

"Experience is the medium through which the sources 'speak' to us, through which we can receive them."[40] As Tillich quite correctly points out, the question of experience has been a central problem wherever the nature and method of theology have been discussed. It is of particular importance in Tillich's theology, because the method of correlation requires that there be a connection between its two sides of existential question and theological answer. That connection is established by human experience.

Tillich places himself in the Augustinian-Franciscan tradition, which held (cf. Alexander of Hales and Bonaventura) that truth is existential, a matter of the participation of the knowing subject in spiritual realities. Thus, experience by participation is the only way to truth and real knowledge. It was, however, the theology of Schleiermacher which gave to the principle of experience its classical expression. And it is with Schleiermacher's interpretation of experience that Tillich primarily identifies himself. Tillich defends Schleiermacher's concept of "the feeling of absolute dependence" by pointing out that "feeling" does not refer to one psychological function among others, but rather means the immediate awareness of the experience of something unconditional, something which transcends intellect and will, subject and object. "The feeling of absolute dependence" is, in Tillich's view, much the same as what he calls "ultimate concern about the ground and meaning of our being." But while Tillich accepts Schleiermacher's emphasis on human feeling, or experience, he is critical of its use in the methodology of his *Glaubenslehre*. Schleiermacher erred, says Tillich, when he attempted to derive all the contents of the Christian faith from the experience, or "religious consciousness," of the Christian. "Experience is not the source from which the contents of systematic theology are taken but the medium through which they are existentially received."[42] It is not Tillich's intention to use experience as a source, but only as a medium; whether or not Tillich succeeds in his intention is a question we shall raise below.

Tillich distinguishes three senses in which "experience" is used in modern philosophical and theological discussion: the ontological, the scientific, and the mystical. The ontological sense of experience is the result of philosophical positivism which holds that reality is identical with experience. Ontologically there is nothing "higher" than experience, there is no split between subject and object, there is nothing which infinitely transcends the human category, nothing which is not available to human experience. This means that experience can be used as a source for theology, and that nothing can be used in theology which transcends the whole of experience—thus a divine being in the traditional sense of the word is excluded from theology. But if one asks the positivist which experiences he uses as the source of theology, he must answer that there are special experiences or qualities of experiences which are of ultimate concern. Tillich argues that there is thus another kind of experience which lies behind his ordinary experiences, so that the positivist must admit to some kind of immediate participation in religious reality which does transcend ordinary experience.

The scientific sense of experience arises from the attempts of some empirical theologians to apply the methods of scientific analysis to theology. (Cf. William James, *Types of Religion Ex-*

perience, and Rudolph Otto, *The Idea of the Holy.*) For them experience not only designates the real, but also the knowable. An analysis of religious experience will yield a correct picture of its object. But Tillich maintains that this attempt was and is doomed to failure because the object of theology, our ultimate concern, is not an object within the whole realm of scientific objects. It cannot be derived from detached analysis, but is known only through acts of participation and surrender. And for this reason religious experience cannot be tested by scientific methods of verification. For in science the tester must keep himself outside of (or at least take account of his partial identity with) the object tested. In theology the testing theologian is never apart from his object, he continually participates in it, and risks himself in that participation.

The most important sense of experience, however, is that of mystical experience, which is experience by participation. This, says Tillich, is the real problem of theology. There is no doubt that experience is a matter of participation. Even the empirical theologians of the ontological and the scientific type "secretly" presupposed the mystical or participation type of experience. The question is: What does this experience by participation reveal? The Reformers held that it could not be a source of theology, that the biblical message is never transcended and nothing new is given by the Spirit. Evangelical enthusiasts, however, derived new revelations from the presence of the Spirit in their experience—and these became for them the ultimate source of theology. Recent "experiential theology" (Brightman, Wieman) has carried this concept to its ultimate extremity, claiming that experience is the ultimate and inexhaustible source of new truths. The theologian of this type "is not bound to a circle the center of which is the event of Jesus as the Christ."[45] This, however, is not Tillich's position.[7] He denies that as a

---

[7] It is unfortunate that the context of the above quotation lends itself to the confusion of Tillich's statement of his own position over against that of "experiential theology." One may editorialize that Tillich's theology "is not bound to a circle the center of which is the event of Jesus as the Christ." But he ought not to use this quotation as Tillich's description of his own position, for it is not. Because of the context, a number of writers have been confused on this point. (Cf. Dowey, *op. cit.,* p. 51.)

medium of theology, experience can become a source which is in any way *post*-Christian. "Christian theology is based on the unique event Jesus the Christ ... the criterion of every religious experience. This event is given to experience and not derived from it."[46] On the other hand, Tillich also denies what he calls the neo-orthodox refusal to acknowledge that experience can in any sense be a source of theology. Experience receives and does not produce. But in this reception, experience does transform what it receives, and in this sense it adds to the Christian message, becoming a source itself. Experience as a source of theology "should not be so small that the result is a repetition instead of a transformation, and it should not be so large that the result is a new production instead of a transformation."[46]

The Norm of Systematic Theology

Systematic theology has for its sources the Bible, church history, and the history of religion and culture. These are mediated to the theologian through his experience. But now we must ask: What is the criterion by which the theologian chooses and judges both the sources and his experiences which mediate them? Such a criterion Tillich calls the "norm of theology." Such a criterion or norm is necessary because all sources and all experiences do not have equal value. Unless there is some principle, some touchstone against which sources and experiences can be judged, the Christian faith would have no definite content and theology no organization.

In the early church the material norm, says Tillich, was the creed, and on the formal side the hierarchical authorities were established to safeguard that norm from distortion. In the Catholic Church, however, the formal norm soon achieved predominance over the material, creedal norm and its basis in the Scriptures. Against this development the Reformers asserted the material norm of justification through faith and re-established the Bible as the formal expression of that norm. Justification and the Bible were the norms of the Reformation and were placed in mutual interdependence. Throughout the history of the church one may distinguish various expressions of these norms or points of view. They grow in a historical process in church history and are the result of the collective experience of the church shaped by the sources of theology.

In this generation Tillich feels that a new expression of the norm of theology is necessary, one which expresses the peculiar situation of our time. This situation he describes "in terms of disruption, conflict, self-destruction, meaninglessness, and despair in all realms of life."[49] Tillich argues that the question arising from this situation is not the question of a merciful God and the forgiveness of sins as in the time of the Reformation. Rather, "it is the question of a reality in which the self-estrangement of our existence is overcome, a reality of reconciliation and reunion, of creativity, meaning, and hope. We shall call such a reality the 'New Being'. . . ."[49] The New Being for Tillich is based on what Paul calls the "new creation," and it answers the question implied in human existence. And if we then ask, "Where is this New Being manifest?", theology gives the revelatory answer, "In Jesus the Christ." Tillich's norm then for theology is "The New Being in Jesus as the Christ." And if this norm is combined with the critical and protective principle of theology, which we found above to be "ultimate concern," then "the material norm of systematic theology today is the New Being in Jesus as the Christ as our ultimate concern. This norm is the criterion for the use of all the sources of systematic theology."[50]

If one says that the Bible itself is the norm of theology, Tillich argues, he says nothing definite, because as a collection of religious writings, canonized by the church and edited through the centuries, the Bible itself can only be understood in relation to some criterion by which it is studied and read. "The Bible as such never has been the norm of systematic theology. The norm has been a principle derived from the Bible in an encounter between Bible and Church."[50] Thus Luther in the church situation of his time derived the principle of "justification through faith" from the Bible and then used it as a criterion for judging the Bible and the biblical books. The Bible can be called the norm of theology only because the norm is derived from the Bible. A norm, or perhaps we may say a hermeneutical principle, is derived first from the Bible and then in turn becomes the criterion for reading and studying the Bible. That this happens in every theology, Tillich insists, is obvious, even if biblicist and fundamentalist theologians will not admit it. The fact that the church canonized the Bible, that this canonization took place rather late, that there is still no universal agreement as to its composition, that Luther himself argued for the exclusion of certain books— all these are evidence that the church actually does approach the Bible with a norm or principle which, although derived from the Bible, is not identical with it.

For Tillich, the relation of the norm to church history is similar to its relation to the Bible. Although the Bible produces the norm, it produces it in an encounter between the church and the biblical message. But beyond this the church cannot be said to be a norm for theology. Against Catholicism and in line with the Protestant tradition, Tillich maintains that the theologian must apply the norm of theology against the history of the church, whether that history is expressed by the Church Fathers, councils, creeds, or popes. The relation of the norm to the theological source of religion and culture is obvious—it stands over against it. But Tillich is careful to point out that religion and culture also played their parts in the establishment of the norm, because the encounter between church and biblical message was and is always partially conditioned by the religious and cultural situation. But although it is derived from the sources of theology and is shaped and colored by the mediation of experience, the norm of theology which is the principle of the New Being in Jesus as the Christ always stands over against the sources and the medium, as criterion and judge.

The Rational Character of Theology

The sources, the medium, and the norm of theology are related to its foundation in history. They form the historical basis for the materials the theologian uses in applying the method of correlation. But now if we ask *how* they are used, we must raise the question of the rational and systematic character of theology. Perhaps the greatest hindrance to the acceptance of the work of

the theologian by other sciences is the fact that in the act of
faith, which certainly must be part of theological activity, there
is an extra-rationality, or at least a different quality of rationality at work than in other human thought. Tillich does not
avoid this problem, but he insists on two points: first, the act of
faith is in no case irrational. We remember that in Tillich's
ontological view the universe is a rational whole, and it would
therefore be impossible for the *logos*, God's rational word, to be
or to create anything outside the bounds of rationality. But although the act of faith is not irrational, it is not rational in the
ordinary sense. Reason, used in the act of faith, is self-transcend-
ing, or ecstatic. "Ecstatic reason is reason grasped by an ultimate
concern. Reason is overpowered, invaded, shaken. . . . Reason
does not produce an object of ultimate concern. . . . The contents
of faith grasp reason."[53]

But second, Tillich insists that the theologian, in addition to
participating in the ecstatic reason of faith, must express the
truth of his faith in a methodical way; he must use formal, technical reason. In neither the case of the ordinary believer nor the
systematic theologian does reason create the contents of theology,
but also in neither case is faith or formal theology irrational.
Ecstatic reason receives the contents of the Christian faith, and
technical reason conceives those contents in systematic, theological formulations. Tillich offers the following directing principles
for the protection of the rational character of theological conception.

First, theology must be *semantically rational*. A favorite theme
which Tillich repeats again and again throughout his system is
that theology (and philosophy as well) must define its terms and
be careful that the word symbols which it uses are adequate and
reasonable for their task. He insists that "all connotations of a
word should consciously be related to each other and centered
around a controlling meaning."[55] Second, theology must be
logically rational. Theology is often irrational when it uses dialectical and paradoxical concepts. But this need not be the case.
"Dialectics follows the movement of thought or the movement of
reality through yes and no, but it describes it in logically correct

terms."[56] Thus, for instance, in the doctrine of the Trinity, theology is not dealing with the "logical nonsense" that three is one and one is three, but is simply stating the inner movement of the divine life of separation and return. It does this in dialectical terms. But "theology is not expected to accept a senseless combination of words, that is, genuine logical contradictions."[56] Similarly, the use of paradox in speaking of the Christian faith should not be interpreted as irrational, or illogical. When Paul describes the tensions of the Christian life in a series of paradoxes,[8] when John says that the Logos became flesh, when Luther says *simul peccator et iustus*, they are not dealing in logical contradictions, but are only expressing "the conviction that God's acting transcends all possible human expectations and . . . preparations."[57] Paradox (*para-doxa*) means simply "against the opinion." And if human opinion goes against divine activity, it is because technical reason has not been grasped ecstatically by the power from above which breaks into and through its own expectations. But this divine activity is never outside the realm of the rational. "For God acts through the Logos which is the transcendent and transcending source of the *logos* structure of thought and being. God does not annihilate the expression of his own Logos."[57]

And third, theology must be *methodologically rational*. It must follow a method, it must derive and state its propositions in a definite way. It must be "systematic." By a "system" Tillich does not mean a "deduced" collection of assertions. The existential nature of Christian truth denies such a possibility. Nor does he mean to imply any kind of closed body of material which is not open to new insights and truth. By "systematic" Tillich means a way of writing theology which follows a certain method, and remains consistent with certain principles.

As we have seen, the method which Tillich uses is the method of correlation. This method determines the outline of the whole of *Systematic Theology*. Paul Tillich's theological system contains five parts, each of which has two sides, which correspond to the existential question and the theological answer respectively.

[8] 2 Corinthians 6:8-10.

Part I, Reason and Revelation, deals with the doctrine of revelation. It seeks to clarify the nature of reason and show in what way it may approach revelation. And it seeks to explain the nature of revelation, the ultimate source of all theological statements. "Reason" expresses the human situation, and "revelation," the theological answer to it.

Part II, Being and God, again according to the method of correlation, begins with man as he *essentially* is, his being. Such a study raises the question of the basis of man's being, to which the theological answer is given: God as the ground of being. *Part III, Existence and the Christ,* distinguishes between what man essentially is and what he is in existence, his estranged nature, his separation from God. A description of this estrangement, the separation from our essential being and the threat of non-being, raises the question of the possibility of New Being. And the theological answer to this question is the appearance of the New Being in Jesus as the Christ. *Part IV, Life and the Spirit,* recognizes that both essential and existential being are abstract concepts and that actual life is experienced as an ambiguous mixture of both. This ambiguity is the result of man's imperfect unity with God and the universe, and the answer to it is expressed theologically in the uniting work of the divine Spirit. And finally in *Part V, History and the Kingdom of God,* that dimension of life which we call history, with all its contradictions and ambiguities, is given the answer, the direction, and the hope of the kingdom of God.

SUMMARY AND ANALYSIS

Tillich begins his *Systematic Theology* with a definition of theology as "apologetic." He defines theology thus because his beginning point is neither with theology as such nor with the object of theology, but rather with its subject—man. This particular perspective which puts man and his situation in the foreground of all theological thinking is the most important fact in this introduction to his system. If one begins with man and the human situation, theology can only be understood as apologetics. It must answer the basic questions of man, questions which express his ultimate concern, his being or non-being.

If we say that theology is "answering theology," and that this expresses both its nature and its function, we imply a certain method. For to "answer," theology must do two things: it must hear the questions of man, and to those questions it must supply the answers of revelation. Theology must deal with human question and divine answer in correlation. To do this, the "method of correlation" demands that theology first analyze the human situation in such a way that it really understands the questions which arise from it, and then interpret the divine revelation in thought forms and word symbols adequate to the situation and the questions. In this way it "correlates" question and answer.

Thus the theologian must on the one hand perform the philosophical function of analyzing existentially the life of man in order to understand his questions, and on the other hand he must fulfill the theological function of interpreting the revelatory answer. This revelatory answer is the content of the Christian faith, and is made available to the theologian from the sources of the Bible, church history, and the history of religion and culture. These sources are mediated to him, and transformed by his personal experience; and source and experience alike are judged against the norm of the Christian faith, the self-manifestation of the divine Logos in Jesus as the Christ.

Tillich's system is tremendously broad in scope. He has said that his whole aim in writing theology is to "make the tradition [the classical expression of Christian doctrine] understandable."[9] And since this task of translation involves under Tillich's method the analysis of human life and its categories, the project which he has chosen for himself seems large indeed. The fact that he has confined his *Systematic Theology* to three fairly small volumes is deceptive. He could have easily, and perhaps with good effect, written three times as much. So large is the area of his concern, and so numerous the various subjects and problems introduced, that even informed readers find it necessary to reread again and again the material he presents. His is a work of remarkable breadth and depth, and commands our respect not only for what it attempts, but what it actually accomplishes.

---

9 From the public lecture, "On the Problem of Authority and Its Limits," delivered in Hamburg, Germany, July 12, 1961.

Specifically, we may ascribe to and applaud Tillich's interest in showing the rational character of theology, and his insistence that it remain relevant to the human situation. That theology should ever retreat to the Pauline expression, "the foolishness of the gospel," when pressed to explain the rational character of its statements, is indeed—to use Tillich's words—a disgrace for the theologian and intolerable for the philosopher. That theology must define its terms and work within the framework of scientific procedure is certainly true and needs to be said. And he is right when he says that there need be no conflict and can be no synthesis between philosophy and theology. In an era when philosophers and theologians for the most part talk completely past each other, Tillich's work is especially useful in suggesting the proper sphere of each and opening the possibility of a real conversation between them.

That Paul Tillich is a philosopher, and that a great part of his *Systematic Theology* is the exposition of a particular philosophical viewpoint, goes without saying. Indeed he has already said that the analysis of the human situation is basically a philosophical task. But Tillich's philosophy as such is not our concern in this study; rather, we are undertaking to study the theological aspect of his *Systematic Theology* and related works. We need not decide one way or the other about Tillich's philosophical position; our judgments need only be concerned with the theological statements which may or may not grow out of them. But while it is not our chief concern, we ought nonetheless to recognize the main features of Tillich's philosophy simply because they do have a direct bearing upon his theological formulations.

Tillich is a philosophic anomaly. Philosophers today have for the most part confined themselves either to an introspective, subjective analysis of "existence" and steadfastly refused to abstract universals, or they have sought to be entirely objective, detached, "scientific," and have confined themselves to those concepts which are open to verification and proof. Against both of these lines, but combining aspects of both, Paul Tillich vigorously asserts the classical and medieval doctrine of ontology.

Ontology is the study of "being." It asks the question: What does it mean that something "is"? Why is it *not*? What is there held in common among all things? And if the answer is given that all things that are have "being," then there is assumed at the same time that by "being" we mean a special quality or power in which all things that are participate, and which accordingly has a ground and a source. Thus ontology naturally leads into and includes metaphysics, it involves the abstraction from "beings" to the power of being, the ground of being, being-itself, which in the Greek and scholastic traditions is called "God." Every *thing* in the universe then is related to every other thing in that it has being, and is related to the power and ground of being. The search for this power, or ground of being, was always the search for that which is all-inclusive, that reality which is the basis (or power of being) for all reality. For Aristotle it was God, who contained in himself as "ideas" the eternal forms, the reflection of which are the objects of our experience. The universe is a whole, and its parts are related in and by the power of being (God).

The Greek classical tradition offered a view of the universe which answered the ontological question. But it did not answer the question of epistemology, it did not describe the way in which it is possible for one part of the universe to "know" another. It did not solve the split between subject (the knower) and object (the known). A solution to this problem of knowledge was put forward in the medieval period by Nicholaus Cusanus (d. 1464) and Giordano Bruno (1548-1600) in their formulations of the "coincidence of opposites." To this solution Tillich largely subscribes. Cusanus and Bruno held that any final antithesis is impossible between subject and object, between the finite and infinite, and between man and God. However great the difference may be, a basic identity must always exist because two things cannot be compared or seen to be in contradiction unless there is some common ground, some identity which allows them to be viewed together. This common ground is of course their ontological relation, their unity in being.

Thus for Tillich ontology not only means a unified and inclusive view of the universe, but is the basis for epistemological assertions as well. The unity of being overcomes the split between the knowing subject and its object and makes knowledge possible. This ontological unity in which everything that is participates in being and the ground of being is seen by Tillich as a rational structure, which structure he calls the *logos*. It is this interpretation of *logos*, following the classical definition rather than the Neo-Platonic, which Tillich uses. And it is this rational *logos* structure of the universe which appears in everything that is. This structure appears in man and is that which allows him to abstract from his own being the unity and universality of being. Thus Tillich can say, again with Cusanus and Bruno, that man has the infinite within himself as concept, as a reflection of the structure of being. Man is thus a microcosmos; in the power of the universal *logos* he can see in his own being a reflection of universal being. This is the basis for Tillich's use of the scholastic principle of the *analogia entis*. For because of the unity of being, what one knows about man, by analogy, he may know about God.

These ontological suppositions are the foundation stones for Tillich's philosophy. And while we do not wish to extend our report of his philosophy beyond these very basic points, yet it may be helpful to mention a few other salient features. As Tillich himself remarks, his philosophic point of departure is the German classical philosophy of the early nineteenth century, especially as it showed him the way of synthesis between classical culture and the Christian tradition. This way of synthesis, Tillich writes, has "remained a driving force in all my theological work. It has found its final form in my *Systematic Theology*."[10]

It was the philosophy of Schelling especially which led Tillich in this direction.[11] The writings of Schelling can only be understood as two distinct systems of thought: the first part of his work produced an idealism (thought precedes being) and the second a realism (being is the antecedent of thought). The first pointed ahead to Hegel's philosophy and its a priori construction

---

10 *The Theology of Paul Tillich, op. cit.*, p. 10.
11 See Tillich's "Mystik und Schuldbewusstsein in Schellings philosophischer Entwicklung," *Beiträge zur Förderung Christlicher Theologie*, Vol. XVI (Gütersloh: Bertelsmann, 1912). For a short survey of Schelling's philosophy, especially as it pertains to existentialism, see Tillich's *The Courage To Be* (New Haven: Yale University Press, 1952), pp. 128 ff.

of the universe of pure thought, and the second to Schopenhauer, the empirical approach to reality, and indeed to the whole existential reaction to Hegel. Tillich acknowledges his debt to Schelling in both periods. From the first period, that of "negative philosophy," Tillich acquired a deep appreciation of Schelling's philosophy of nature. It was Schelling's concept of the "life" of nature, the dialectical movement of all things, even the inorganic, in the process of becoming, which inspired Tillich to include the natural world in his theological formulation of the Fall and salvation. (This will especially be seen in Tillich's analysis of "life" in Chapter VI, Part IV, of the system, "Life and the Spirit.") But it was Schelling's later period, his "positive philosophy," which was the greater influence on Tillich's development. In this period, under the influence of Jakob Böhme, Schelling became more a theosophist than a philosopher. He sought to solve the antinomy between freedom and necessity by saying that they are both aspects of reality and as such exist in God together. God is both freedom and necessity, he is eternal being and becoming. In this way Schelling also sought a solution to the ego-God polarity, for as both being and becoming, God cannot be an object of human knowledge, and thus cannot be properly said to stand over against man as an object. The process of God's becoming is eternal, the stages of the process are fused (the persons of the Trinity) and cannot be distinguished by the human mind. This part of Schelling's philosophy is echoed by Tillich when he speaks of God as including within himself both being and non-being, as eternally overcoming non-being, which is the root of evil and negativity in human existence. We find an echo too in Tillich's concept of the Trinity as expressing this "process of the divine life." And we hear again Schelling's view of God as synthesis when Tillich speaks of God as including within himself the ontological elements of individualization and participation, dynamics and form, and freedom and destiny. (See Chapter IV, Part II.)

Tillich identifies himself with the "existential" reaction to the all-embracing synthesis of Hegel, as found in the writings of Kierkegaard, Marx, and Nietzsche, and which he feels had as its turning point the positive philosophy of Schelling. For this reason Tillich is sometimes spoken of as an "existentialist."[12] But such a designation must be qualified. What does such a designation mean? What acceptable definition of existentialism could be applied alike to Kierkegaard, Sartre, Bultmann, and Tillich? This writer knows of none. If one defines existentialism as the belief "that *existence* comes before *essence*"[13] then perhaps Tillich (and every other philosopher who uses the empirical method) can be said to be, at least methodologically, an existentialist. But Tillich could not possibly follow Sartre, for example, in saying that the first principle of interpreting the above statement is that "Man is nothing else but that which he makes of himself,"[14] and certainly could not and does not follow the atheism incumbent upon that view. For much the same reason he cannot be said to fall into the line of thought represented by Heidegger either. Heidegger would agree with Tillich that an analysis of man's existence informs one about man's being, but he would resist the projection of man's being into a realm of essential being. Existentialism is not a matter primarily of where one begins, but where one ends (or more exactly, where one does not end). To abstract essence from existence necessarily leads to some notion of the divine, of God who as essence must be said to precede man's existence; this the true existentialist refuses to do, and this Tillich does. Tillich begins with existence, but only, it would seem, as a method for obtaining what is essential to it.[15]

[12] Cf. Will Herberg, *Four Existentialist Theologians* (New York: Doubleday & Co., 1958).

[13] Jean-Paul Sartre, *Existentialism and Humanism*, tr. Philip Mairet (London: Methuen & Co. Ltd., 1948), p. 26.

[14] *Ibid.*, p. 28.

[15] For Tillich's own description of his relation to existentialism, see especially *Theology of Culture, op. cit.*, pp. 76 ff., and *The Courage To Be, op. cit.*, pp. 117 ff. Tillich considers himself an existentialist in the broadest possible terms. He is an existentialist in "attitude," meaning a deep involvement and concern with the philosophical object. He is an existentialist as opposed to an essentialist (Hegel), but he numbers with himself in this opposition Plato and the Christian doctrines of the Fall, sin, and salvation! But the determining reason why Tillich should not finally be considered an existentialist in any usual sense of that word is summed up in a conversation which he reports between himself and T. S. Eliot in *Theol-*

A more detailed and deeper analysis lies outside the field of our inquiry, and any judgment of the merits of Tillich's philosophy as such lies outside this writer's competence. But perhaps the above remarks are sufficient to show how Tillich, beginning with the propositions of Platonic and Aristotelian ontology, and adding to them aspects of the philosophic tradition of German classicism, has been able to present an "ontological vision" which includes and unites subject and object, self and world, man and God. For Tillich, the universe is a whole, within it everything, inorganic matter and man alike, is related and united in being, and the whole is related and united with being-itself, the ground of being (which Tillich on theological grounds will call "God"). Because man is bound to, united with, and participating in, God as the ground of his being, and because the structure of this unity is rational and common to man and the universe, man may see in the structure of his own life a reflection of the structure of the universe and by analogy abstract, from his own being, being-itself.

The question naturally arises whether or not this philosophical "vision" is an adequate tool for the task which Tillich has set for himself, namely, the explanation of the contents of the Christian faith. Can Tillich, going his own way, accomplish the task he has set? This is the only meaningful way in which this question can be asked, and it can only be answered when we have studied his system as such, when we have followed him along his own way. But while we should not anticipate the answer, we can at least clarify the question. If Tillich begins his systematics with this ontology, what can he do but apply these presuppositions to his theology and work and think within their framework? What else can he do, as he actually does do, than to view man and the

---

ogy of Culture, op. cit., p. 125. "I believe [said Tillich] that you cannot answer the question you develop in your plays and your poems on the basis of your plays and poems, because they only develop the question—they describe human existence. But if there is an answer, it comes from somewhere else." Eliot replied, "That is exactly what I am fighting for all the time. I am, as you know, an Episcopalian." Tillich's ontology leads to essentialism, his method to existentialism; he wishes to correct the one with the other, and transcend them both.

ground of his being (God) in an ontic relation, which can only mean an application of the *analogia entis*, which, if logical enough under the Catholic scheme, is strangely out of place in a theology built upon a "Protestant principle"? And if his philosophy is directly translated into its theological counterpart, the *analogia entis*, how else will the divine-human relation finally be seen than one of mutual immanence, how else can it then be described than as a general situation, rather than the result of a special, unique event?

And now if we turn from his philosophy as such and consider the introductory theological statements in this chapter, we may put the same question in this way: *Can* theology be apologetic in nature? Can it begin with this ontology (or any other philosophical position for that matter) and then proceed in that context to a correct interpretation of the Christian faith? The answer to that question depends upon whether or not the method of such a theology, the method of correlation, is adequate to its task. Tillich sees exactly the problem involved when he warns that apologetics must not sacrifice the Christian message to the "situation." As Tillich rightly points out, a method cannot be judged apart from its application. And so our question cannot be answered apart from our study of his whole system. But we can nonetheless make these few preliminary and, for our purposes, tentative remarks: It is possible that theology could be written as "apologetics" if we mean by that simply that it answers the questions implied in human existence. Surely theology must be relevant; it must, in presenting the contents of the Christian faith, relate the answers given in revelation to the questions implied in the human situation. If God has addressed himself to man, it behooves the church in its preaching and teaching to point out to man that he is, in fact, addressed—addressed in the totality of his life. This is certainly not new with Tillich. One can think of no theological tradition which has not to some extent, and with more or less success, addressed itself and its message to the human "situation." But the measure of success or failure in this regard has always been the accuracy of the theologian's grasp: first, of the message he has to deliver, and second, of the human situation to which he speaks. And this brings us to the point that if apologetic, "answering" theology is possible as a theological method, it is possible only if it actually does allow man to be addressed, if it does not *always* ask its questions, if it finally listens!

Therefore, while we are sympathetic with Tillich's concern for relevant theology, we cannot but ask whether it is possible for the Christian message to be heard if placed in the correlation which Tillich has described. Will there be a point in his theological method at which the theologian will not ask, but will listen? There are several aspects to Tillich's introductory statements which make us apprehensive.

We are apprehensive because Tillich says that in the method of correlation the questions arising from the human situation control the *form* but not the *content* of the revelatory answers. Is this division between form and content possible when dealing with the Christian message? In any expression of ideas in any medium, there is of course a translation of the thought of one into the thought of another, the analysis of which involves semantics and the symbolic function of language. But this is not to say that the form of the content has been changed, rather the form of our expression of that content. Obviously Tillich wishes to say more. We read that "God does not answer questions which have not been asked," or that while "God in his abysmal nature is in no way dependent on man, God in his self-manifestation to man is dependent on the way man receives his manifestation."[61] As we have pointed out above, Tillich can only mean, in spite of his intention to the contrary, that there exists between man and God, between the questions of the former and the answers of the latter, a relation of necessity to which both are bound. Is there not a danger that such a concept will inhibit the freedom of God? Does it not fail to take seriously the fact that in the Bible, at least, God's willing and his doing, his Word and his actions, the content and the form of his address to man, are always the same, and cannot be separated?

Again, Tillich is right when he says that the fact that the Logos became flesh is the basic paradox of the Christian religion. But if the divine Logos took this form, then how can this form be said to have been determined by the questions of men if it is true *paradoxa* (against and counter to human expectation)? We can only say that insofar as Tillich holds fast to this paradox, the divine self-manifestation in Jesus as the Christ, the Logos become flesh, he indeed has *not* allowed the human question to change the revelatory answer—but then, neither has he controlled its form! But if his theology does not hold fast at this point, to this Man, will it not have changed the content of the Christian message, as well as have imposed its form? In either case it is difficult to see how the method of correlation can actually separate form and content, and remain true to itself and the Christian message.

We ask again, can theology be apologetic in Tillich's sense of that term? Can it proceed with the method of correlation from the analysis of the human situation and the questions which arise therein to a statement of the Christian faith which answers those questions? To this we may answer "yes," *if* two conditions are met: if the divine answer is really God's answer and if the human questions are really man's questions. The first condition we indicated above when we said that in order for the answer side of the correlation to be a real answer, one based upon God's self-revelation of himself, it must remain steadfastly dependent upon God's self-revelation in Jesus as the Christ, and him alone. The second condition for a correct "apologetic theology" is that the existential questions really do reflect the "human situation," that they actually arise from a correct analysis of who and what man is. This may seem to be a strange requirement to place upon a theology which claims to begin with man. We state the matter thus because the thing that has been taken for granted in most commentaries on Tillich, but which is not at all obvious, is that Tillich in his desire to begin with man has actually succeeded in doing so, has really succeeded in analyzing the human situation. For where finally must Christian theology find its interpretation of man? Where must its anthropology begin? Is it actually the case that a philosophical analysis of the ontological polarities, the conflicts and tensions in existence, or the ambiguities of life, will render a final and accurate interpretation of the human situation?[16] Is man's situation over against God really available to this approach? Is anthropology strictly the function of philosophy and not of theology? In this connection it may be fair also to ask whether or not so-called "kerygmatic theology" is really so irrelevant to the human situation after all. Might not the kerygma, the central message of the New Testament of the divine self-manifestation in Jesus as the Christ, also have something to say about the human situation? Indeed might not it be just there that we finally, and definitively, discover what that situation actually is? Can any analysis of the ambiguities of life say more about man's estrangement from the ground of his being than the Cross? Is not this the correlate question to the answer found in the Resurrection and the New Being?

We shall let these questions stand as preliminary to Tillich's further development of his system. We are under no obligation to reject either his definiton of theology, or his method, but we shall have to ask in every section whether there has been an actual correlation, whether the questions are based upon an accurate interpretation of man and his situation, and whether the answer of God's self-manifestation in Jesus Christ is actually heard. In this way we will study Tillich's systematics, with great admiration for his erudition and respect for the deep concern which he has for the gospel. And if he teaches us in a negative as well as a positive way, he will nonetheless have taught us, and we will nonetheless have learned.

[16] George Thomas has seen this problem clearly when he asks, "Can a philosophical reason which has not been fully 'converted' by the Christian faith correctly formulate the . . . deepest 'questions' implied in existence?" (*The Theology of Paul Tillich, op. cit.*, pp. 103-104).

III

REASON AND REVELATION

Reason . . . is subject to the conditions of existence . . . [to]
disruption and self-destruction.[82-83][1] *This experience drives*
men to the quest for . . . revelation. Reason does not resist
revelation. It asks for revelation, for revelation means the
reintegration of reason.[94]
Revelation has an unshakable objective foundation in the event
of Jesus as the Christ . . .[146] *Reason is not excluded from*
the healing power of the New Being in Jesus as the Christ. . . .
its essential structure is re-established . . . fragmentarily, yet
really and in power.[155]

REASON

Paul Tillich's *Systematic Theology* begins with an analysis of
reason and the doctrine of revelation. Thus, from the first, he
establishes the criteria, basis, and verification of his philosophical
and theological assertions, and shows the rationality and intelli-
gibility of revelation.

In our study of Tillich's theology, we are following his own
method of correlation, and we are using that method as an outline. Thus, in each chapter we begin with an analysis of the
human situation (in this case its rationality), discover the questions which it raises, and then see how the questions raised from
the human side are answered.

The Nature of Reason

Tillich draws a distinction between ontological and technical
reason. "According to the classical philosophical tradition,"

[1] Numbers in parentheses in this chapter refer to page numbers in
Tillich's *Systematic Theology*, Vol. I.

ontological reason "is the structure of the mind which enables
the mind to grasp and to transform reality."[72] This concept
of reason includes every function of the human mind in which it
seeks meaning in and from reality; it includes cognition and
aesthetics, theory and practice, detachment and passion, the subjective and the objective, intuition and criticism. It expresses the
totality of the rational structure of the mind and the universe.
The rational structure of the universe Tillich calls *logos*, which,
in this sense, is synonymous with ontological reason. Technical
reason, on the other hand, reduces reason ". . . to the capacity
for 'reasoning.' Only the cognitive side of the classical concept
of reason remains, and within the cognitive realm only those
cognitive acts which deal with the discovery of means for
ends."[73] The proper function of technical reason is to supply
the scientific methods of "reasoning" for ontological reason, and
it thus fulfills the useful function of establishing consistent and
logical thought. But if technical reason denies the validity of
ontological reason, it is confined to a shallow description of human life and is irrelevant for any deep understanding of man
and his ultimate concern. Thus reason for Tillich cannot be
merely technical, but is understood as ontological—which includes the technical.

Technical reason is neither a problem nor an aid for theology,
because it operates on a different level. The theologian must concern himself with the problem of ontological reason, for ontological reason, as an expression of the universal *logos*, is identical
with the content of revelation, the self-manifestation of the Logos.
But it is a mistake to identify actual ontological reason with the
divine Logos.

Tillich distinguishes within ontological reason its essence and
its existential actuality.[2] For while "the essence of ontological

---

[2] The terms "essence," "existence," and "actuality" or "life" must
here be distinguished in a preliminary way. They will be treated at length
in Chapters IV, V, and VI. "Essence" indicates the original unity of all
being in God, the ground of being. It is perfection, creation before the
Fall. "Existence" is the logical opposite of essence; it points to separation, estrangement of beings from God. But both essence and existence, so
defined, are abstractions and do not point to any real state. Therefore
Tillich distinguishes thirdly "actuality," or "life," which is a combination of essence and existence, union and separation, sin and salvation.

reason, the universal *logos* of being, is identical with the content of revelation, still reason, if actualized in self and world, is dependent on the destructive structures of . . . existence; it is subjected to finitude and separation . . ."[74] Thus, as is all of life, reason is subject to the Fall, to sin and error, but also, as all of life, it participates *fragmentarily* in salvation. It is never completely cut off from its original unity and perfection with being-itself. Tillich admits that according to its fallen state, reason is subject to "blindness" (the traditional criticism of theology), but he insists that according to its original and actual fragmentary union with the universal *logos*, reason is a necessary and useful tool of theology. The distinction between the essential and existential nature of reason is thus an important insight for systematic theology. In any case, when throughout his system Tillich speaks of "reason" in correlation with revelation, it is ontological, "fragmentarily saved" reason which is meant.

Reason has both a *subjective* and *objective* character. Subjective reason enables the mind to grasp and shape reality, and objective reason is the rational structure of reality which can be grasped and shaped. Reality and the mind have in common a rational structure. Subjective reason (the rational structure of the mind) in the philosopher grasps the objective reason (the rational structure of reality) of the universe. Subjective reason in the artist grasps the objective reason (meaning) of things. Subjective reason in the legislator shapes society according to the objective, reasonable structure of social balance. This double nature of reason is consistent with and follows from Tillich's ontological presupposition that the world and man are equally related to the rational structure of the universe, the *logos*.

Reason, as expressed in both its subjective and objective form, points to what Tillich calls "the depth of reason." Here his debt to the Platonic tradition is seen most clearly. In spite of the fallen nature of reason, every rational function points to the ultimate and is transparent to it. What Tillich means by the depth of reason sounds very much like Plato's eternal forms, or, perhaps more accurately, the Aristotelian "ideas" in the divine mind. Tillich, however, would say that the depth of reason is simply that which *points* to truth-itself, beauty-

itself, justice-itself, or love-itself. But the depth of reason is not
these as such, but is the *quality* of reason which points to these
essences. This depth of reason which points reason beyond itself
is most clearly seen in the rational functions of myth and cult.
Tillich maintains that myth is not primitive science, nor is cult
primitive morality. Rather, they both show that even under the
conditions of actual existence, even in its fallen state, reason has
within it a depth and power which points it beyond itself to
essential being.[3]

We have said that essential reason is reason united with its
ground. Now we must turn to Tillich's concept of existential
reason, fallen reason, finite and actual reason, as we experience
it. "Being is finite, existence is self-contradictory, and life is
ambiguous. Actual reason participates in these characteristics of
reality." [81] But in spite of its finitude, contradictions, and
ambiguities, finite reason is not without the infinite. We see this
intimated in Tillich's concept of "the depth of reason," which
even in its distorted and hidden form of myth and cult is nevertheless present to fallen reason. We also noted in the short sketch
of Tillich's philosophy in the first chapter that Tillich follows
the *docta ignorantia* (learned ignorance) of Cusanus, which held
that although human reason cannot grasp (is ignorant of) its
infinite ground, in recognizing this situation it becomes aware
of that infinity which it cannot attain, and this realization is
(learned) true knowledge. This is the principle of the "coincidence of the opposites," which states that the contradiction
between the finite and the infinite implies their unity. For if
there were no common ground between the two, finitude would
have no concept of the infinite against which it could place itself.

---

[3] Tillich's conception of 'myth'' is important for his theory of the symbolical nature of revelation. Myth is symbolical language about the divine.
It is unavoidable and universal, because man cannot express the infinite or
the divine except indirectly, through symbols. Thus, ''If the Christ—a
transcendent, divine being—appears in the fullness of time, lives, dies and
is resurrected, this is an historical myth'' (*Dynamics of Faith, op. cit.,*
p. 54). But the Christian myth is ''broken myth,'' i.e., it is seen as myth,
as symbolic, and thus points beyond itself to the infinite and inexpressible
which it symbolizes. One sees beyond it, looks through it. Tillich does not
mean by myth something ''that is not true,'' and he should not be
criticized at that level.

Thus two things are said about finite reason: it is separated from its infinite depth, and is thus distinguished from essential reason which is not; and it is united with its depth, being-itself, because, realizing its finitude, it becomes aware of infinitude and its essential structure.

The same situation, says Tillich, is described by Kant in his analysis of the categories of finite reason. These categories, especially that of time, show that reason is imprisoned in finitude and can not break through its limits. It tries to do so, but it fails. Tillich, perhaps going somewhat beyond Kant, would, in agreement with Cusanus, maintain that the knowledge of this failure necessarily *implies* an awareness of the infinite which reason cannot grasp. Tillich argues that Kant himself sees one point at which finitude is open for the infinite, for in the concept of the categorical imperative Kant has allowed the unconditional to break through the prison of finitude. But this point where the unconditional command is apprehended is only a point; the mind does not grasp the infinite, but reason, sensing the unconditional in the moral imperative, becomes aware of its own depth. Actual reason is finite, and as such is separated from its ground. But Tillich's interpretation of Cusanus and Kant seeks to show that reason is not merely finite. "In the actual life of reason its basic structure is never completely lost . . . essential and existential forces, forces of creation and forces of destruction, are united and disunited at the same time." [83] Essential reason is lost, and existential reason is "fallen," cut off from its ground. But the essential structure of reason is never completely lost, never completely cut off from its depth. For, says Tillich, if this were not so, mind as well as reality would have been destroyed in the very moment of coming into existence, because there can be no life which is not to some degree related and united with being-itself and its rational structure. This is certainly a consistent ontology, and we cannot but admit the truth of it. But a theological problem arises when Tillich goes on to say that it is this presence of the infinite within finite reason which enables reason to ask for revelation. If reason—fallen, estranged reason—is said to include within itself the infinite, the unconditional, then the question arises: In what sense can it be said that reason actually asks the question of revelation? Would it not already contain within itself the answer?

We will have more to say about this problem below, but now it is important to understand Tillich's concept of reason, its essential and existential character, for it is out of the tensions and contradictions resulting from this split that the questions arise which point to the answer of revelation.

The Question of Reason

Reason under the conditions of existence is in a state of conflict between its various structural elements. It is out of these conflicts that the quest for revelation arises. Tillich analyzes these conflicts under three main headings, the first being that of autonomous reason against heteronomous reason. "Autonomy means the obedience of the individual to the law of reason, which he finds in himself as a rational being." [84] It is a mistake to think of autonomy as being a law to one's self, or willfulness. Autonomy is the serious attempt to be obedient to one's own essential structure. This kind of thought is usually represented by liberal and humanist traditions. But in man's fallen state, autonomy loses its depth, its dependence on the rational structure of being-itself, and becomes shallow and meaningless. Thus, heteronomous reactions take place which are intended to restore authority and depth to reason. "Heteronomy imposes a strange (*heteros*) law (*nomos*) on one or all of the functions of reason. It issues commands from 'outside' . . . But . . . it represents, at the same time, an element in reason itself, namely, the depth of reason." [84] Like autonomy, heteronomy is not simply a "mistake" of reason. It represents a legitimate aspect of reason, authority. It tries to speak in the name of the ground of being and reason, and therefore inevitably speaks in an unconditional and ultimate way. However, as a mere reaction to autonomy, it is destructive to reason, for it denies reason the right to express its own inner structure. Heteronomy is represented by all authoritarian movements of thought and is most clearly seen in its destructive form in the totalitarian state.

Both autonomy and heteronomy are rooted in theonomy. "Theonomy" is one of the most important words in the Tillichian vocabulary. It means, generally, the unity of actualized being with being-itself. It is the result of the saving process of revelation and occurs whenever and wherever man as finite being is united transcendentally with God, the ground and power of being. For our present subject, theonomy means "autonomous reason united with its own depth." [85] The "situation of theonomy" is one in which the conflict between autonomy and heteronomy is overcome, for, having depth, there is no need for authority to be imposed upon reason from the outside. But under the conditions of existence, complete theonomy never appears; the split in reason remains. Thus, the question of a reunion of autonomous and heteronomous reason arises out of the existential situation of reason, and it can only be answered by revelation.

The second heading under which Tillich analyzes the conflict in existential reason is relative reason against absolute reason. In a penetrating study, Tillich shows how absolutism is found in both conservative and revolutionary traditions. Conservatism is clearly absolutistic because it identifies reason with special morals, political forms, aesthetic and philosophical principles. But revolution is no less absolutistic, "Because the attack [upon tradition by revolution is] victorious through the strength of an absolute claim. . . . Revolutionary reason believes just as deeply as traditionalism that it represents unchangeable truth."[87]

Relativism comes as a reaction to absolutism and may take either a positivistic or cynical form. Philosophical positivism (with which Tillich carries on a continuous debate throughout his system) has, since the time of David Hume, attacked absolute norms and criteria with pragmatic tests. Truth becomes relative to a group, a concrete situation, or an existential predicament. Cynical relativism reacts primarily to the failure of utopian absolutism. In its reaction it is wholly negative; it denies every principle of reason and "cynically" uses reason to deny reason. But its attack fails, because its negativity produces a vacuum into which ever new absolutisms may intrude.

Because the reaction of relativism is the reaction of the particular against a universal in which it loses itself, or of the concrete against an absolute which would swallow and destroy it, the conflict between absolutism and relativism can only be overcome by that which is absolute and concrete at the same time. Therefore, says Tillich, reason requests the answer of revelation, because only in revelation is there offered the absolutely concrete.

The third conflict which expresses the situation of existential reason is between formalism and emotionalism. The formal element of reason is seen primarily in its cognitive and legal functions, while the emotional element is expressed in the aesthetic and communal. Actually, of course, they appear in combination in all of these. Formalism in cognition results in intellectualism, which is the use of the intellect without philosophical *eros*.[4] But emotional reactions do not heal the split, because they forget the necessity for strict and technically correct thinking in all of knowledge. Formalism in aesthetics results in what Tillich calls "connoisseurship," which is expressed in the phrase "art for art's sake." Emotional reactions to such dead art are right in insisting upon a spiritual substance to art, but unfortunately are usually wrong in their aesthetic judgment. The same conflict between the formal and emotional functions of reason could be described in the legal and communal realm; this conflict is tragic because just as form without emotion lacks life, so emotion without form lacks those structural elements which give strength and power—it falls easy prey to irrationalism and fanaticism, it becomes demonic. Reason, therefore, seeks the reunion of the formal and the emotional, and this it can only find in revelation.

We have described the conflicts of reason generally as they appear in autonomy versus heteronomy, absolutism versus relativism, and formalism versus emotionalism. Under the latter conflict we must give special consideration to the particular function of reason called "cognition." ". . . for revelation is the manifestation of the ground of being for human knowledge . . .

---

[4] Tillich means by *eros* that kind of love which seeks to fulfill its own being by the pursuit of truth through all the levels of reality to truth and being-itself. He means Platonic *eros*. See Paul Tillich, *Biblical Religion and the Search for Ultimate Reality* (Chicago: The University of Chicago Press, 1955), pp. 70-72.

[therefore] theology must give a description of cognitive reason under the conditions of existence.'' [(94)] Formal knowledge is achieved through detachment and separation; ''emotional'' knowledge is the result of union with the object. ''Knowing is a form of union . . . the gap between subject and object is overcome. . . . But the union of knowledge is a peculiar one; it is a union through separation.'' [(94)] Separation is necessary, because in order to ''know'' a thing it must be ''looked at,'' and one can only look at a thing from a distance. For true knowledge, union and separation must appear together in the act of cognition, but under the conditions of existence they are split. Dogmatism, for instance, expresses the union side of cognition, and becomes dangerous when it unites with distorted elements of reality. But it is right in expressing commitment to the object of its knowledge. Liberal reactions, although sometimes wrong in neglecting the aspect of unity and identification, are right in stressing the need for detachment, honesty, and openness for true knowledge. In a technological age such as ours, the power of the detached type of knowledge enjoys the greatest public confidence, but its results in the areas of anthropology and history, to mention just two, are shallow, if not misleading. History becomes mechanics, and man becomes a ''cog'' in the machine. Knowledge gained through detachment has certainty, but in its verification it treats its object as only an ''object,'' as a thing, and thus ''kills'' it, taking away its subjective quality, its self-relatedness which constitutes its life. Knowledge gained through union goes deeper into the essence of its object, it ''intuits,'' it becomes aware of the life and subjectivity of the other through union. But it is not able to prove or scientifically demonstrate its knowledge. Thus cognitive reason asks for revelation, because, says Tillich, revelation claims to achieve union with that which is revealed, and at the same time satisfies the demand for detachment and analysis.

We have seen that reason, for Tillich, is not only the act of ''reasoning'' by which the mind grasps reality, but it has also an objective quality; it is the structure of reality which allows itself to be grasped by the mind. These two aspects of reason are united in being-itself, in essential reason. The most important point in Tillich's understanding of reason is that even under the conditions of existence, "fallen" reason is not totally separated from its depth, God, and the *logos* structure of being. Tillich maintains that it is this awareness of its depth and origin that enables reason, even under the conditions of existence, to ask for revelation.

But in spite of the faint awareness of its depth and essential unity with the ground of being, reason under the conditions of existence finds itself in a state of conflict—it is out of this conflict that it asks for revelation, and it is in terms of this conflict that revelation must answer. Out of the conflict between autonomy and heteronomy, reason asks for that which can establish theonomy and unite the rational structure of man with its own depth, the eternal *logos*. This it can only find in revelation. Out of the conflict between relativism and absolutism, reason asks for that which can unite the absolute and the concrete (or the relative). Only revelation offers that which is absolute and concrete at the same time. Out of the conflict of the formal and the emotional, reason asks for that which unites detached (formal) knowledge and united (emotional) knowledge. Only revelation can give it. Therefore, Tillich affirms, "Reason does not resist revelation. It asks for revelation, for revelation means the reintegration of reason." [94]

We have satisfied the first half of the method of correlation by analyzing the existential situation of rational man and discovering the questions which arise out of that analysis. We must now turn to the second half of Tillich's method, the theological answer, examine the nature of revelation itself, and show how it answers the questions of reason.

REVELATION

Tillich divides his discussion of revelation into three parts: a phenomenological study of revelation as such; a dogmatic description of what he calls "actual," or "final," revelation; and an analysis of how revelation answers the questions of reason.

The Nature of Revelation Generally

Tillich attempts a phenomenological description of revelation before raising the question of its truth or reality. He does this because he believes that theology must force "its critics first of all to see what the criticized concepts mean and also [force] itself to make careful descriptions of its concepts . . ." [106] Phenomenology would seem a strange tool for Tillich to use, especially in the light of the sharp criticism he has directed toward empiricism generally. He readily admits that while a description of appearances is adequate for the definition of objects, it hardly can be so for revelation, because in this case there is no universal agreement as to which appearances are genuine. A critical principle is needed. One example of the appearance of revelation must be the norm by which all others are judged. And so Tillich calls his approach "critical phenomenology" and takes the appearance of Jesus as the Christ as the "classic example" of revelation. "Each example of revelation is judged in terms of this phenomenological concept, and this concept can be employed as a criterion because it expresses the essential nature of every revelation." [108]5

Using the revelation of Jesus as the Christ as his criterion, Tillich proceeds to examine the phenomena of revelation generally. In this examination he finds three "marks" which are present in every revelation: mystery, ecstasy, and miracle. Tillich points out that the word "mystery" (*muein*, "closing the eyes or mouth") indicates the transcendence of ordinary cognition. "Mystery," by definition, remains hidden. And so when religion claims that in revelation a mystery is "revealed," it is not stating a paradox, but is simply saying that the reality of the mystery and our relation to it have become matters of experience. "Whatever is essentially mysterious cannot lose its mysteriousness even when it is revealed." [109] Genuine mystery reveals to reason its "ground" in being-itself. But it remains mysterious. This mysterious character of revelation has a subjective as well as an objective character. It "appears objectively in terms of what traditionally has been called 'miracle.' It appears subjectively in terms of what has sometimes been called 'ecstasy.' "[111] For

---

5 The circular nature of such a "critical phenomenology" (the selection of descriptive phenomena being controlled by a prior decision as to the nature of the object under study) was explained and defended in Chapter II where we reported Tillich's concept of the theological circle and the necessity of an a priori in all spiritual matters.

revelation to take place, there must be a correlation between God's act and man's, between miracle and ecstasy.

"Ecstasy" should not be confused with over-excitement. Nor should it be thought irrational. Ecstasy for Tillich points to a state in which the mind is grasped by revelation, is taken out of its ordinary situation of subject-object relationship, and is united with the ground and meaning of being-itself, or God. Negatively, ecstasy is an "ontological shock"; the mind feels its ground falling away, man asks seriously, "Why am I not?" It is the threat of non-being. Tillich insists that ecstasy is no more emotional than intellectual—in fact it is neither, for it transcends every function of the mind. In the encounter of revelation, man is momentarily lifted out of his condition of finitude, existence, and estrangement. "Ecstasy is not a negation of reason; it is the state of mind in which reason is beyond itself . . ." [112]

If ecstasy describes the subjective state of the receiving mind in revelation, "miracle" describes the objective side, the transformation of reality in revelation. Tillich resists any interpretation of miracles as happenings that contradict the laws of nature. Such an interpretation, says Tillich, splits God. God as the manifestation of the ground of being would destroy God as the structure of being, which in the *logos* is also the structure of natural law. For Tillich, miracles are "sign events" which take place within the natural order, but which are filled with transcendent meaning and are received as such. Thus the marks of revelation are mystery, ecstasy, and miracle. And they appear in every revelation.

What are the media by which revelation comes to man? "There is no reality, thing, or event which cannot become a bearer of the mystery of being and enter into a revelatory correlation." [118] Negatively, nothing is excluded from being a medium of revelation because nothing is "good enough" or worthy of that function. Positively, everything is able to be a medium of revelation, because "every thing participates in being-itself." [118] Thus, of course, Tillich maintains that nature is a medium of revelation. And he means that natural objects such as a stone, water, or the sky, or natural events such as life and death or health and ill-

ness, have special qualities which are used by the divine in revelation. But at the same time he is careful to say that "Revelation
through natural mediums is not natural revelation. . . . Natural
knowledge about self and world cannot lead to the revelation of
the ground of being." [119] The thing, or the event as such, does
not have revelatory character, but it is used by that which it
reveals. Similarly, history, groups, and individuals can be
bearers of revelation. In themselves they have no revelatory
power, but they are used. Groups and their history can become
mediums of revelation if, under special circumstances, they point
to a quality of being-itself, and if they are received as revelation.
Individuals may be vessels of revelation if, through some aspect
of their personalities, they show aspects of the divine. This, says
Tillich, is the meaning of "sainthood." A saint is one "transparent" to the ground of being; others "see" in and through
him some aspect of the divine. "Transparency" is a good word
to describe Tillich's understanding of revelation and its media,
for it involves the divine power which "shines through" the
medium, and it involves the recipient's willingness and ability to
look through and beyond the thing, event, or person which bears
revelation. It involves miracle and ecstasy.

For Tillich a basic medium of revelation is "the word." This
concept of "word" is distinguished from "Word of God," because, says Tillich, "the symbols 'Word of God' and 'Logos'
cannot be understood in their various meanings without an insight into the general nature of the word." [122]

Approaching the matter in this way, Tillich seeks to show how
the phenomenon "word" has special qualities which make it
usable as a medium of revelation. Words generally have a deno-
tative power which goes beyond ordinary definition and points
toward existential meaning. And they have an expressive power
which goes beyond what is possible to express, and points to the
inexpressible. Thus words are naturally endowed with a kind of
transcendence. They point beyond themselves. But words used
in revelation are "transparent"; through them one may see the
depth of being and meaning. Since nothing is communicated to
man or revealed to man except through words (for every actual-

ized thought must use words), "the word is not a medium of revelation in addition to the other mediums; it is a necessary element in all forms of revelation." [124]

Revelation gives knowledge, but what kind of knowledge? "Knowledge of revelation is knowledge about the revelation of the mystery of being to us, not information about the nature of beings and their relation to one another." [129] Thus there should be no conflict between revelatory knowledge and ordinary knowledge; neither can add to or take away from the other. This statement is perhaps not so obvious as it sounds. For instance, in the realm of historical research, conflicts have arisen with the biblical narrative. Tillich maintains that such a conflict is wrong, because "knowledge of revelation, although it is mediated primarily through historical events, does not imply factual assertions . . ."[130] Revelation does not offer facts, but it tells us of our relation to a mystery.

The knowledge which revelation gives "is knowledge of God, and therefore it is analogous or symbolic . . . this certainly refers to the classical doctrine of the *analogia entis* between the finite and the infinite."[131] In our discussion of Tillich's philosophy in the second chapter, we saw that his ontology leads him naturally to affirm this doctrine. But just as he was anxious to avoid the onus of natural revelation when he spoke of revelation through nature, so here Tillich is careful to point out that "the *analogia entis* is in no way able to create a natural theology." [131] It should not be thought a method by which one may discover truth about God, but rather, like the word "symbol," it points to the necessity of using finite reality to give content to what is revealed in revelation about the infinite. We shall have to ask later in our analysis whether this understanding of *analogia entis* really solves the problem and avoids the danger of natural theology.

The Nature of Actual Revelation

The above description of revelation has dealt with revelation generally, revelation as an object, the attributes of which may be studied and catalogued. We come now to Tillich's dogmatic assertion of the specific content of the Christian revelation, which he calls "actual" revelation.

He begins with the statement that actual revelation is final revelation. And he means that insofar as revelation has to do only with what concerns us ultimately, if one is grasped by a revelatory experience, that experience is "final" for him; if he looked for other revelations he would look at the revelation he has in a detached way, and thus he would no longer be in the revelatory situation of ultimate concern. But final does not mean "last"; it means "the decisive, fulfilling, unsurpassable revelation, that which is the criterion of all the others." [133] That Jesus as the Christ is the final revelation in this sense, Tillich says, is the claim of Christianity and is the basis of a Christian theology.

Now the fact that any revelation received as actual must be held by the receiver as final is merely a psychological truth, and applicable to every religion. Therefore Tillich asks whether there is in the revelation of Jesus as the Christ itself a criterion which would demonstrate its finality. And he sets forth the following: "A revelation is final if it has the power of negating itself without losing itself." [133] This criterion is necessary, says Tillich, because under the conditions of existence every revelation is distorted by the medium through which it appears. Thus, if a particular revelation is said to be final, decisive, "completely transparent to the mystery it reveals," it must overcome and sacrifice its finite medium. Jesus as the Christ fulfills this requirement. He sacrifices his finitude (that which was Jesus in him). He sacrifices himself. But Jesus could not surrender himself completely unless he possessed himself completely. "And only he can possess—and therefore surrender—himself completely who is united with the ground of his being and meaning without separation and disruption." [133] We shall go into the whole matter of Christology in detail in Chapter V. But now we must confine ourselves to the implication of Tillich's view of Christ for revelation. In the first place, Tillich maintains that Christ's finitude (his identity as Jesus) is distinguished as a *medium* of revelation and is not simply the revelation itself. Secondly, he holds that it was the complete unity of Jesus as the Christ with God which allowed him to sacrifice his finitude. But since Tillich does not think that this unity alleviates the necessity of sacrificing the finite Jesus, it can only be that it is not Jesus as Jesus who is thus united with God, but Jesus as the Christ. The finite Jesus as the medium of the revelation of Jesus as the Christ is not for Tillich completely united with the God whom he reveals, otherwise he would not distort the revelation of the Messiah and would not, like every other finite medium, have to be sacrificed. And the third mark of Tillich's Christology, as it applies to revelation, is that he places emphasis on the Crucifixion at the expense of the Resurrection. Revelation, the work of Christ, the healing and reunion of the estranged, is said by Tillich to take place through the destruction and sacrifice of the medium rather than by its victory. "In his cross Jesus sacrificed that medium of revelation. . . . For us this means that in following him we are liberated from the authority of everything finite in him. . . . Only as the crucified is he 'grace and truth' and not law. Only as he who has sacrificed his flesh, that is, his historical existence, is he Spirit or New Creature. . . . And he is the Christ as the one who sacrifices what is *merely* 'Jesus' in him" (italics mine). (134)

We can see here the results of the method of correlation. Because man's questions demand a sacrifice of the medium of revelation, the revelatory answer must take the form of the Christ who sacrifices Jesus, and not the form of Jesus Christ, in eternal and indissoluble unity. And we shall have to ask whether or not such a dictation of form does not in the most radical way also affect and change the content of the answer.

But to continue our analysis of actual revelation: Tillich maintains that revelation has a history. It is not an isolated event, it was prepared for, and it was received, it has both a before and an after. But the history of revelation is not a historical survey of all revelations which have taken place. This is because of its special and "final" character. "The event of final revelation establishes itself as the center, aim, and origin of the revelatory events which occur in the period of preparation and in the period of reception." (138) Tillich insists upon a period of preliminary revelation. He places himself against humanistic theology which identifies the history of revelation with the history of religion and culture, and against what he calls "neo-orthodox" theology which says "that there is only *one* revela-tion, namely, that in Jesus the Christ." [138] The latter position Tillich objects to as unable to explain how the final revelation could be received. Without preparation, he says, it would fall as a "strange body" into the world and could not be assimilated into man's spiritual life. Tillich calls the revelation of Jesus as the Christ the only "actual" revelation. Nevertheless there is for him such a thing as "universal revelation" which is real revela-tion and can be found in myth and cult throughout history. But because this universal revelation invariably turns into idolatry, it cannot be said to be directly preparatory for final revelation. Only under the impact of the prophetic criticism of the Old Testament could universal revelation be transformed into a con-crete revelation which points toward the Christ. "The revelation through the prophets of Israel is the direct concrete prepa-ration of the final revelation, and it cannot be separated from it."[142] But because Israel could not sacrifice the medium of its revelation, its national life, it in turn was rejected and trans-formed by the New Testament.

The receiving period of revelation is of course the period of the church, and its constant point of reference is Jesus as the Christ. It is always dependent upon the original event.

To close this section on the nature of revelation, we should examine what Tillich means by "Word of God." By Word of God he means simply God's revelation of himself. And since revelation may take any form, "The 'Word of God' is every reality through which the ultimate power breaks into our present reality . . ."[6] We have seen above that Tillich requests a strict interpretation of "word" as language which is "transparent" to the ground of being. But if one uses the phrase "Word of God," Tillich insists that this "word" be understood in the classical sense of *logos*, the rational structure of the ground of being. Against Ritschl and Harnack, Tillich maintains that the Greek concept of *logos* is not intellectualistic, but rather a de-fense against it. For the Greeks always considered knowledge to

6 *The Protestant Era, op. cit.*, p. 81.

imply participation; it was "existential." Tillich finds the intellectualization of the *logos* idea not in Greek philosophy, but in every "theology of the word" which views the *logos* of revelation as spoken word. That the Word of God should not be confused with the spoken word has been a constant theme in Tillich's theology. In 1924 he wrote, "Word is not only present where it is spoken and conceived, but Word is also present where it is made visible and acted in powerfully operative symbols. *Verbum* is more than *oratio*."[7] And in 1929 he made the very explicit statement: "It is quite wrong . . . to mix up God's word with the word of Scripture or the word of preaching."[8]

For Tillich, "the elaboration of a theology of the spoken or the written word . . . is *the* Protestant pitfall."[(157)9] Therefore to avoid this "pitfall" he sets forth six different meanings of the term "Word of God," all of which are consistent with his broader concept of *logos*. (1) The Word is the "principle" of the divine self-manifestation. For the ground of being itself has the char-

---

[7] Paul Tillich, *Kirche und Kultur* (Tübingen: J. C. B. Mohr, 1924).

[8] Paul Tillich, *Religiöse Verwirklichung* (Berlin: Furche, 1929), p. 48.

[9] If it is a pitfall, it is one which appeared early in Protestantism, for even Calvin did not hesitate to follow Erasmus' translation of John 1:1, "*In principio erat Sermo, et Sermo erat apud Deum, et ille Sermo erat Deus,*" interpreting Logos as *sermo* or human speech. "*Nam ut sermo character mentis dicitur in hominibus, ita non inepte transfertur hoc quoque ad Deum, ut per Sermonen suum dicatur nobis se ipsum exprimere*" ("For just as the word is said to be the character of the mind of man, so it is not inappropriate to apply this to God, so that he may be said to reveal himself to us through his Word") (*Ioannis Calvini in Novum Testamentum Commentari*, Vol. III, Berolini, apud Gustavum Eichler; cf. *Corpus Reformatorum* 75.1). Of course Tillich is right when he warns against the degeneration of the concept of the Word into that form of verbal inspiration which argues for verbal inerrancy. But what he does not see is that such fundamentalistic positions may be closer at their base to his view than to the views of Calvin or of Barth. For the problem hangs not so much on intellectual detachment over against existential participation as it does on whether one views revelation as a general situation or a specific event. If one says that God has "spoken" to man in Jesus Christ (which we certainly must do if for no other reason than that this happens in the proclamation of the church and the written word of Scripture) the specific event-character of revelation is indicated. God *does* something, there is movement and life. But if one interprets the *logos* (as did the Greeks and as Tillich insists) as the rational structure of being-itself, then one is faced not with an event, but with a general situation. This situation, in spite of Tillich's wish to show its inner dialectical movement, must appear as static, as a given. And the idea of revelation as a "given" deposit of truth is certainly characteristic of fundamentalism in any form.

acter of self-manifestation. It reflects God's nature as one who reveals himself. (2) The Word is that by which God creates. It is dynamic and spiritual. (3) The Word is manifest in the history of revelation; it is the revelation of God received as such. (4) The Word is therefore identical with final revelation. "The Word is a name for Jesus as the Christ." [158] (5) The Word is also the Bible. It is the document of final revelation and its preparation. (6) The Word is finally "the message of the church as proclaimed in her preaching and teaching." [159] We cannot fail to notice that there is a deliberate order in this listing. The first three meanings have to do with general and preliminary revelation, while the last three have to do with concrete and final revelation. And the question naturally arises whether or not, in the light of the first chapter of John, the interpretation of "the Word" as Jesus as the Christ is not the only place where the first three meanings of "the Word" can be understood.

The Answer of Revelation

We must now proceed to an analysis of the way in which revelation answers the questions of reason and must take special note of how in each case the form of the revelatory answer is dictated by the question.

We remember that Tillich described the problems of reason in terms of conflict between autonomy and heteronomy, absolutism and relativism, and formalism and emotionalism. Now he must show how revelation solves these conflicts. Autonomy was described by Tillich as the self's allegiance to its own inner rational structure at the expense of the depth of reason. Heteronomy was seen as any finite claim of ultimate authority imposing itself upon autonomy. "Revelation overcomes the conflict between autonomy and heteronomy by re-establishing their essential unity." [147] This essential unity is expressed in what Tillich calls "theonomy." Final revelation, which is the revelation of Jesus as the Christ, creates theonomy by avoiding the shallowness of autonomous reason left to itself. For the true depth and basis of autonomous reason shines through the transparent medium of that revelation. Also the tendency of heteronomous reason to establish itself as ultimate authority is overcome by the sacrifice of the medium of that revelation. The mind which tends to assert its autonomous rational power according to its own rational structure is able, under the influence of Jesus as the Christ, to see the source, ground, and authority of its own life and reason. It is thus protected from the demonic attacks of heteronomous reason. Any authority is heteronomous which claims ultimacy for the finite. Such tendencies are counteracted by final revelation which does not claim ultimate authority for its finite medium, but sacrifices it. " 'He who believes in me does not believe in *me*,' says Jesus in the Fourth Gospel, destroying any heteronomous interpretation of his divine authority." [148]

Final revelation in Jesus as the Christ, by its transparency to the ground of being, and by its sacrifice of its finite medium, overcomes the shortsightedness of autonomy and the arrogance of heteronomy. It creates theonomy, the state of union with the ground of being.

The second conflict which we found in reason and which is solved by revelation is that between absolutism and relativism. Absolutism was characterized as either conservative or revolutionary traditions which claim to speak in behalf of unchangeable truth. Relativism, either pragmatic or cynical, refuses in the name of the particular and the concrete to be swallowed by the general and universal concepts of absolutism. Reason always stands in this dilemma; either it takes the form of absolute, general law, and thus overlooks and does violence to the special and the concrete, or it takes the form of a relativism, which, concentrating on the concrete and particular, is powerless to claim any kind of universal validity. "Final revelation . . . liberates reason from the conflict between absolutism and relativism by appearing in the form of a concrete absolute." [150] The concrete side of final revelation is the picture of a personal life in Jesus as the Christ. And the paradoxical claim of Christianity is that at the same time this concrete picture has unconditional and universal validity. But it is not absolutistic and is therefore not subject to the attacks of pragmatic or cynical relativism. Jesus does not give absolute ethics, doctrines, or ideals. He points to the absolute, but he is not the absolute itself. "The absolute side of the final revelation, that in it which is unconditional and un-changeable, involves the complete transparency and the com-plete self-sacrifice of the medium in which it appears." [151] In this way the absolute character of the Christ results from the transparency and sacrifice of his concreteness. An absolutism which involves its own sacrifice is not subject to the reactions of relativism. In Jesus as the Christ, in final revelation, absolutism and relativism meet and their conflict is overcome.

The power which overcomes this conflict is love. Love "is abso-lute because it concerns everything concrete. . . . Love is always love; that is its static and absolute side. But love is always de-pendent on that which is loved [and that is its relative side]." [152] Tillich offers this example of the way love overcomes the con-flict between absolutism and relativism: every action includes the conflict of absolutism and relativism. Every decision to act is absolutistic in that it resists the relative arguments of other possibilities. And the struggle between absolute action and rela-tive possibilities is tragic, because the excluded possibilities "take their revenge" in the way of disappointments, errors, etc. Final revelation overcomes this conflict, alleviates the anxiety of de-cision and makes it possible to act by showing that there are no "right" decisions; there are only decisions which are rooted in love. And such decisions are not absolutistic, nor are they merely relative. They are not exposed to the revenge of excluded possi-bilities because they are still open to them. Final revelation over-comes the conflict between absolutism and relativism through love, for love is absolute as love and relative in every love relationship.

The third and last conflict which Tillich finds in his analysis of reason under the conditions of existence is that between for-malism and emotionalism. We have seen how formalism is ex-pressed in all of life (e.g., in cognition as intellectualism and in aesthetics as connoisseurship) and we also saw that emotional reactions are always present. But, says Tillich, "When the mys-tery of being appears in a revelatory experience, the whole of the person's life participates. This means that reason is present both structurally [formally] and emotionally and that there is no conflict between these two elements." [153] We remember that it was the cognitive function of reason which most clearly showed the conflict between formalism and emotionalism. For in the cognitive function there is the conflict between detached (formal) knowledge and knowledge gained by union (emotion). Tillich requests that theology return to the early Alexandrian doctrine of *gnosis*, which he says means cognitive as well as mystical and sexual union, and which therefore is the only adequate word to express that kind of knowledge which comes with revelation, which contains both formal and emotional elements. This original sense of *gnosis* claims that there can be no contradiction between these poles because the same Logos which teaches the philosopher teaches the theologian. Tillich argues passionately for a view of revelation and salvation which includes not only the healing of the estranged "heart and soul," but also the mind of man. Final revelation conquers the conflict between theological (emotional) knowledge and scientific (formal) knowledge. For final revelation claims that "that which can be grasped only with 'infinite passion' (Kierkegaard) is identical with that which appears as the criterion in every act of rational knowledge."[154] Emotional knowledge implies unity. Formal knowledge implies separation. In the figure of Jesus as the Christ, Tillich sees both separation and unity appearing together in the Logos. And the Logos is the basis for every type of knowledge, formal or emotional.

And so the correlation is complete. The conflicts and tensions found in reason are answered by revelation. Moreover, the answer has been given in the form in which the question was asked.

SUMMARY AND ANALYSIS

We began our study of the nature of reason with the distinction which Tillich makes between the subjective and objective aspects of ontological reason. Subjective reason is the function of the mind in grasping and shaping reality. Objective reason is the structure of reality which allows itself to be grasped and shaped. This distinction is important, for *essentially* these two aspects of reason are united, but *existentially* they are separated. And it is this separation of subjective reason from the objective rational structure of the universe which causes the conflicts in actual reason. This situation causes reason to ask for revelation, to ask for an answer which can unite its divided functions. And for our study the most important supposition which Tillich makes in his examination of reason is that reason is *able* to ask for revelation, because ". . . in the actual life of reason its basic structure is never completely lost. . . . Therefore, the quest for a reunion of what is always split in time and space arises *out* of reason and not in opposition to reason." [83,85]

Following the method of correlation, we then moved from the analysis of the situation of reason and the questions arising from it to consider the nature of the answer found in revelation. In the phenomenological description of revelation as such, Tillich finds the experiences of mystery, ecstasy, and miracle always present; he finds that revelation may come through the media of nature or history, and that it always uses "the word," the expression of the rational structure which is the only way of communicating with or to man. Particularly important in this phenomenological description is Tillich's attempt to use revelation through nature and the *analogia entis* without implying a "natural revelation" or "natural theology." Tillich insists that the *analogia entis*, rather than allowing one to abstract the infinite from the finite, points to the necessity of using symbols taken from the finite to speak of the infinite, for that is the way of revelation.

We turned from Tillich's phenomenological description of general revelation to the criterion of revelation, the final revelation in Jesus as the Christ. And here arises the most critical point in this chapter, a point which indicates perhaps a basic flaw in the method of correlation. For basic to the method of correlation is the expectation and demand that the revelatory answer to man's questions take the form of those questions, fulfill their demands, and answer the questions in the terms in which they are asked. Man's question of reason was expressed in the three great conflicts: autonomy versus heteronomy; absolutism versus relativism; and formalism versus emotionalism. Thus the question of reason demands an answer which contains in itself the sacrifice of finitude to the infinite and demonstrates the transparency of the medium of revelation to the ground of being. Such an answer resolves the conflict between autonomy and heteronomy, and between absolutism and relativism. This answer must also contain the elements of both union and separation. For only then can it overcome the conflict between formal, detached reason and emotional, united reason. Such an answer to the conflicts of reason Tillich finds in the final revelation of Jesus as the Christ. And because he had to express that revelatory answer in the forms dictated above, he had to say, formally, that ". . . Jesus of Nazareth is sacrificed to Jesus as the Christ . . ."[135] and maintain at the same time that the material meaning of revelation remained unchanged.

Paul Tillich, by his own assessment, stands on the border between philosophy and theology. Such a position naturally brings him into conflict with those who remain on one side or the other of that line and who perhaps feel that there is little useful commerce possible between them. Such a prejudice from the theological side should be resisted, for there seem to this writer to be valuable insights for theology in Tillich's philosophical analysis of the conflicts of reason. The depth of his understanding of man's intellectual life will certainly find appreciation and expression in the work of any theologian or preacher who attempts to address himself to the human situation. For instance, the conflict between autonomy and heteronomy finds its religious expression in the problem of man's lack of faith on the one hand and his tendency for idolatry on the other. Other homiletical applications are possible, of which many examples are to be found in Tillich's own sermons. Furthermore, Tillich is quite right when he points out that union is necessary for real knowledge. The importance of this concept for the doctrine of revelation is obvious; because it has been ignored, Christendom is largely divided between those who view revelation as a deposit of truth in an ecclesiastical structure and those who see it as a

deposit of information in the written words of the Bible. Tillich
has emphasized correctly that the knowledge of revelation is
not the reception of information, but is the participation in an
encounter between man and God, and as such is synonymous
with salvation.

We also cannot but agree with Tillich that revelation, being
salvation, is healing, even if fragmentary, and that this saving
power of revelation heals also the conflicts of reason. For can
not and does not God in the self-manifestation of himself in the
Christ lead man to faith, break down his idols, and thus overcome in the realm of reason both autonomy and heteronomy?
Does he not unite man with himself, and at the same time affirm
and accept him as he is? He does, and Tillich is right in pointing out that the benefits of grace apply also in the realm of
reason.

Thus we can accept and applaud Tillich's description of the
conflicts of reason and their healing under the impact of revelation. But at the same time we must raise a question regarding
the way he finds it possible to move from one to the other. This
movement from existential question to theological answer, from
human reason to divine revelation, turns on two foci: the ability
of reason to ask for revelation, and the conformity of revelation
to that question.

Reason is able to ask for revelation because, Tillich argues,
"In the actual life of reason its basic structure is never completely lost . . ."[83] This "basic structure" he has called "the
depth of reason." This presence of the depth of reason, he feels,
is necessary because if reason were entirely cut off from the
eternal *logos* of being, it would have no basis in being and would
be destroyed in the very process of coming into existence. Tillich
is saying that God addresses himself to man as his creature,
and that man does not cease to be a part of creation in his
fallen state of existence. And he is saying that this creatureliness of man enables him to sense (or become aware of) his
ontic relationship to God, the ground of his being. Thus man
can ask for God, for revelation. Certainly we agree that man
does not cease to be God's creature. But the point is, how does

man know himself as creature—from an analysis of his own being, or from the fact that he is addressed as such? This is the real problem of natural theology which Tillich has not been able to escape. For has not natural theology always held, as Tillich does, that an analysis of man yields a general truth which explains his natural capacity for knowing the Word of God? Has it not always been the mark of natural theology that it has started with a general revelation of God in creation and moved from that point into the inner circle of specifically Christian theology based upon special revelation? Was this not true for Schleiermacher, who held that religious experience is the realization of a religious potentiality in man, quite apart from the special revelation of God in Christ?

Of course Tillich does not wish his concept of the depth of reason and man's natural ability to ask for revelation to be extrapolated beyond that specific meaning, or to be interpreted in such a way that it gives the content of revelation. But is not the ability simply to ask for revelation already saying too much? Dare we move beyond the interpretation of the *imago Dei* as *recta natura* to a *rectitudo* or even a *potentialiter*? If one says one more word than this, or goes one step further, it is difficult to see how he can avoid a natural theology. It is clear that Tillich repudiates natural theology in its more extreme pantheistic form. He does not believe that nature "reveals" anything about God to man. But is not the question as to whether revelation is found in, or apprehended through, nature a secondary one? Is not the question of natural theology one of anthropology? Is not the question that of whether man has within himself the knowledge of himself as a creature related in a particular way to his creator so that he may ask for him, or whether he learns this because, and only because, he has first been addressed as such? The former alternative is certainly the position of every natural theology and would seem, moreover, to be the position of Tillich. Again, when Tillich affirms the *analogia entis* with the qualification that it is in no way able to create a natural theology, we have to ask: Does it not in fact do just that when it enables man to say anything at all about God? Of course Tillich is

correct when he says that there must exist an analogy, a simili-
tude, between the infinite and the finite which allows man to
apply his language to God. But the question is whether this
analogy is one of being, preceding revelation, or whether it is
created by revelation and man's response to it in faith.

In defense of his position Tillich argues that if one abandons
the concept of the depth of reason, if reason has no innate ability
to ask for revelation, if the unity of being does not establish an
analogy which allows man to speak of God, then the knowledge
of revelation is rendered inexplicable.[10] But we must ask in return whether the above propositions do not render the fact and
reality of revelation inexplicable. If man asks for God, must
he not already know that it is "God" for whom he asks? In
this sense the question implies the presence of the answer, indeed
the question *is* the answer! Tillich maintains that while reason
can ask for revelation, the content of revelation must come from
somewhere else. But must it? Why is it not possible for reason
to abstract from its perception of the infinite within itself the
contents of the answer it seeks? In fact has not Tillich already
begun this process when he sees man's questions as determining
the form of the revelatory answer? And if we find that this
determination of form has radically altered and affected the
content of revelation, will not that abstraction be complete?
Our interest in this study is certainly not to find fault with
Tillich, still less to carry on a polemic against him, but rather
to learn from him and to understand him. But what are we to
take more seriously, his abhorrence of natural theology, his
sense of the estranged and fallen state of creation, or his concept
of the depth of reason and his use of the *analogia entis*?

The other problem which we find in the movement from reason
to revelation concerns the accommodation of revelation to this
movement. The method of correlation rests on the proposition
that revelation necessarily takes the form of the questions of

10 From a purely philosophical standpoint, John Herman Randall holds
that Tillich's definition of reason does not really lead to a need for revelation, insofar as its problems (i.e., the need for a concrete absolute) seem
solvable within itself (see *The Theology of Paul Tillich, op. cit.*, pp. 141 ff.;
see also Dorothy Emmet's comments, p. 210).

men and yet remains independent as to content. Regarding the relationship between reason and revelation, Tillich's thesis is that because the conflicts of reason require the sacrifice of the finite to the infinite in revelation, final revelation in Jesus as the Christ appears in the form of him who sacrifices Jesus of Nazareth to Jesus as the Christ. This formulation of revelation raises two closely related questions: Can the form and content of revelation be so distinguished as to be divided in this way, and does the self-manifestation of God in Jesus as the Christ actually appear in terms of the sacrifice Tillich has described?

It is certainly true that Jesus sacrificed himself, thus accomplishing the work of his office as the Christ. And it is certainly true that Jesus pointed away from himself to God the Father. But what is not certain at all is that this sacrifice can be correlated or even paralleled with what Tillich calls the necessity of sacrificing the finite medium.[11] Thus final revelation

---

[11] The single citation from Scripture which Tillich presents in support of this view is from John 12:44, where Jesus says, "He who believes in me, believes not in me . . ." ("*O pisteuon eis eme, ou-pisteuei eis eme*"). It depends of course upon which *eme* the emphasis is given, and the interpretation of that emphasis. The matter can be simply put: Is Jesus pointing away from himself at the expense of himself, or rather as an affirmation of himself? The latter interpretation would seem necessary simply because of the context. In the next verse we read, "And he who sees me sees him who sent me," and above, in verse 32, "and I, when I am lifted up from the earth, will draw all men to myself." And moreover, in the preceding chapter, at the tomb of Lazarus, it is this same Jesus preparing for his own sacrifice who says, "I am the resurrection and the life; he who believes in me, though he die, yet shall he live . . ." (11:25). Far from paralleling the need for the sacrifice of the finite medium of revelation, this sacrifice of Jesus would seem to be a very definite affirmation and glorification of that medium.

This was certainly the view of Luther, who, commenting on this passage, took the affirmation of Jesus for granted and even applied it to the ministers of his Word. "*Wir aber sagen, dass einer Predigers Wort . . . nicht einer menschen Stimme, sondern Gottes Stimme . . . ist . . .* [and then he adds!] *Da soll Gott und Mensch nicht metaphysich von ein-ander gesondert werden, sondern ich will den Einfältigen sagen, Dieser Mensch . . . ist die Stimme Gottes*" ("The word of the preacher . . . is not the voice of man, but the voice of God. Here God and man should not be metaphysically separated from each other, rather I say to the simple in heart that this man . . . is the voice of God") (Erwin Mülhaupt, *Martin Luthers Evangelien Auslegung*; Göttingen, 1954, Vol. IV, pp. 360-361).

The only alternative to seeing Jesus as affirmed in his sacrifice would be to distinguish in the New Testament between those occasions when Jesus speaks of himself as finite, and those when he speaks of himself as united

must sacrifice the form Jesus to the content of the Christ. But has it not always been the case in the Christian church that in this matter especially it can not and will not accommodate the form in which it received its gospel to any necessity? Was it not in the name of this demand that the Jews took up stones in order to bring about in their own way the sacrifice of Jesus to the Christ?[12] Could Peter have been more explicit in his refusal to accommodate this form when he preached "Jesus of Nazareth, a man . . ." was indeed sacrificed but "this Jesus, . . . God raised . . . up"?[13] Has not the church since the Council of Chalcedon held with more or less accuracy and seriousness that it is exactly and precisely in this man and no other, in this finite, human being that God reveals himself; that the eternal *logos* took this form and no other, that the Christ appears not only through, but in and with this man in such a way that they cannot possibly be separated? Is this man not more than a medium, is he not the revelation himself? Was Jesus sacrificed on the cross, but not the Christ? Was the Crucifixion any more an offering of humanity than divinity? Far from being the negation of finitude and humanity, was not the "lifting up" of this man its affirmation and glorification? It is most difficult to see how the form of revelation in Jesus as the Christ can possibly be interpreted in terms of an inner necessity of sacrificing its finite medium and not have violence done to its meaning and content.

Our point here is not to question Tillich's Christology as such, but only to see what it means for his view of revelation. This meaning becomes clear when we read that by sacrificing "Jesus," the finite medium, the Christ "becomes completely transparent to the mystery he reveals."[(133)] That is to say, another picture, a clearer image, is given apart from the man Jesus. And what is this picture, what is this image which shines through the "com-

---

with his identity as the Christ. That such a division is impossible has been generally accepted since the fourth century. Only because he was already from the beginning the Christ, could this Jesus say, "He who believes in me, believes not in me . . . ," because he was also that Other, which as yet they did not know.

[12] John 10:33.
[13] Acts 2:22-24.

pletely transparent" Christ? It is the picture of a "mystery"!
Here Tillich is perfectly consistent, for we have seen above
that for him the first mark of revelation is its mystery, and that
a mystery cannot cease to be mysterious. Its "revelation" indicates only our relation to its mysterious character, but it does
not cease to be a mystery. Is this really the function of revelation, to point us to a mystery? And insofar as revelation does
have a mysterious element, how will our relation to that mystery
become clear if our attention is averted for even one minute
from Jesus to the abyss which lies beyond him? Has not Tillich
made explicit what unfortunately was implicit in Calvin's view
of God as *Deus nudus absconditus*, namely, that behind and
removed from his self-manifestation in Jesus as the Christ, God
remains inscrutable and hidden?[14] And as was true in Calvin's
doctrine of predestination, will not this hidden and mysterious
God of Tillich be for man a danger and a threat rather than
salvation and promise? Of course there is mystery in revelation,
mystery enough in Christmas, Good Friday, and Easter! But the
point is that it is there where the mystery lies, there in the birth,
life, death, and Resurrection of that man, and not in the abyss
which lies beyond. The thing to which Christian theology must
hold fast is that in the event Jesus as the Christ, God's willing
and his doing are revealed. Both his purpose for man and its
accomplishment are seen only in him, and whatever may remain
mysterious, that much is clear. It is difficult to see how Tillich
can hold fast to this point if he conceives of the man Jesus as a
transient medium for an eternal principle called the Christ,
which only points beyond itself to a God about whom the most
that can be said is that he is both the abyss and the ground of
being. Such a view of revelation can only leave man in the most
radical doubt as to whether he will stand on that ground or fall
into that abyss.

[14] Such is clearly the case in an early lecture in which Tillich argues,
"Certainly for the Christian, Christ is the definite and concrete name of
God, the picture of the *Deus revelation*. But he is this only upon the basis
of the *Deus absconditus*" (Paul Tillich, "Rechtfertigung und Zweifel,"
Vorträge der theologischen Konferenz in Geissen; Geissen: Alfred Töpel-
mann, 1924, p. 27).

We have had to ask whether or not Tillich's concept of the depth of reason, which allows reason to ask the question of God, does not lead to and express a natural theology; and we have had to ask whether his conception of final revelation as the sacrifice of Jesus to the Christ does not change the form and thus the content of revelation in such a way as to make the fact of revelation inexplicable and ambiguous.

At this stage of our study, at least, we are not able to understand Tillich in this matter in the way we believe he wishes to be understood. He would want it differently, for in private conversation and public preaching, he voices the conviction that the beginning and end of any theology, his included, must be the self-manifestation of God in Jesus as the Christ and that this event is the necessary basis of every theological assertion. Moreover, there seems to be implied in the theology of Paul Tillich itself an a priori acceptance of God's saving revelation in Jesus as the Christ. This a priori is hinted at when the basis of the method of correlation is described thus: "... God answers man's questions, and under the impact of God's answers man asks them." [61][15] In this present chapter we hear echoes of this priority of God's action when Tillich says that Jesus as the Christ is given to experience and not derived from it. We hear it when he says that the content of faith grasps reason. It is certainly not Tillich's intention to present reason in such a way that it is seen to create its own "revelation"; rather he is trying to explain how it is possible for reason to hear the Word of God. Neither is it his intention to "do away with" the finite nature of Jesus as the Christ; rather he is seeking to indicate the depth and infinite significance of this event for man. Indeed he can speak of Jesus as one "who is united with the ground of his being and meaning without separation and disruption." [133] Tillich does not want to be understood as a natural theologian,

[15] John Dillenberger has also noted this a priori. "The marvel of Paul Tillich's theology is not that theological answers and philosophical . . . questions fit together so well. After all, why shouldn't they? Tillich has forged the questions, and he has formed them in the light of the answers . . ." ("Man and the World," *The Christian Century*, Vol. LXXVI, No. 22, June 3, 1959, p. 669).

still less as a Gnostic. And yet his *Systematic Theology* inevitably leads to such an understanding, because this a priori, this precedence of God's revelation, explicitly expressed elsewhere, remains hidden and is barely implicit in his system. Nor is this suppression accidental. He feels it is necessary for the relevance of theology. In describing how the systematic theologian proceeds with the method of correlation, Tillich writes that he must formulate the questions of man, "as though he had never received the revelatory answer . . ."[16]

But man, the systematic theologian included, has in fact received the answer. A Word has been spoken to him, and we cannot help but feel that any suppression or ignoring of that Word must have not only the gravest consequences for a correct interpretation of revelation, but must distort and obscure the actual human situation as well. Therefore, in spite of our acceptance of and appreciation for much of Tillich's presentation, we have had to understand him in a way which is perhaps basically against his own intention.

[16] Paul Tillich, *Systematic Theology*, Vol. II (Chicago: The University of Chicago Press, 1957), p. 15.

IV

BEING AND GOD

[This] part of the system must give an analysis of man's essential nature (in unity with the essential nature of everything that has being), and of the question implied in man's finitude and finitude generally; and it must give the answer which is God.[(66)1]

" 'God' is the answer to the question implied in man's finitude. [(211)] *[For] the being of God is being-itself . . . he is the power of being in everything and above everything, the infinite power of being.* [(261)]

We come now to the heart of Paul Tillich's theology, his ontology. Ontology is the study of being, and it is with being, man's being, that Tillich begins, and it is being-itself, God's being, to which he relates every part of his system.

Understanding this ontology is difficult because we stand (more so than Europeans) in the general tradition of nominalism, deriving the contents of thought from specific and particular objects of experience. Thus, such ontological and abstract concepts as "being-itself," "universals," "essences," and "categories" fall strangely on our ears, and only with the greatest difficulty can we ascribe any real meaning to them. But we must make the attempt, for Tillich's "vision" of ontology is the key to any understanding of his system of thought. We call this ontology a "vision" because Tillich's view of "being" is not something that can be "proved"; it is something that can only be intuited and accepted. It is a priori to all specific objects of man's experience. Thus if we are to follow and learn from him, our attitude toward his ontological analysis must be one of "a willing suspension of disbelief." We must accept and try to

---

[1] Numbers in parentheses in this chapter refer to page numbers in Tillich's *Systematic Theology*, Vol. I.

participate in his understanding of "being." If we do this we will be in a position to understand more fully what was meant in the last chapter when reason was called the "structure of being," and we shall be able to understand what Tillich means when he calls God "being-itself," or Christ the "New Being," or the Holy Spirit "the unity of the power and meaning of being."

One further word of introduction: We must always keep in mind the development of the method of correlation as it applies to each part of Tillich's system. In this part of his theology the question side of the correlation consists of an ontological study in which the situation of man in being is set forth, and the question arising from this situation is stated. The answer side consists of a general definition of "god" and then, specifically, the Christian doctrine of God as the ground and power of being which answers the question of man's being.

THE NATURE OF BEING

What is ontology? It is the study of "being." It is the attempt to understand the question: What does it mean that something "is"? This is the most basic question which can be asked. Thought does not arrive at this question through any logic or observation, it begins here. Thought cannot go behind, or find anything prior to, this question of "being." Moreover, this question itself implies some understanding of what "being" is. Thought then must begin with some preconceived notion of being. It cannot begin with "nothing," even "if one asks why there *is* not nothing, one attributes being even to nothing." [163] Ontology asks for the one thing held in common by all things insofar as they are said to be. What does it mean that a thing is or that a thing is not? This question is called by Tillich "first philosophy" and is therefore the basis of all philosophy.

But how can this question be answered? How can one discover the nature of "being"? What more can be said about a thing than that it simply *is*? The problem is this: usually, when we ask a question we base the question and judge any answer on some prior knowledge or experience. Thus, if for

instance I ask about the nature of my pipe, I must include in my
question a knowledge of what a pipe is, an acquaintance with
other pipes, and perhaps even some knowledge of the brier from
which they are made. On the basis of these special and definite
objects of knowledge, I can ask an "informed" question and find
or receive an answer. My knowledge of other things makes possible my question and gives the criteria upon which to judge the
answer. But if I ask about the "being" of a thing (my pipe),
this does not hold true. My question about "being" as it appears
in my pipe necessarily includes the question of the "being" of
every and all pipes, brier, metal, tobacco, or anything else I
might ordinarily use as a cognitive entrance to the knowledge of
pipes. The ontological question, the question of "being," differs
from all other questions in that it does not allow the questioner
to base his question or the reception of his answer on any prior
knowledge of particular and special things. For the question of
being as it appears in one thing implies the question of the
being of all other things. How then is the ontological question
possible—is it not reduced to the empty tautology that being is
being?

To this question nominalism would answer "yes!" Nominalism holds that man can only know particular objects of his
experience and so-called "universals" ("being-itself," "being-
as-such") are mere abstractions from particulars with no reality
in themselves. They are only tools for grouping particulars.
Thus a concept like "being-itself" would simply be the highest
possible abstraction, and one would not learn anything real from
it.

But, Tillich argues, nominalism cannot explain how one can
know even particulars. It cannot explain this because the possibility of knowledge implies some structure which unites subject
and object in the act of cognition, and such a structure transcends the particulars of experience, for it is grounded in being-
as-such, or being-itself. One can and must ask about the nature
of being, Tillich maintains, because reason cannot be confined to
the realm of the particulars of experience, but must ask about
the structure of being which makes such experience possible.

Again, nominalism claims that ontology is impossible because it is based on the pure abstraction of universal being, which abstraction has no basis in experience and which, therefore, cannot be known. But Tillich claims that "Ontology is possible because there are concepts which are less universal than being but more universal than any . . . concept designating a realm of beings." [164] Such concepts are called "principles" or "categories," and they tell something about the nature of being. They give reason some place to stand when asking the ontological question. They cannot be "proved"; they are not derived logically from experience; they are strictly a priori, and can only be accepted. But they can be accepted, says Tillich, because, while not derived from experience, they appear in experience and are thus self-evident. "Man is able to answer the ontological question himself because he experiences directly and immediately the structure of being and its elements."[169] Tillich distinguishes four levels of such ontological concepts: (1) the basic ontological structure; (2) the elements which constitute that structure; (3) the characteristics of being found in existence; and (4) the categories of being and knowing. An elaboration of these concepts renders a definition of "being" and gives basis and content to the ontological question.

The Structure of Being

What is this structure of being which man "experiences"? The very fact of the ontological question implies that being has a subject-object structure. If a question is asked, there is an asking subject and an object about which it asks. This subject-object structure of being is immediately experienced by man in terms of his own self and the world. "A self," Tillich argues, "is not a thing that may or may not exist; it is an original phenomenon which logically precedes all questions of existence."[169] By "self" he means a centered structure (*Gestalt*) which includes both the central point from which actions and reactions occur and the environment, area, or world in terms of which the center is defined. Thus everything has centeredness and selfhood. Tillich says that in Descartes' famous formula, "*Cogito, ergo sum,''* the "self" is not established by the fact of thought. The self is rather the basis and self-evident a priori of thought. However, the "I" in Descartes' formula is established through thought. Man is qualitatively different from other "selves" in that through thought or self-consciousness, he has an "I-self." "Man is a fully developed and completely centered self. He 'possesses' himself in the form of self-consciousness. He has an ego-self." (169-170)

But the self does not stand alone; man experiences himself as having a world to which he belongs. It now becomes clear what was meant in Chapter I when we said that Tillich begins with man—man in the relation self-world. Man cannot be considered as an isolated "point"; he is always related to his world either dependently or independently. He has an environment (which he may change and shape) and he belongs to an environment (which changes and shapes him). "The interdependence of ego-self and world is the basic ontological structure and implies all the others." (171)

The Elements of Being

The elements which constitute the self-world and subject-object structure of being are: individualization and participation, dynamics and form, and freedom and destiny. These elements, like the basic structure of being, appear as polarities, and are always apprehended in their polar relation. The reader's attention is especially directed to these three polarities because they, together with the categories, form the structure within which Tillich analyzes the human situation in the other three parts of his system.

The first pair of ontological elements is individualization and participation. We have defined the self as a structural center, and have said that everything that is has such a center, or self. Individualization therefore is not a special characteristic of some beings, but is also a quality of everything that is and is therefore an ontological element. But individualization implies participation. Man, for instance, is an individual because he participates in his world. The individual self is a part of the world. This means that a self includes within itself that in which it participates. As "an individual leaf participates in the natural structures and forces which act upon it" and therefore has "microscopic qualities," so also, Tillich claims, "man . . . is *microcosmos*." [176] Man contains within himself the universe because he participates in the universe through his ability to grasp universal structures, forms, and laws. As we have seen, upon this concept of man as microcosmos Tillich bases the possibility of both revelatory and natural knowledge, and a view of man as the proper object of ontological analysis.

The next two elements of being are dynamics and form. " 'Being something' means having a form." [178] It is impossible to conceive of anything without some constitutive structure. In this sense, "form should not be contrasted with content. The form which makes a thing what it is, is its content, its *essentia*. . . . The form of a tree is what makes it a tree." [178] Now form is not a dormant or static concept. "Every form forms something. The question is: What is this 'something'? We have called it 'dynamics,' . . ." [179] "Dynamics" is a difficult concept to grasp due to the fact that if one names a thing, it must have being, and therefore form. How then can something be put in a polar relation to form if everything that is has form? The answer is that although he gives it a name, Tillich does not consider dynamics "to be," it is not something that "is." It is something about-to-be. Dynamics is "the potentiality of being, which is nonbeing in contrast to things that have a form, and the power of being in contrast to pure nonbeing." [179] This importance of the distinction between potential being, which Tillich calls *me on*, and pure non-being, which he calls *ouk on*, will be discussed below.

In man the polarity of dynamics and form appears as the polarity of vitality and intentionality. "The dynamic element in man is open in all directions; . . . Man is able to create a world beyond the given world; . . . This is his vitality . . ." [180] But man's vitality does not go in all directions; it is directed and formed toward meaningful contents by his intentionality. Neither vitality nor intentionality can exist alone; "They are interdependent, like the other polar elements." [181]

The third pair of ontological elements is freedom and destiny. This polarity is most important for Tillich's theology, for it is largely in terms of his understanding of these two concepts that he interprets the doctrines of creation, the Fall, and providence. And although we shall find all three polarities treated throughout his system, it is Tillich's understanding of freedom and destiny upon which his argument most often rests. "Man is man because he has freedom, but he has freedom only in polar interdependence with destiny."[182] Freedom is usually spoken of in contrast to necessity. This Tillich feels is wrong because when freedom and necessity are put together, necessity is thought of as mechanistic determinancy and freedom as indeterministic contingency. This either/or of chance and necessity does not correspond to what man actually experiences in terms of freedom. "Man experiences . . . freedom within the larger structures to which the individual structure belongs. Destiny points to this situation in which man finds himself, facing the world to which, at the same time, he belongs."[182-183] Another reason that Tillich objects to the traditional discussion between determinism and indeterminism is that both sides assume that there is a "thing" called "will" which may or may not be free. It is one of the insights of Tillich's ontology that a "thing," as pure object, is completely determined and therefore, by definition, lacks freedom. "The *freedom* of a *thing* is a contradiction in terms."[183] Thus determinism always wins its argument, but all that is proved is that a thing is a thing.

Tillich insists that it is not something called "the will," but man who is free. And man is not a thing. Freedom is experienced by man as deliberation, in which he weighs arguments and motives, being free of all of them; it is experienced as decision, in which real possibilities are "cut off"; and it is experienced as responsibility, which reflects man's awareness that his decisions are not determined by anything outside of himself, or any part of himself, but his whole, centered self. In each case freedom is bound to the situation in which it is experienced.

If freedom is seen in this way, Tillich maintains that the meaning of destiny becomes understandable. Destiny is the environment of the self; it is the situation or context out of which decisions arise. "Destiny is not a strange power which determines what shall happen to me. It is myself as given, formed by nature, history, and myself. My destiny is the basis of my freedom; my freedom participates in shaping my destiny."[185] Destiny is not the opposite of freedom; it rather sets its conditions and its limits. "Only he who has freedom has a destiny. Things have no destiny because they have no freedom."[185] Neither can exist without the other. They constitute a basic polarity of being.[2]

The basic structure of being is the polarity of self and world, or subject and object. This basic structure is expressed in the ontological elements, which appear in the polarities of individualization and participation, dynamics and form, and freedom and destiny. We must now continue our investigation of the nature of being through a study of terms which we have used in Chapters II and III, but which now require a more detailed definition.

Being and Non-Being, the Infinite and the Finite, Essence and Existence

(1) Being and Non-Being: When a man asks, "What is the basis of my being, why *am* I *not*?", he has envisaged nothingness and has applied it to himself, to his own being. But as the use of the verb in the question indicates, he attributes being even to nothingness. The absolute opposite of being cannot be expressed. For this reason Parmenides excluded it from rational thought. But Tillich does not mean by non-being this inexpressible opposite. If an anticipated event does not appear, one makes a negative judgment that the awaited event and conditions are non-existent. This negative judgment implies the distinction between that which is and that which is not, between being and non-being. Non-being is that which makes it possible for man to step back from and look at being, his own being, and make this distinction.

Non-being is a part of being, but what kind of being is it? We have spoken of dynamics and have said that it expresses what

---

2 In commenting on the debate over humanism between Luther and Erasmus, Tillich says, "Luther's assertion that man's will is in bondage to demonic structures is meaningful only if man, in his essential nature, is free" (*The Protestant Era, op. cit.*, p. 129).

the Greeks called *me on* or the potentiality of being. Non-being is
me on. It is that which does not yet have being, but which can
become being. This is opposed to *ouk on*, by which the Greeks
meant that kind of nothing which has no relation to being. *Ouk
on* is a name for the *nihil* out of which God created the universe;
it is the absolute negation of being. But the non-being of which
Tillich speaks, *me on*, is different. Augustine referred to it when
he spoke of sin as "non-being." He did not mean that sin has
no reality, but rather that it has only a negative ontological
standing, it perverts and resists being. This is Tillich's understanding of non-being, which concept he finds necessary in the
doctrine of God, for ". . . if there is no negative principle in
addition to [God] which could account for evil and sin, how can
one avoid positing a dialectical negativity in God himself?"[189]
But this implies no Manichaeistic dualism, for while non-being
stands over against being, it is a part of being, it is a part of
being-itself. Non-being does not stand alongside of being-itself,
for in God non-being is continually overcome by his power of
being.[3] In man, however, non-being is not overcome. It exists in
polar tension with his being and is always present as a danger
and a threat. For man may lose his being, he may succumb to
non-being and die, or he may fail to realize his potentiality and
not develop. This in fact happens. Finite being, man, is a mixture
of being and non-being.

(2) The Infinite and the Finite: The mixture of being and
non-being in which non-being is not overcome, but limits being,
is called by Tillich "finitude." "Nonbeing appears as the 'not
yet' of being and as the 'no more' of [finite] being."[189] This
negative and limiting effect which non-being has upon man constitutes his finitude. But at the same time man is more than
finite. "In order to experience his finitude, man must look at
himself from the point of view of a potential infinity."[190] One
could not see his whole life moving toward death unless he were

---

[3] Tillich says that if God's "No" were not overcome in himself, his
"Yes" would have no meaning. See *The Courage To Be, op. cit.*, pp. 169 ff.
He also says, "Being 'embraces' itself and nonbeing. Being has nonbeing
'within' itself as that which is . . . eternally overcome in the process of
the divine life" (p. 34).

able to transcend himself as finite and look upon himself as possibly infinite. This power of imagining infinity "is an expression of man's belonging to that which is beyond nonbeing, namely, to being-itself."[191]

(3) Essence and Existence: The distinction between essence and existence is absolutely central in Tillich's ontology and lies at the heart of all his work. By "essence" Tillich means that which makes a thing what it is and that against which a thing is judged; it is the power of being and the criterion of being. By "existence" he means actuality; it is that which is "fallen" from essence. "Whenever the ideal is held against the real, truth against error, good against evil, a distortion of essential being is presupposed . . ."[202] But the question arises, "How can being, including within it the whole of its actuality, contain its own distortion?"[202] And the only possible answer is that there must be within being-itself a distinction between what is essential and what is distorted, or existential. Tillich follows the mediating position of Aristotle between the ontology of Plato, who judged existence negatively, holding that the essential was the only good, and Ockham, who held the nominalist thesis that only existence is real and dismissed the concept of essences altogether. Christianity, Tillich insists, must (against Plato) view existence as the fulfillment of creation, as the actualized expression of being-itself in God's creativity. But at the same time it must (against Ockham) emphasize the split between created goodness and distorted existence. It must see the unity and estrangement of essence and existence. "The distinction between essence and existence, which religiously speaking is the distinction between the created and the actual world, is the backbone of the whole body of theological thought."[204]

We have analyzed the nature of being and have found that it has a polar structure which is expressed in the correlates, self and world, and subject and object. This structure contains the elements of individuality and participation, dynamics and form, and freedom and destiny. We have also noted the distinction which Tillich makes between being and non-being, the infinite and the finite, and essence and existence. Essential being includes within itself non-being, but is not disrupted or split by this inclusion. Finite and existential being, however, is split, disrupted, and threatened by non-being. It is the purpose of this part of *Systematic Theology* not only to analyze being but to show how this threat to finite and existential being raises the question of God. It is to this question which we now must turn.

THE QUESTION OF FINITE BEING

The basic question of finitude arises from the situation of finite being, which, having less than the power of being-itself, is threatened by non-being. This threat may take the form of approaching and inevitable death; it may take the form of the limitation imposed upon the self by the world; or it may take the form of an existential awareness of the disruption between what we are and what we should be, between our essential and actual being. In this situation, finite being can do nothing but courageously affirm itself over against and in spite of the non-being which threatens it. The fact that finite being does not succumb to non-being, but continues to be, proves that this "courageous" affirmation in fact takes place. But where is the basis for such a courage to be found? Because the answer to this question is to be found only in the ground and power of being, it is the question of God. This question is asked in many different ways, some of which are presented by Tillich in the following study of finitude in relation to the categories and the ontological elements.

The Categories and the Question of Finitude

"Categories are the forms in which the mind grasps and shapes reality."[192] They are "ways of speaking"; one cannot express a rational thought without using some category, be it time, space, causality, or substance. These are forms of finite being, and as such they participate in the mixture of being and non-being which we have described above. They unite a positive and a negative element, and the tension between them raises the question of God.

Time, looked at negatively, is the movement ". . . from a past that is no more toward a future that is not yet through a present which is nothing more than the moving boundary line between past and future."[193] If a thing is said to be, it must be "present"; therefore, "if the present is illusory, being is conquered by nonbeing."[193] Looked at positively, time has a creative, direct, and irreversible character. It can symbolize movement and life. The conflict between the positive and the negative attributes of time becomes critical on the level of human awareness. Man experiences the anxiety of transitoriness; he knows that time is moving him toward death, toward non-being. And so "he affirms the present through an ontological courage . . ."[194] This "courage" to affirm being over against non-being is "ontological"; it is not a product of faith or hope. If this "courage" did not exist naturally in man, Tillich argues, man would give up his being in the very moment of coming into existence. If he did not naturally affirm temporality, man would surrender to the annihilating character of time; he would resign from having a present. But still one must ask upon what basis man has this courage, and this is the question of God.[4]

Space is closely related to time because to be present means to be present someplace. All beings must have space, and they protect their being by protecting and cultivating their space, be it a home, a country, a group, or a vocation. But the very fact that all beings must have space means that they are threatened by non-being, for man is constantly losing his space. He moves from one place to the other, and ultimately he knows he will lose every space, for he will die. "The loss of space includes the loss of temporal presence, the loss of the present, the loss of being."[195] Thus man is faced with the anxiety and insecurity of spacelessness, but in the face of this threat he nonetheless "courageously" affirms his space, he fights to protect it and enlarge it. But what is the basis for this ontological courage? This is the question of God.

Causality also expresses the mixture of being and non-being

---

[4] Tillich does not mean to imply that this ontological courage, in which man affirms his being in spite of the threat of non-being, establishes his being in such a way that it does not need saving. The elaboration of the nature of this courage and its basis in God as the ground and power of being is the whole aim of *The Courage To Be*. This book, apart from his *Systematic Theology* itself, is a most important source for Tillich's theology.

found in finitude. "If something is causally explained, its reality is affirmed. . . . The cause makes its effect real . . . To look for causes means to look for the power of being in a thing."[195-196] But at the same time causality expresses non-being, for if a thing has a cause, it is not its own cause; it does not possess its own power of being. This negative side of causality is expressed in man in the anxiety "of not being in, of, and by one's self." This is man's ". . . anxiety about the lack of necessity of his being. He might not be! Then why is he? And why should he continue to be?" [196] But again, man is endowed with an "ontological courage" to face the fact of his contingency and at the same time to rest in and depend upon himself. Such a courage is necessary and true for all of life. But how is it possible? What is the basis for such a courage? This is the question of God.

Substance is "something underlying the flux of appearances, something which is relatively static and self-contained."[197] Everything that is has substance and accidents. The accidents depend upon their substantial basis in being, and the substance of a thing is dependent upon the accidents through which its being finds expression. The problem of substance is seen in the problem of change. The process of change (changing accidents) threatens the substantiality of a thing; it may lose its power of being; it is threatened by non-being. This is the root, says Tillich, of man's fear of change; it is not that he fears the change itself, but the threat of non-being which accompanies change. But man accepts this threat and meets it with a natural or ontological courage in which he affirms the attributes of his identity, which are really accidental, by attributing to them substantiality. The four categories of time, space, causality, and substance show the dialectical nature of finitude. "They express the union of being and nonbeing in everything finite. They articulate the courage which accepts the anxiety of nonbeing. The question of God is the question of the possibility of this courage."[198]

The Elements and the Question of Finitude

Finitude is that form of being which is threatened by nonbeing. We have seen how that threat is expressed in the categories; we shall now see how it is expressed in the ontological elements. The ontological elements appear in finite being in tension and conflict. This lack of balance arises from the fact that finite being is not the whole of being; it may express one side of the polarity more than the other. Thus man sees that he is not what he essentially is, namely a balanced whole. He sees that he is threatened by a disruption and break in the polarities of being, which would be a destruction of the very structure of his own being.

The polarity of individualization and participation appears in finitude as the threat of loneliness over against the threat of collectivization. On the one hand the outer-relatedness of the self to the world and other people is threatened, and on the other hand the collective swallows individuality and self-relatedness. Man "oscillates anxiously between individualization and participation, aware of the fact that he ceases to be if one of the poles is lost, for the loss of either pole means the loss of both."[199]

The polarity of dynamics and form as it appears in finitude also appears in a tension which threatens to split one pole from the other. Dynamics must produce form, otherwise being has no actuality. "But at the same time dynamics is threatened because it may lose itself in rigid forms, and, if it tries to break through them, the result may be chaos, which is the loss of both dynamics and form."[199-200] Man is thus made anxious that his vitality may be lost in formalism (law and custom). And on the other hand he experiences the anxiety "of a chaotic formlessness in which both vitality and intentionality will be lost."[200]

The polarity of freedom and destiny perhaps shows most clearly the tension between the elements incumbent upon finitude. The necessities of destiny threaten man's freedom, and the contingencies of his freedom threaten his destiny. Man is always "in danger of trying to preserve his freedom by arbitrarily defying his destiny and of trying to save his destiny by surrendering his freedom."[200] This split is disastrous, for without freedom man becomes a determined "thing" and loses his power of being. Without destiny he loses the meaning of his being; there is no direction for his life. This is why absolute freedom, if put in opposition to destiny, becomes mere arbitrariness, which always in the end falls victim to natural law. "The loss of a meaningful destiny involves the loss of freedom also."[201]

Finitude, the mixture of being and non-being, is threatened by disruption and destruction. But this threat need not become an actuality, and if it does not, the question arises: What power of being can save it from final disruption and the loss of being? This is the question of God.

The Logical Argument for God

Before proceeding to that answer, Tillich asks on what basis man is able to ask about God, and whether finite being, as it appears in human reason, can answer this question. Is there a way from finite being to the infinite? Can reason "prove" the existence of God? Let us use as an example Anselm's classic ontological proof.

> ... thou [God] art a being than which nothing greater can be conceived ...
>
> ... even the fool is convinced that something exists in the understanding, at least, than which nothing greater can be conceived. ...
>
> And assuredly that, than which nothing greater can be conceived, cannot exist in the understanding alone. For ... then it can be conceived to exist in reality; which is greater.
>
> Therefore, if that, than which nothing greater can be conceived, exists in the understanding alone, the very being, than which nothing greater can be conceived, is one, than which a greater [that is, real] can be conceived. But obviously this is impossible.
>
> Hence, there is no doubt that there exists a being, than which nothing greater can be conceived, and it exists both in the understanding and in reality.[5]

What Anselm is saying is simply this: if one "thinks" God, and calls him the "greatest," God must have objective as well as subjective reality, for if God (the greatest) existed only in the

5 St. Anselm, *Proslogium*, tr. Sidney N. Deane (Chicago: Open Court, 1903), chs. 2-4, pp. 7-8.

mind, he would not be the greatest, because the mind can conceive of a "greater," that is, a God who also exists, objectively, really. For Anselm the idea of God prohibits his being confined to mere subjectivity. If he is the greatest, he *must* have objective as well as subjective standing in being. All arguments for God's existence turn on the presupposition that "existence," objective reality, is somehow an "addition" to being, and that as such it can be applied to God.

Tillich, however, maintains that existence is a part of being-itself; it is not an addition. On the other hand, God is not a being who "exists," because "The ground of being cannot be found within the totality of beings. . . God does not exist. He is being-itself beyond essence and existence. Therefore, to argue that God exists is to deny him."[(205)] The Anselmic proof, then, does not "prove" God, but it does, Tillich argues, demonstrate that finitude can ask the question of God. Such "proofs" "are expressions of the *question* of God which is implied in human finitude. This question is their truth; every answer they give is untrue."[(205)] Man can ask the question of God because, being aware of his finitude, he is aware of infinity; being aware of his contingency, he is aware of the unconditioned. Therefore Tillich defends these ontological arguments, not as arguments, but as analyses, because they show what is so important for his own theology, namely that "The question of God is possible because an awareness of God is present in the question of God. This awareness precedes the question."[(206)6]

This concludes the first half of the method of correlation as it applies to this part of the theological system. We have analyzed man's situation in being, and we have seen how this situation

---

6 Tillich is both philosophically and theologically correct in rejecting the Anselmic "proof" for the existence of God. But can it be said that this proof demonstrates a natural "awareness" of the unconditional in man? After all, was not Anselm's argument *"Fides* quaerens intellectum"? Indeed, he addresses himself to God in whose reality he already believes, for the whole "proof" appears in the context of a prayer! Has not Tillich perhaps missed the point that in Anselm's argument we are at least given an example of the correct method of theology, namely, that the question of God's being may not proceed from a general "awareness" of an unconditional element in man, but rather can only arise from and follow faith in and acceptance of the reality of the specific God of revelation?

raises the question of the ground and power of being which can be the basis of man's courage to be. This question can only be answered by the second half of Tillich's method: the exposition of the answer of God.

A GENERAL DEFINITION OF "GOD"

In the last chapter we saw that Tillich gave a phenomenological description of "revelation" in order to establish a definition of the object of his study. This methodology is also followed here. Before answering the question of being in the doctrine of God, Tillich offers a description of what men mean by "god." He believes this aids in the interpretation of the reality of God and gives the theologian a ". . . tool with which an interpretation of the nature and the development of the phenomena which are called 'religious' may be fashioned."[212] The main theme found throughout this discussion is the necessity of concreteness over against ultimacy and transcendence in the idea of god. Whatever man holds as his ultimate concern he calls "god." But he can be concerned only with that which he encounters concretely, and he can only be concerned ultimately with that which transcends every concrete and finite concern.

This ambivalence between the concrete and the ultimate is seen in that characteristic of the divine called "holiness." "Only that which is holy can give man ultimate concern, and only that which gives man ultimate concern has the quality of holiness."[215] The holy always appears concretely in holy objects; something or someone is holy. But this entails the risk of the loss of ultimacy, which is the idolatrous and demonic identification of man's ultimate concern with the mere objective medium of the holy. The holy loses its character of transcendence when identified with the secular, but on the other hand, "the holy needs to be expressed and can be expressed only through the secular, for it is through the finite alone that the infinite can express itself."[218] Whenever man experiences the divine, he is met with the ambivalent situation of the ultimate appearing in the concrete, which very concreteness threatens the ultimate character of the divine.

Tillich considers this conflict between the concrete and the ultimate in the concept of god to be the key to the whole history of religion. In a brilliantly concise analysis, he argues that polytheism arises from the need of concreteness in religion; that the need for ultimacy, or the absolute, causes a reaction toward monotheism; and that "the need for a balance between the concrete and the absolute drives [man] toward trinitarian structures."[221]

Polytheism expresses the concrete side of man's concept of the divine, and is not so much a matter of a number of gods as it is a concept of "god" which lacks a unifying principle. Tillich distinguishes three types of polytheism: the universalistic, the mythological, and the dualistic. The "universalistic" type of polytheism (e.g., pantheism) expresses a view of "god" as a universal and all-pervading power which appears in special persons, places, or things. It does not lack a sense of the absolute and therefore does not degenerate into separate gods, but neither does it conceive of the divine as one. It is neither fully concrete nor fully universal. The "mythological" type interprets the divine in various gods who represent broad realms of value and meaning. The necessity of concreteness is served by the "personal" aspect of each god. They partake fully in finitude and afford man the person-to-person relationship he requires. But, on the other hand, they express ultimacy and universality by transcending finitude in either a superhuman or subhuman way. This expression of ultimacy is a reaction within polytheism to the reduction of the divine to human finitude. The need for the absolute is also seen where a particular god is raised above the rest or where all the gods are made subject to a higher principle— such as fate in Greek mythology. The "dualistic" type of polytheism seeks to solve the ambiguity of the demonic and the holy in the divine by splitting divinity, giving to one god the qualities of goodness and creativity and to the other the qualities of evil and destruction. Dualism, by its very nature, denies the ultimacy of one God. But even here monistic and absolute elements intrude insofar as the good god is usually considered the more powerful and is ultimately victorious over evil. In every type of polytheism there is a movement toward monotheism, toward the absolute without which man's concrete god could not have ultimate significance.

The mark of monotheism is not that it allows only one god, but that the principle of ultimacy prevails over the concrete. Within monotheism Tillich distinguishes the monarchistic, the mystical, the exclusive, and the trinitarian types. "Monarchistic monotheism lies on the boundary line between polytheism and monotheism."[225] One god rules over and is the ontological basis of all the others. But he is threatened by these other gods; the concreteness of polytheism threatens the ultimacy of monotheism. Tillich sees the phrase "Lord of Hosts" in the Old Testament as indicative of a residue of this type of religion in Judaism. "Mystical" monotheism transcends the gods "in favor of the divine ground and abyss from which they come and in which they disappear."[226] The demonic application of divine power to concrete finitude is overcome by the establishment of an absolutely transcendent One. But because of man's desire for a personal god, this type of monotheism leaves itself open for the intrusion of concrete gods. This happened in Hinduism where the ultimate, Brahman-Atman, came to be expressed in the various gods of Hindu piety. "Exclusive" monotheism alone is able to resist polytheism. It is ". . . created by the elevation of a concrete god to ultimacy and universality without the loss of his concreteness and without the assertion of a demonic claim."[227] This God (and here Tillich changes to the uppercase *G*) is absolute over against every other god, and he is concrete in his self-manifestation in the nation of Israel. And this concreteness does not dissolve his ultimacy and degenerate into polytheism because the concrete medium, Israel, is not raised to ultimacy. But because God's ultimate and universal character tends to obscure his nature as a living God, "exclusive monotheism needs an expression of the concrete element in man's ultimate concern. This posits the trinitarian problem."[228]

"Trinitarian" monotheism is not a matter of the number three. "It is a qualitative and not a quantitative characterization of God."[228] It is the quality of God which allows man to speak of him as living; it is the concept which unites the ultimate and the concrete in God. "Trinitarian monotheism is concrete monotheism."[228] Tillich sees the movement toward trinitarianism in monarchical monotheism when the highest god makes himself concrete in incarnations. He sees it in mystical monotheism when, for instance, in Hinduism the Brahma is separated from the Brahma principle and united with Shiva and Vishnu to form a divine triad.

What does Tillich seek to show by this survey of religious history? He is not seeking to demonstrate, as did some forms of nineteenth-century liberalism, that there is a line of religious progress in human history, and he should not be attacked as if he were. What he is trying to prove is that progress has been made in the "idea of god."[7] There has been progress in overcoming the conflict between ultimacy and concreteness in man's conception of the divine, a progress which culminates in the trinitarian ideas found in various religions. That man's interpretation of his ultimate concern should show this development is most important for Tillich's system. For it is one of the cardinal points of the method of correlation that God does not answer questions which have not been asked: he does not address himself to man in "strange" forms, but in forms which are acceptable to man's interpretation of his own situation. If God is seen as one who is both ultimate and concrete, there must be an acceptance of this idea of "god" before he can reveal himself as such. That this prior understanding of the phenomenon of "god" actually exists is the point of this study.

To recapitulate: We have seen that man's situation in being causes him to ask for the ground and power of all being, and for the basis of his own courage to be. We have seen that man's ability to ask the question of God is based on his knowledge of his own finitude. And he expects an answer in the form of a god, who is both concrete and absolute. Thus we now are ready for the

---

[7] Such an "idea of god" is seen by Tillich as a function of religion, but not revelation. This distinction makes understandable such statements as ". . . revelation is not possible without the preceding religious experience of mankind . . ." (Paul Tillich, "Natural and Revealed Religion," *Christendom*, Vol. I, No. 1, Autumn, 1935, p. 165).

second half of the method of correlation in which the dogmatic
assertion of God as the basis of being is given, and the way in
which he answers man's question of his own being is explained.

THE DOCTRINE OF GOD AND THE ANSWER
TO THE QUESTION OF BEING GENERALLY

God as Being

The fundamental proposition of Paul Tillich's theological
system is that "God is being-itself."[(235)] He has being, he is
being, but he is not a being. "Even if he is called the 'highest
being' . . . When applied to God, superlatives become diminu-
tives."[(235)] God is the ground and power of being; he cannot be
placed in a category with other beings, even if elevated above
them.

"As being-itself God is beyond the contrast of essential and
existential being."[(236)] God is not threatened by non-being but
includes it as that which he overcomes. Thus God's being is
"prior" to the split between essential and existential being. God
is not "essence"; that is to say, he is not the totality of finite
possibilities. Even less should God be identified with existence.
To say that God "exists" makes him "a being whose existence
does not fulfill his essential potentialities; . . . It is as atheistic
to affirm the existence of God as it is to deny it."[(236-237)8] God
does not exist as a being. He is the ground and power of being
and as such is the answer to the question of being generally.
Everything that is has both its origin and its power to be in him.

God as Knowable

Man is finite, and whatever he knows he knows in terms of
finitude. He escapes from his finite prison only by his awareness
of what Tillich has called the depth of reason, by his ability to
"imagine" the infinite. But he cannot describe or have any cog-

---

[8] John H. Hick has pointed out that when Tillich says that God does not
exist, he means that God does not exist in the way that man exists. He is
simply trying to formulate a discrimination between the necessary and
unconditional being of God and the contingent being of man. See Hick's
very fine article, "The Idea of Necessary Being" in *The Princeton
Seminary Bulletin*, Vol. LIV, No. 2 (Nov., 1960), pp. 11-21.

nitive relation with the infinite except through that which he really knows, the categories of finitude. Thus the question arises: How can man "know" God? How can he legitimately apply segments of finite knowledge to the infinite? He can, answers Tillich, because "that which is infinite is being-itself and because everything participates in being-itself."[(239)] This, as we saw in the last chapter, is Tillich's understanding of the *analogia entis*. He insists that while it does not give us knowledge of God, the *analogia entis* does explain the *possibility* of knowing and saying anything about God.

If man can only approach God through the categories of finitude, this means that everything that he says about God is necessarily symbolic except "the statement that God is being-itself . . ."[(238)9] Every other statement about God is necessarily symbolic, for it points beyond itself. A symbol differs from a sign in that it participates in that to which it points; the possibility of this participation has been explained in the statement that all being participates in being-itself.

Naïve criticism of symbolism has often been based either on the belief that symbols are not "true" or that they indicate something "not real." Tillich objects to both criticisms. "The truth of a religious symbol has nothing to do with the truth of the

---

[9] Unless symbols indicate that which is known directly and unsymbolically at some point, symbolic knowledge is emptied of all "real" content and is reduced to the circular argument of a thing being a symbol of a symbol of a symbol, ad infinitum. This point has been raised by both Charles Hartshorne and John Herman Randall (in *The Theology of Paul Tillich, op. cit.*, pp. 160-161, 195), who ask from different points of view whether even Tillich's concept of "being-itself" is non-symbolic.

Tillich has acknowledged their criticism and has amended the above statement to read: ". . . the statement that everything we say about God is symbolic . . . . is not symbolic" (*Systematic Theology*, Vol. II, p. 9). But at the same time he admits that this correction does not solve the logical problem of symbolism. He knows that "if we make *one* non-symbolic assertion about God, his ecstatic-transcendent character seems to be endangered" (*ibid.*); and the whole rationale for the necessity of symbolism is lost. This "dialectical difficulty" cannot be resolved, and so we must content ourselves with the picture of the human situation which Tillich is trying to present through its use.

He is trying to show that "Although man is actually separated from the infinite, he could not be aware of it if he did not participate in it potentially" (*ibid.*). There is no way out of or around this dialectical situation, for it is the human situation.

empirical assertions involved in it . . ."[240] A symbol can only be judged on the accuracy with which it expresses that to which it points. "A symbol *has* truth [if] it is adequate to the revelation it expresses. A symbol *is* true [if] it is the expression of a true revelation."[240] Those who distrust symbols as "non-real" have usually identified the real with empirical reality (as in the nominalist tradition). But as we have seen, Tillich rejects such a view. He certainly does not intend to weaken the reality of religious terminology by insisting upon its symbolic nature. Again and again he attacks the phrase "only a symbol." Much criticism of Tillich's symbolism has been irrelevant because it has overlooked his intention, which is ". . . to give to God and to all his relations with man more reality and power than a nonsymbolic and therefore easily superstitious interpretation could give them."[241]

God as Living

If we speak of God as "living," we use a symbol taken from man's finite being. But God can and must be said to live, for as the ground of being he is also the ground of life. Thus, theology may describe the nature of being-itself, the divine life, in terms of the structure of being as it appears in human life. We remember that this structure is composed of the "ontological elements," individualization and participation, dynamics and form, and freedom and destiny. God's life may be described symbolically in these terms. But there is a difference; while in finite being these elements are in tension and conflict, in the divine life their polarity is one of inclusiveness and rest. This is so, again, because in God there is no threat of non-being to disrupt the essential unity of the polar elements of being.

The divine life includes the polarity of individualization and participation; God is a "personal God." He may be called the "absolute individual," but if he is called this he must at the same time be called the "absolute participant." The one cannot be applied without the other. ". . . both individualization and participation are rooted in the ground of the divine life and . . . God is equally 'near' to each of them while transcending them both."[245] As we could not call God *a* being, so we cannot call him *a* person. He is not a heavenly, perfect person, he is not *a* person, but he is not less than person, he is the ground of everything personal.[10] Similarly, if God is said to "participate" this does not mean that something exists alongside of him with which he has to do. "God participates in everything that is . . . But the divine participation creates that in which it participates."[245]

The polarity of dynamics and form may also be applied to God as his potentiality and actuality. Tillich objects to the classical understanding of God's potentiality and actuality as *actus purus*, that is, that God is the pure form in which everything potential is actual. This, he says, violates the dynamic element in God by placing it in an all-embracing form. God includes dynamics and form, potentiality and actuality, in perfect balance. ". . . this dynamic element . . . includes a 'not yet' which is, however, always balanced by an 'already' within the divine life."[246] It would be inconsistent with the concept of God as being-itself to imply that there is a potential being which exists over against his actual being and that he must continually strive to "realize" himself. This is the human situation, but it is not the situation of him who is the ground of all being. Potentiality implies a lack, but God lacks nothing, therefore potentiality can only be applied to God analogously, symbolically.

The polarity of freedom and destiny may also be applied to the life of God. There is hardly a word said about God in Scripture which does not affirm his freedom. He creates, saves, reveals, and punishes without being influenced in any way. In more abstract terms, God is free because he has "aseity," he is *a se*, self-derived. There is nothing prior to him which could in any

---

[10] "*Against* Pascal I say: The God of Abraham, Isaac, and Jacob and the God of the philosophers is the same God. He is a person and the negation of himself as a person" (*Biblical Religion and the Search for Ultimate Reality*, op. cit., p. 85). Also in *Theology of Culture*, op. cit., pp. 127 ff., Tillich argues for a view of God as "supra-personal," referring to Schelling's statement that "Only a person can heal a person." In the light of these and many other statements in Tillich's works, the often voiced charge against him of impersonalism seems to be unjustified. For Tillich, God transcends the personal, but he nonetheless includes it. He is person.

way condition him. God is certainly free. But how can he be said
to have a destiny? Tillich argues that it is possible to apply this
element of being to God ". . . provided the connotation of a
destiny-determining power above God is avoided and provided
one adds that God is his own destiny and that in God freedom
and destiny are one."[248-249]

God as Spirit and as Trinity

If God is a living God, he is both Spirit and Trinity. Tillich
defines "spirit" as "the unity of power and meaning."[249] In
the realm of the spirit the ontological elements are united, the
first element in each polarity being indicated by power (self,
dynamics, freedom) and the second by meaning (participation,
form, destiny). Spirit is then the *telos* or fulfillment of life, for
it expresses the reunion of the estranged elements in finite being.
Thus "spirit" is a necessary and all-embracing symbol for the
life of God. "The statement that God is Spirit means that life as
spirit is the inclusive symbol for the divine life."[250] Tillich
acknowledges that to speak of the Christian doctrine of the
Trinity, one must begin with Christology, but he believes that
there are presuppositions for trinitarian thinking inherent in
the doctrine of God which are prior to specific Christian doctrine.
These presuppositions, he maintains, are incumbent upon the
definition of God as Spirit. "God's life is life as spirit, and the
trinitarian principles are moments within the process of the
divine life."[250] Because God is Spirit, one may distinguish
within the divine life the principles of "power," "meaning,"
and their unity. Power naturally refers to God's creativity, the
"abysmal" power of being. Meaning refers to what we have
called the structure of being or the *logos*; it channels the creative
power of God to rational structures. The idea of God as Spirit
unites these two concepts, indicating the nature of the divine life
as power which takes on a meaningful structure. It is not difficult to see the application of these principles to the Christian
doctrine of the Trinity, but Tillich warns that they must only be
seen as a "preparation for it, nothing more."[251]

THE DOCTRINE OF GOD AS THE ANSWER
TO THE QUESTION OF FINITE BEING

God as the ground and power of being, as being-itself, is the answer to the general question of all beings, of being as such. We now turn to the specific application of this answer to the question of finite being. We turn to the answer of God as the basis of man's courage to be.

God as Creator

"The doctrine of creation . . . answers the question implied in man's finitude and in finitude generally."[(252)] It is not a story of an event; it describes the basic relation between God, man, and the world. God's creativity is not contingent; it is not something that might or might not happen. It is identical with his life. He is Creator because he is God, and he is God because he is Creator. Tillich distinguishes between God's originating, sustaining, and directing creativity.

God's originating creativity: The Christian doctrine of *creatio ex nihilo* means that there is nothing prior to or alongside of God with which, or in terms of which, he creates. It is the ultimate protection from any kind of dualism. There is no second power or material co-eternal with God out of which he creates. In the Nicaean Creed, there appears the formula that God created "all things visible and invisible." This refers directly, says Tillich, to the church's fight against the Platonic doctrine that God co-exists with eternal forms and essences. It is true that Tillich takes the classical idealist position that above and beyond the particular and the concrete there are universal concepts which make the structure of being knowable. But his point here is that God is not identical with these essences and forms. He creates essential beings and is therefore as "prior" to them as he is to existence and concrete phenomena.

This gives insight into Tillich's doctrine of the Fall. This doctrine itself will be treated in detail in the next chapter, but now we must see its connection with God's creative activity. God creates man as he essentially is. "In the creative vision of God the individual is present as a whole in his essential being and inner *telos*.''[255] But man is not this essence; he exists as a particular, finite being, separated from his essence, his unity with being-itself. "Man has left the ground [of his being in the divine life] in order to 'stand upon' himself, to actualize what he essentially is, in order to be *finite freedom*. This is the point at which the doctrine of creation and the doctrine of the fall join.''[255] Tillich admits that this statement is highly dialectical, and we shall see that it is one of the most problematic in his whole system. He is certainly saying that creation involves the movement from essence to existence, from what man "was" in the creative eye of God to what he is, a finite being, estranged from his creator and the ground of his being. Creation and the Fall coincide. "Fully developed creatureliness is fallen creatureliness.''[255] Tillich, however, resists what could seem to be a logical conclusion to this view of the Fall, namely, that it is an unavoidable and necessary part of human destiny. It is part of man's destiny, says Tillich, as is shown in its universal application, but the important thing is that it is the result of actualized freedom. Tillich insists upon these two points: The Fall is not contingent, neither is it a matter of structural necessity. "Every theologian who is courageous enough to face the twofold truth that nothing can happen to God accidentally and that the state of existence is a fallen state must accept the point of coincidence between the end of creation and the beginning of the fall.''[256]

What does Tillich's view of creation mean for his doctrine of man? Traditionally, theology has considered man the "end" of creation, who is distinguished from all other creatures by what has been called the *imago Dei*, the image of God in him. For Tillich, the image of God in man must be distinguished from his created goodness. The latter was lost in the Fall, but not the former. But at the same time he is careful to avoid the inference that the image of God includes an existent relation between God and man, that it creates a special communal relation. Rather, "Man is the image of God in that in which he differs from all other creatures, namely, his rational structure.''[259] Tillich, of course, does not mean man's ability to "reason" in a technical sense. He is speaking here again of ontological reason, the *logos* structure of being which is part of the divine life. This structure appears in all finite beings, but only in man completely, for only in man is there the awareness of this structure. This awareness is seen in man's knowledge of himself as a self that has a world, it is seen in his ability to transcend his finitude by imagining infinity, but most importantly, and following from these others, it is seen in his ability to actualize his freedom, to transcend the causal chain of his environment. The image of God is the *logos* (the structure of reason) in man. "[Man's] *logos* is analogous to the divine *logos*, so that the divine *logos* can appear as man without destroying the humanity of man."[259]

God's sustaining creativity: In older theologies this has been called the doctrine of preservation. Original creation, as we have seen, has as its fulfillment the actualized freedom of man, in which man "stands on his own." But this does not mean, Tillich argues, that man (or the rest of creation) is "independent." It is necessary that the creation remain dependent on the creator because "only in the power of being-itself is the creature able to resist non-being."[261] This is the basis for the doctrine of preservation. Tillich, following Augustine, asserts that "Preservation is continuous creativity, in that God out of eternity creates things and time together . . . giving the power of being to everything that has being. . ."[262]

God's directing, or providential, creativity: Tillich maintains that creation has no purposes beyond "itself." It should not be thought of as serving the purpose of God's glory (as in Calvinism) or as providing an object for the divine love (as in Lutheranism). Such concepts, says Tillich, imply a "lack" in God, which creation is supposed to fill. Rather, one should speak of the *telos* of creation, which is to drive every creature toward its own fulfillment. Such directing creativity is called "providence."

The meaning of the word "providence" is ambiguous. It is often interpreted as "fore-seeing," in which God is mere spectator, or as "fore-ordering," in which God is seen as a planner and his creation nothing but a great machine which runs its foreordained course. Tillich rightly rejects both views. God "never is a spectator; he always directs everything toward its fulfilment. Yet God's directing creativity always creates through the freedom of man . . ."[266] Providence works through the elements of being; it works through all the conditions of human life and includes man's individuality, his participation, his anxiety, his finitude, his freedom, and his destiny. "Providence is not interference; it is creation . . . It is the quality of inner directedness present in every situation."[267][11]

Providence is paradoxical. One believes in God's directing creativity in spite of the seeming meaninglessness and tragedy of life. This consideration brings Tillich to the discussion of "theodicy." It is the insuppressible question: "How can an almighty God be justified (*theos-dike*) in view of realities in which no meaning whatsoever can be discovered? . . . why [is] it . . . that some beings are excluded from any kind of fulfilment . . ."[269] Tillich insists that this question cannot be asked in a non-existential way, for "all theological statements are existential . . ."[269] One may only ask about his own fulfillment. But at the same time the individual always exists in polarity with participation, and thus one must include "others" in every question and answer concerning his own fulfillment. But the question of theodicy is finally answered for Tillich in the unity of individualization and participation in the ground of being. And in giving this answer he certainly seems to be pointing toward a kind of universal salvation based on the unity of all and every being in God. "The confidence of every creature, its courage to be, is rooted in faith in God as its creative ground."[270]

We began this chapter with Tillich's analysis of being and we learned that finite being is distinguished from essential being in that the threat of non-being disrupts and splits the structure of

---

[11] This interpretation leads Tillich to a most interesting concept of prayer. He denies that "prayer can mean that God is expected to acquiesce in interfering with existential conditions." [267] Rather, prayer requests that God direct the situation toward fulfillment. But prayer is nonetheless efficacious, because the prayer itself constitutes an element in the situation, that of surrender to God's will, which is most open to God's directing creativity.

being in finitude. Man's finite being is threatened, its unity with being-itself is lost, and yet man continues to be. He continues to be because he has what Tillich calls "ontological courage" to affirm his being in spite of the disruption and death which threaten it. But how is such a courage possible? This is the basic question of being and the determining question for this part of Tillich's theology. We are now able to give the answer: Man's courage to be "is rooted in faith in God as [his] creative ground." The fact that God, who is being-itself, is the origin of finite being, that he sustains it, and that he directs it toward a final fulfillment in unity with himself is the basic answer to man's situation in being. We saw above that the question of finite being, while always the same, appears in different forms when applied to the categories of being. In like manner the basic answer of God as creative ground finds different expressions in his various attributes. But in every case the point is the same. The answer to the question of man's being is found in God who is the ground of being.

God as Omnipotent

The fact that the Christian creed begins with the affirmation of "God, the Father Almighty" separates exclusive monotheism from every other religion. If God were anything less, he could not be God and he could not be the object of man's ultimate concern. The religious meaning of the term is clear, but its theological expression often involves a contradiction. If God's omnipotence is thought of as his ability "to do whatever he wants," then it is denied because God would become a being alongside other beings, a being who, faced with various possibilities, chooses one. But as we have seen, in God potentiality and actuality are united. Therefore Tillich suggests, "It is more adequate to define divine omnipotence as the power of being which resists nonbeing in all its expressions and which is manifest in the creative process in all its forms."[273] Faith in the power of God to overcome non-being is the answer to the question of finitude. The ultimate power of being overcomes the anxiety of non-being and gives the courage to be.

God as Eternal

Eternity is omnipotence in respect to time. Tillich's discussion of this subject is one of the best examples of the beautiful clarity of his thought and the depth and incisiveness of his philosophical insight. He begins by rejecting two misinterpretations of eternity. "Eternity is neither timelessness nor the endlessness of time . . . rather it means the power of embracing all periods of time."[274] Eternity is not timelessness; it is not simultaneity. There is no time without past, present, and future. Just as potentiality and actuality are united in the divine life, so are the elements of time. "Eternity is the transcendent unity of the dissected moments of existential time."[274] "To elevate the dissected moments of time to infinite significance by demanding their endless reduplication is idolatry in the most refined sense."[275] What then is the relation of eternity to the modes of time? Tillich suggests that we must use for our example man's experience of his own finite time, which includes both past and future, but which is predominantly experienced as "present." Therefore eternity must be seen as an eternal present. "The eternal present is moving from past to future but without ceasing to be present."[275] This means that God is open for the future, for the new, but at the same time he anticipates the future, it "already" exists in his being beyond the split between potentiality and actuality. God "has" the future, but the new can actually happen. Neither is God tied to the past; for him the past is not complete, it contains potentialities which are actualized in the future. "The past becomes something different through everything new which happens."[276]

Man's time is threatened by a past which is no more and a future which is not yet, and his present is nothing more than the moving point between the two. Thus he experiences a radical threat to his being in time. This threat ". . . is conquered by the freedom of God toward the past and its potentialities. The anxiety of the future is conquered by the dependence of the new on the unity of the divine life."[276] God as eternal is the basis for man's courage to be in time.

God as Omnipresent

God's omnipresence expresses his relation to space. Pantheism extends God into all spaces, but this, says Tillich, subjects God to dissected spatiality; space becomes coexistent with God, rather than a part of his being. Nor can God be relegated to a particular space, for he is everywhere, since his power and creativity act at every place. Tillich maintains that God's relation to space can only be seen in his participation in the spatial existence of his creatures. Thus "God's omnipresence overcomes the anxiety of not having a space for one's self. . . . In the certainty of the omnipresent God we are always at home . . ."[278] God's omnipresence is the answer to the question of man's being in space.

God as Omniscient

Knowing a thing implies the separation of the knower and the known; it implies the subject-object structure of being. But God is not "separate" from anything, and he is not a participant in the subject-object scheme. He is above it. How then can we speak of God's omniscience? Tillich suggests that just for the above reasons, omniscience cannot mean that God is "all-knowing." Rather, it "expresses the spiritual character of the divine omnipotence and omnipresence."[278] This fact of the divine life overcomes the anxiety of the dark and the hidden in the life of man, for nothing is hidden to God.

God as Love

Love, says Tillich, is primarily an ontological and not an emotional concept. ". . . God is love. And, since God is being-itself, one must say that being-itself is love."[279] Love is the unity of individualization and participation. It is the longing of the individual for reunion and participation with the other. And since God includes in perfect unity the polar elements of individualization and participation, he is love. Tillich distinguishes four types of love. "Love as *libido* is the movement of the needy toward that which fulfils the need. Love as *philia* is the movement of the equal toward union with the equal. Love as *erōs* is the movement of that which is lower in power and meaning to that which is higher."[280] The fourth type of love, *agape*, differs from these in that it represents the desire, not for one's own, but for the other's, fulfillment. It is independent of any contingent reactions of the loved one; it is unconditional. This characterizes God's love for man. The other types of love are also included in the love relation between God and man—indeed Tillich declares that man's love for God must be described as *eros*. But *agape* is the norm and standard for every other type of love because it expresses the ontological basis for all love in being-itself.[12]

One of the valuable insights in Tillich's conception of love is that it forms the basis for an understanding of divine justice. God's reaction to the creature who violates justice and love, and therefore the structure of being, is called judgment and condemnation. But it is nonetheless an act of love. It is ". . . God's loving power against that which violates love. Condemnation is not the negation of love but the negation of the negation of love."[283]

This understanding of God's love and judgment is also significant for Tillich's doctrine of predestination. To speak of a "double predestination," Tillich insists, is to establish "an eternal split within being-itself."[285] Non-being would then have coexistence with God. Predestination can have only one quality: it "is providence with respect to one's ultimate destiny. It has nothing to do with determination . . ."[286] That we are "predestined" simply means "that, in relation to God, God's act always precedes and further, that, in order to be certain of one's fulfilment, one can and must look at God's activity alone."[286] Predestination of course is based on God's grace, which is his love. In the later parts of Tillich's system we will note a growing

---

12 Tillich describes this function of *agape* as that which makes sexual love (*libido*) seek the fulfillment of others, makes aesthetic love (*eros*) become involved and united with the loved object, and causes communal love (*philia*) to accept in love that which is unacceptable. It should be noted that Tillich distinguishes *eros* from *epithymia*, that is, from sensual desire, and speaks of it in the Platonic sense of *eros*: it is the desire for unity with higher values. See Paul Tillich, *Love, Power, and Justice* (New York: Oxford University Press, 1954), pp. 116 ff.

emphasis on grace and to that extent an evolution in his thought. But we should not lose sight of the fact that such an emphasis is also to be found in this early part of his theology. "... 'grace' qualifies all relations between God and man in such a way that they are freely inaugurated by God and in no way dependent upon anything the creature does or desires."[(285)]

The doctrine of God as love is the final answer to the question implied in man's finitude. It is the final answer because only as man sees the other attributes of God in the light of this attribute can they serve as a basis for his courage to be. We can courageously affirm our creatureliness only if we know that he who is the power of creation draws us toward himself in love. We who lack power, who pass out of time, and whose space is threatened can only affirm ourselves courageously if our beings are united in love with him who is omnipotent, eternal, and omnipresent. God as love is the final answer to the question of the courage to be. But this love is manifest only in the appearance of Jesus as the Christ. Therefore the doctrine of God both presupposes and points to the doctrine of Christ.

SUMMARY AND ANALYSIS

For Paul Tillich, Christian theology must be apologetic theology; it must answer the questions implied in the human situation. In this second part of his system, the question of man's situation in being is asked. This is the ontological question: "What does it mean to be?" The structure of being is experienced by man in a subject-object, or self-world, polarity, and contains the elements of individualization and participation, dynamics and form, and freedom and destiny. This structure of being always includes "non-being," which is a negative element perhaps best described as the "not-yet and the no-more of being." It is the unrealized potentiality of being and it is the possibility of ceasing to be. Because man has less than the power of being-itself, his being is threatened by non-being. This threat is experienced in the imbalance and tension which occur in the elements of finite being; if freedom is overcome by destiny, or if the polarity of any of the other elements is broken, the structure of being is destroyed and man ceases to be. This threat is also seen in the categories of finitude, in which time, space, causality, and substance manifest a negative power which can destroy man's being. But man's being is not destroyed; he continues to be because he affirms himself in spite of this threat with what Tillich calls "ontological courage." But what is the basis for this courage to be? What power of being is there available to and undergirding man's being which causes him to be in the face of non-being? This is the question arising out of man's situation in being. It is, according to the method of correlation, the human and philosophical question which can only be answered by the theological affirmation of God.

One of the main propositions of the method of correlation is that the human question determines the form of the revelatory answer, so that the answer is given in terms of the question. Thus if God is the answer to man's quest for that which undergirds, protects, and supports his being, then God must be called the power of being which overcomes non-being. He is the ground of being for everything that is; he is being-itself. This means that he is not *a* being or *a* person, for he transcends all particular beings. But God can be spoken of as person, because he is the basis of, and includes, all personality. This participation of all being in God is the ontological basis for the symbolical application of finite categories to the divine. Thus God can be said to be a living God, for although he does not live as man lives, he includes in himself the elements of being which are the criteria for finite life.

That God is the ground of being implies the assertion that he is the creator of the universe. Tillich distinguishes among God's originating, sustaining, and directing creativity, the latter two types representing the traditional doctrines of preservation and providence. Thus, God as being-itself is the answer to the general question of being, for he is the creative ground, the sustaining power, and the guiding will for everything that is.

But how does this doctrine of God answer the specific question of man's finitude? How does this God give to man the courage to be in spite of the threat of non-being? Here again the answer is given in the form of the question. Tillich describes man's situation in being in terms of the categories of time, space, causality, and substance. Thus God's time, eternity, gives man the courage to be in time, and God's omnipresence gives man a "home" wherever he is and is thus the basis for his courage to be in space. Similarly, God's omnipotence and omniscience overcome the threat of non-being implied in causality and substance and give to man the courage to be.

But above all of these attributes of God is his being as love. God's love, *agape*, draws man to himself and unites his being with the power of being-itself. The divine love is sometimes judgment, but it is always grace. The God who is the ground and power of being is the answer to the question of being and the basis for man's courage to be, because he is also the God of Love.

This part of Tillich's theological system offers perhaps the best example of the beautiful symmetry and consistent logic which characterize all his work. The depth of his insights and the originality of many of his concepts contribute alike to the importance of this material not only for the philosophical problem of ontology, but for the theological doctrine of God as well. Tillich's analysis of being is most convincing, and seems a more adequate basis for philosophical anthropology than the materialistic and empiricist attempts of recent thought. We wholeheartedly accept Tillich's description of God as the ground and power of being-as-being-itself. Moreover, Tillich's ontology offers clarification of many concepts which must be included in the theological doctrine of man. Particularly his view of the distinction and unity of individuality and participation, and dynamics and form, can only add to the theologian's understanding of human existence. In the same way theology should find most useful Tillich's treatment of the categories of time, space, causality, and substance. We have already expressed appreciation for Tillich's brilliantly concise survey of religious history and the conflict between concreteness and ultimacy, polytheism and monotheism, in man's idea of the divine. If we heed Tillich's warning that this history shows a development only in man's *idea* of god and not an evolution in God's revelation of himself, then it could and should serve as a useful key to the understanding of the various religions.

The greatest problem which this writer sees in Tillich's ontological analysis of being is one which we have already noted in
the last two chapters. It is the question of a natural relation
between God and man which causes an awareness of God in man
and which allows man to apply finite categories to God. This is
the old question of natural theology. The question is not of man's
apprehension of the unity of being nor his realization that there
is a power of being beyond himself. Nor is the question whether
or not God can be called the power of being, the ground of
being, or being-itself. Certainly he can. The question is: Does
man's knowledge of his own being carry with it even an "awareness" of the God of Christian revelation as the ground of his
being? Tillich obviously thinks that it does. This extra-revelatory
awareness was found in the last chapter in "the depth of reason"; it is the basis for the *analogia entis* and indeed is the
foundation of Tillich's whole system insofar as the method of
correlation requires an ability on man's part to ask the question
of God prior to the reception of his revelatory answer. Now
Tillich tries to avoid the stigma of natural theology by asserting
that this awareness is not a real knowledge of God. But is this
distinction between an awareness of God and the knowledge of
God possible? It is hard to escape the fact that as soon as the
object of awareness is named, a certain knowledge is assumed.[13]

This same problem of the knowledge of God is seen in Tillich's
theory of symbolism. It is clear that he does not wish to be confused with the Roman Catholic position regarding the possibility
of natural knowledge of God.[14] That position, however, sounds

[13] It is true that Tillich does not name the object of this awareness. Indeed, he says that man's ultimate concern as the criterion for theology
cannot, apart from revelation, be called "God," and that man is "aware"
only of the unconditional in human thought. But insofar as he maintains
that this awareness is the basis for the question of "God," it is certainly
implied that the object of the question of man's awareness is known.

[14] In the Vatican Council of 1870 the dogma was promulgated that
"*Eadem sancta mater Ecclesia tenet et docet, Deum, rerum omnium prin-
cipium et finem, naturali humanae rationis lumine e rebus creatis certo
cognosci posse*" ("The same holy mother church holds and teaches that
God, the beginning and end of all things, can be known with certainty
from his creations by means of the natural light of human reason")
(*Enchiridian Symbolorum*, ed. Henrici Denzinger; Freiburg: Herder, 1946,
No. 1785).

very much like Tillich's in that it is based on mutual participation in being of both God and man. We cannot but agree with Tillich on the necessity of the symbolic nature of all finite terms applied to God. But the question is: On what basis may we apply our symbols? Tillich argues that we can do so on the basis of the *analogia entis*, on the basis of the unity of being in God. Thus, because man's being in which he experiences love is related to God's being, man may symbolically apply the word "love" to God. But is it not just the other way around? Is it not just because man's love contains far too much lovelessness that he cannot apply his concept "love" to God, whether that idea be transcended or not? Is it not rather that because God has shown man what love really is in Christ that man may apply it to God and seek after it himself? In other words, is not the power of religious symbolism grounded in grace rather than ontology, and in revelation rather than awareness?

It is very strange that this section of Tillich's theology, which seems to us to involve a natural unity between God and man, is meant to underline God's transcendence. The whole point and purpose of his doctrine of God is, in Tillich's own words, to offer a view of God beyond "naturalism and supernaturalism."[15] Both views err, Tillich rightly claims, in that they do not see the infinite distance between the creator and the created. God is the "God above the god of theism."[16] Certainly this needs to be said, especially to those naïve as well as sophisticated forms of theology which do not take cognizance of the fact that God is wholly other. The power and effectiveness of Tillich's purpose in this regard cannot be denied and commands our wholehearted agreement.

But in spite of our basic agreement with many of Tillich's dogmatic assertions concerning the nature of God, there remains just below the surface of every point the nagging question: How do we know? How do we know that God is love? How do we know that he sustains and directs his creation? The thing that is most striking about Tillich's doctrine of God is that nowhere are his assertions said to be based upon God's acts as they are revealed in Christ, still less are they based on any exegesis of the record of those acts in Holy Scripture. In fact, at only one place in this doctrine is the character of the divine life said to be "manifest in revelation."[243] In this situation is there not bound to arise in the reader's mind a suspicion that the content of Tillich's doctrine of God is deduced from his analysis of being rather than received from revelation itself?

Tillich would answer that God's revelatory acts are assumed and implied throughout his doctrine, and this would be in line with what we have called the "hidden a priori" in his thought. While it is true that the analysis of the human situation will affect the form of the doctrine of God, Tillich is anxious that the relation between question and answer in the method of correlation should not be seen as one in which the human situation has the whole determining function. "God answers man's questions, and under the impact of God's answers man asks them."[61] This determination from the side of revelation is made much more explicit in the introduction to the second volume of *Systematic Theology*. There Tillich speaks again of the "circle" in which the theologian works, that is, his commitment to final revelation in Christ, and describes it as an ellipse, the two foci of which are the existential question and the theological answer.[17] Thus both question and answer are subsumed under and conditioned by the Christian faith. Certainly this chapter on being and God shows this double determination. For why should Tillich have chosen just those elements of being, why especially did he choose just those categories? Obviously because they are in harmony with the traditional attributes of God, he chose them within the "theological circle." Therefore if we say, as we certainly must, that the existential question determines the form of the theological answer, we must also see that the form or structure of the question is affected by the prior theological commitment of the writer. But the very important difference is this: Tillich systematically begins with the question and systematically develops its determination of the form of the theological answer. But he does

[17] *Systematic Theology*, Vol. II, pp. 14-15.

not analyze the theological commitment which affects that question, nor does he describe the way in which it determines the form of the answer. Thus in his doctrine of God we can note similarities between both his questions and his answers and the biblical witness to the nature of God. But we cannot find anywhere, explicitly stated or elaborated, that fundamental relation between revelation and the question or the answer to which Tillich lays claims. It remains strictly a priori to his thought and hidden in his system.

And if it remains hidden, how much more likely and dangerous becomes the possibility that this concept of the depth of reason and the unity of being will be seen as the actual basis of his speaking of God! If the first and decisive thing that must be said about God, namely that he is the one who reveals himself to man in his Word, is not said, at least not said in such a way that this attribute of God determines the method of doctrine which must be applied, then is there not the greatest danger that all of the other attributes which can in truth be applied to this God will be seen as mere extensions of the elements and categories of man's being? And would not a god so described be an idol? This is why the questions of the knowledge of God and revelation are so important to the doctrine of God. Faith in God's self-revealing act must precede and form the basis for any analysis of his being. This was the truth we found in St. Anselm's argument, but which we cannot find in Tillich's systematic development.

At the beginning of this study we said that, in spite of inherent difficulties, we need not and ought not reject Tillich's definition and method of theology out-of-hand. His intention to show how the questions of human existence are answered by God's revelation is certainly a legitimate one. The only question which we must ask is whether he succeeds; and this depends upon whether or not he can, following his own method, accurately describe the human situation and faithfully report the revelatory answer. In this regard we have had to ask whether Tillich's concepts of the depth of reason and the unity of being have not caused him to describe the human situation in such a way that man's radical separation from God has been overlooked. And we have had to ask whether the "unconditional" which appears in the depth of man's reason and of which he is aware in his own being can possibly be identified with God, even to the extent of expressing man's quest for him. We leave these questions open because we must allow for the possibility that within Tillich's system as a whole an understanding of man's situation in estrangement and the character of God's revelation in Christ will be stated which will give a positive interpretation to those negative elements we have found in his doctrines of revelation and God. Such a backward reading would be entirely consistent with the method of correlation and with the interdependence of all the parts of his *Systematic Theology*. Therefore if we are to find an interpretation of man's existence which will enable us to avoid the implication of natural theology found in the concepts of the depth of reason and the unity of being, and if we are to find an interpretation of God which will show him as really and decisively revealed in Jesus Christ, then we must look with much care and anticipation to the central and absolutely determining part of Tillich's system, "Existence and the Christ," to which we now turn.

V

EXISTENCE AND THE CHRIST

The state of existence is the state of estrangement. Man is estranged from the ground of his being, from other beings, and from himself. The transition from essence to existence [the Fall] results in personal guilt and universal tragedy.[(44-45)][1] *Attempts to overcome estrangement within the power of one's estranged existence lead to hard toil and tragic failure. . . . Only a New Being can produce a new action.*[(80)]

New Being is essential being under the conditions of existence, conquering the gap between essence and existence.[(118-119)] *For it is the Christ who brings the New Being, who saves men from the old being . . .* [(150)] *. . . in Jesus as the Christ the eternal unity of God and man has become historical reality. In his being, the New Being is real, and the New Being is the re-established unity between God and man.*[(148)]

Because he is a Christian theologian, the aim and purpose of all of Tillich's work is the elucidation of the meaning of Christ for man. Thus this part of his system is determinative for the evaluation of the whole, for here the basic concepts of his theology are applied to his central concern and thus reveal their adequacy for their task.

We have divided this chapter into four sections which parallel Tillich's own outline and express his method of correlation. First we will give his analysis of man's existential situation, from which analysis he expounds a doctrine of man. Second, we will present the question arising out of this situation, which is the quest for New Being. Third, the revelatory answer will be given as the New Being in Jesus as the Christ in which Tillich's dogmatic assertions concerning the being of Christ will be pre-

---

[1] Numbers in parentheses in this chapter refer to page numbers in Tillich's *Systematic Theology*, Vol. II.

sented. And fourth, we will consider the way in which the Christ fulfills the quest of man for New Being in his death and Resurrection.

The Meaning of Existence

"To exist," "*existere,*" means to "stand out." "Immediately one asks: 'To stand out of what?' [and] the general answer to the question . . . is that we stand out of non-being."[20] We remember that Tillich distinguishes between two kinds of non-being, that which is the absolute negation of being (*ouk on*) and that which is relative, that is, potential being not yet actualized (*me on*). To exist means to "stand out" of both types of non-being. An existent being is, rather than is not (*ouk on*), and it has left the state of potentiality (*me on*) and has become actual.

All being, potential or actual, essential or existential, stands out of absolute non-being in the sense of *ouk on*. Therefore, the decisive understanding of existential, or actual, being lies in its contrast to meontic being, that is, to potential or essential being. This distinction achieved its classic expression in Plato's doctrine of essence and existence, in which potential being or essential being was "real" being and existence was only a shadow world of unreality, error, and evil. The ultimately real, true, and good was found in the realm of ideas, or essences, of which the actual or existential could at best be only a poor approximation. Thus, for Plato, existence was being, "fallen" from the realm of essence. This negative evaluation of existence continued, in spite of the mediating attempt of Aristotle, through the ancient and medieval world. Under the impact of the spirit of humanism which arose in the Renaissance and found its fullest expression in the Enlightenment, the gap between essence and existence was closed and existence was seen not as a fall from essence, but as the actualization and fulfillment of one's essential potentialities. This is what Tillich calls "essentialism," which means that "in existence, man is what he is in essence."[23] This view reached its apotheosis in the philosophy of Hegel. In his all-embracing the negativity of non-being inherent in existence was swallowed by the actualization of essential being in the universal process. For Hegel, "the world is the self-realization of the divine mind; existence is the expression of essence and not the fall away from it."[24]

The philosophical movement called "existentialism" arose in direct revolt against this essentialism of Hegel. It expressed the view shared by such otherwise different thinkers as Schopenhauer, Kierkegaard, Marx, and Nietzsche "that man's existential situation is a state of estrangement from his essential nature."[25] They held that Hegel was in error when he claimed that man, though estranged, was reconciled with his true being. In the existentialists' appraisal of life in terms of conflict, destruction, anxiety, and meaninglessness, Tillich finds an appropriate definition of existence for theology, ". . . namely, the predicament of man and his world in the state of estrangement."[27]

The Fall

We come now to one of the most crucial and at the same time difficult points in Tillich's whole theological system. As we have seen, Tillich maintains that existentialism and theology hold in common a view of existence as "fallen" from essence. The Fall as a concept is equally near to both philosophy and theology because it describes the universal situation of man. Therefore, "theology must clearly and unambiguously represent 'the Fall' as a symbol for the human situation universally, not as the story of an event that happened 'once upon a time.' "[29] To aid in this understanding of the Fall, Tillich speaks of it as the "transition from essence to existence."

The first question is: How is this transition possible? And the answer is, "It is finite freedom which makes possible the transition from essence to existence."[31] The marks of man's freedom, says Tillich, are his language, whereby he creates universals which liberate him from the concrete and particular, his ability to ask questions and thus penetrate into the deeper levels of life, his power of deliberation and decision, and his creativity.[2] But,

---

[2] Tillich has also defined freedom as "that faculty of man by which he is able to determine his being through history" (Ruth N. Anshen, ed. *Freedom: Its Meaning*; New York: Harcourt, Brace, 1940, p. 124).

"Finally, man is free, in so far as he has the power of contradicting himself and his essential nature. Man is free even from his
freedom; that is, he can surrender his humanity."[32] We shall
see that much of Tillich's argument hangs upon this definition
of freedom. The Fall is possible because man has finite freedom.
But as we saw in the last chapter, freedom always appears in
polarity with destiny. "In man freedom and destiny limit each
other, for he has finite freedom."[32] Thus even man's freedom
to deny his freedom is conditioned and limited by his destiny.
And this destiny is not only his own. "The transition from
essence to existence is possible because finite freedom works
within the frame of a universal destiny."[32] The possibility of
the Fall is not, Tillich argues, an unfortunate aspect of man's
freedom, as Calvin asserted; rather it is identical with his freedom; it is the expression of the image of God in man. Man
would not be man without the possibility of the Fall.

What is this state of essential being from which man falls?
Tillich calls it a state of "dreaming innocence." This is not an
actual stage of human development; rather it is, as the word
"dreaming" indicates, a state of pure potentiality. It did not
"happen"; it is not temporal; it is not real. But it contains both
the real and the actual in terms of anticipation. It is a stage
of innocence, an example of which Tillich finds in the child's
original innocence of his sexual potentialities, which is gradually
replaced by experience, responsibility, and guilt. The state of
dreaming innocence is lost.

But dreaming innocence is not a stage of perfection; it is a
state in which temptation is experienced. This temptation is
experienced as the desire of man to actualize his freedom; it is
present in the creature as such. This natural or creaturely
temptation explains the fact of God's prohibition not to eat of
the fruit in the story of the Fall. Such a prohibition presupposes
a split between the creator and creature *before* the Fall—it presupposes the desire to sin which Tillich calls "aroused freedom."
This temptation "occurs in the moment in which finite freedom
becomes conscious of itself . . ."[35] Man wishes to use his freedom
     ualize his independent self; at the same time he is com-

manded to preserve his dreaming innocence. "He experiences a double threat . . . of losing himself by not actualizing himself and his potentialities and . . . of losing himself by actualizing himself and his potentialities."[35-36] Man must and he does actualize himself, or else he would cease to be. But this entails his fall from essential being, which, Tillich maintains, is the fall into sin.

Tillich admits that the Fall, so explained, blends the logical sequence in a most confusing way. It is not an event in the past; it did not "happen"; but it is the original fact from which all other facts proceed. Tillich speaks of the "transcendent Fall," indicating that "the very constitution of existence implies the transition from essence to existence."[38] The myth of Adam's Fall contains not only the ethical thrust of personal responsibility, but the implication of its universal tragedy. Therefore, Christian theology must "simultaneously acknowledge the tragic universality of estrangement and man's personal responsibility for it."[39]3

A most important point in Tillich's doctrine of the Fall is that man and nature are equally involved in the transition from essence to existence; neither is "innocent." This is supported by the impossibility of pointing with certainty to the boundary between man and nature. The relation between individual guilt and the evolutionary and the maturational processes, the fact that one cannot say exactly when the evolving individual becomes guilty, proves, Tillich argues, that both man and nature partake mutually of the estrangement of existence from essence. The universal fall of nature indicates the element of destiny in

3 We cannot agree with R. A. Killen that "perhaps the best simile to express [Tillich's] view of the pre-historical fall is that of the unconscious struggles of the babe in its mother's womb before it is born. Can the babe be held responsible for what it does in coming to birth? Surely not!" (Killen, *op. cit.*, p. 260). In the first place Tillich does not speak of a "pre-historical" Fall, for that would be an event in history. He speaks of a "transcendent" Fall by which he seeks to indicate an ontological quality and not an act, a state of being and not an event. However, insofar as this state of finite being called the Fall is expressed in human beings in temptation, desire, or "aroused freedom," it requires self-consciousness in man— at least a consciousness of his finite freedom. Thus, the prenatal simile is out of place.

man's actualization of his freedom and subsequent estrangement. But Tillich denies that he has substituted Manichean tragic destiny for Pelagian moral freedom, for there always exists a strict polarity of mutual dependence between freedom and destiny. This highly dialectical concept of freedom is everywhere described by Tillich in words similar to these: "Freedom is the possibility of a total and centered act of the personality, an act in which all the drives and influences which constitute the destiny of man are brought into the centered unity of a decision."[43]

Does not this relation between freedom and destiny make sin and the Fall ontologically necessary and therefore part of the creation so that the creation can no longer be considered good? In answer, Tillich again insists that the creation is good in its essential character. But at the same time he says that, "Creation and the Fall coincide in so far as there is no point in time and space in which created goodness was actualized and had existence."[44] Essential creation is good, but "actualized creation and estranged existence are identical."[44] Thus actual creation is not good. By way of example, Tillich speaks of the newborn child which, being created, falls into estrangement. But this point of coincidence between creation and the Fall is not, he insists, a logical necessity. It is simply a fact which "the child, upon growing into maturity, affirms . . . in acts of freedom which imply responsibility and guilt."[44]

In order to understand what Tillich is proposing, it is necessary to distinguish between essential creation, which is God's work and which is, to use Tillich's own word, "merely" potential, and actual creation (e.g., the conscious man), which is the result of man's actualization of his freedom. And it is further necessary to conceive of this freedom as conditioned by destiny in such a way that while man must choose to actualize himself in order to be, he nonetheless is personally responsible and guilty for the estrangement which follows upon this choice.[4]

---

[4] Reinhold Niebuhr has attempted to explain the relation of possibility and necessity (or freedom and destiny) in Tillich's description of the Fall by suggesting that Tillich uses "essence" in two ways: "All finite existence represents at least a partial contradiction to essential being, since essential being is undifferentiated being. But in addition man has the possi-

The Doctrine of Sin

The human situation is one of both universal and personal estrangement from essential being and from God. We have seen the cause of this situation in the free and yet destined Fall of man and the world from essence to existence. We must now analyze this "fallen" situation itself in terms of sin (or estrangement) and its result, the structure of evil.

Man's situation is one of "estrangement," which means that "man as he exists is not what he essentially is and ought to be."[45] Tillich prefers "estrangement" to the traditional word "sin" because it expresses the truth "that one belongs essentially to that from which one is estranged."[45] "Sin," however, cannot be abandoned because it expresses "personal freedom and guilt in contrast to tragic guilt and the universal destiny of estrangement . . . Man's predicament is estrangement, but his estrangement is sin."[46] Sin or estrangement may be described as "unbelief," "*hubris*," or "concupiscence."

Unbelief is not the rejection of church doctrine. It "means the act or state in which man in the totality of his being turns away from God"[47] and toward himself in the actualization of his freedom. When man turns toward himself, he becomes involved in the universal tragedy of human life which the Greeks called *hubris*. *Hubris* is the self-elevation of finite man to the realm of the infinite. The possibility of this self-elevation is man's greatness; Tillich calls it the image of God in man. But the danger is that man will refuse to acknowledge his finitude. He "elevates himself beyond the limits of his finite being and provokes the divine wrath which destroys him."[50] Man turns away from

---

bility, not the necessity, of contradicting . . . his own essential being" (*The Theology of Paul Tillich*, *op. cit.*, p. 222). The first, "partial contradiction," is a matter of necessity or destiny; the second, self-contradiction, is a matter of possibility or freedom. But this explanation ignores the fact that, for Tillich, essential being *includes* particular or differentiated being, although it transcends it. In the same way, God as being-itself includes man's finite being although he transcends it infinitely. Thus finite particularity per se does not contradict being-itself (God) and therefore cannot represent the element of destiny in the Fall. But Niebuhr is right in pointing to Tillich's distinction within the category of finitude as essential and existential, created and actual, being.

God in unbelief and toward himself, because he is then in a position to draw the whole world to himself. The poverty of man's particularity creates the natural desire for union with the whole of reality. This desire is not bad in itself, but if it is unlimited it becomes "concupiscence," which is not simply unrestrained sexuality, but unlimited desire in all of man's relations. Sin is man's turning away from God (unbelief) and toward himself (*hubris*) in order that he might make himself the center and focus of all reality (concupiscence).

Theology has always made a distinction between "original" and "actual" sin. Tillich rejects the Augustinian interpretation of original sin as being in any way hereditary or, for that matter, original. It is both inconsistent and absurd, he argues, that Adam should have been able to commit an original act in freedom, disassociated from the universal destiny of man. The concept of original sin (*Erbsünde*) must include the element of destiny in Adam's fall and the element of freedom in the fall of his heirs. "Adam must be understood as essential man and as symbolizing the transition from essence to existence. . . . The unity of destiny and freedom must be preserved in the description of every condition of man." [56] "Original" and "actual" sin are translated by Tillich into sin as "fact" and "act." The fact is original and precedes the act; the fact conditions the act and forms its destiny. As act, "sin is a matter of freedom, responsibility, and personal guilt."[56] But since freedom and destiny cannot ultimately be separated, "it is impossible to separate sin as fact from sin as act."[56] As we have noted above, the resolution of this dialectic finds in Tillich no more understandable formulation than the eternal polarity of freedom and destiny.

The Doctrine of Evil

In the state of estrangement, man contradicts his essential being and destroys its structure. This destruction is the result of "evil," which Tillich calls "the structure of destruction." In the last chapter Tillich described the ontological elements, their polar relations, and the tensions which arise between them in finitude. Here he shows their destruction and disruption under the conditions of estrangement. Also in the last chapter we found in the tension of the structure of being the root of the question of being-itself, or God. Here, in the analysis of the destruction of the structure of being, we find the root of the quest for New Being, which is the question of the Christ.

The polarity of the ontological elements, self and world, is the basic structure of being, and its destruction means the destruction of all the elements of being. This destruction takes place because man actualizes his freedom, he sins. "The attempt of the finite self to be the center of everything gradually has the effect of its ceasing to be the center of anything. Both self and world are threatened."[62] And this in turn threatens the polarity of freedom and destiny. "In the moment of aroused freedom a process starts in which freedom separates itself from the destiny to which it belongs."[62] Under the control of *hubris*, freedom does not relate itself to "the objects provided by destiny," but to "an indefinite number of objects" which are contingent. And, as existentialism has taught us, "if no essential relation between a free agent and his objects exists, no choice is objectively preferable to any other . . ."[63] Freedom becomes arbitrariness, and to that extent "destiny is distorted into mechanical necessity."[63] *Hubris* and concupiscence destroy the polarity of dynamics and form. "Dynamics are distorted into a formless urge for self-transcendence. . . . Yet form without dynamics is equally destructive. . . . it becomes external law."[64] Dynamics without form is chaos. Form separated from dynamics is oppressive and suppressive. The estrangement of sin also disrupts the polarity of individualization and participation. The more a being is individualized, the more it can participate, transcend itself, and embrace the whole universe of being. But, as we saw in the loss of self, if man in his estrangement turns inward toward himself alone, then he ". . . is shut within himself and cut off from participation. At the same time, he falls under the power of objects which tend to make him into a mere object without a self."[65]

This "structure of destruction," says Tillich, raises the question of New Being, or the Christ. But the reader may wonder if the above is not simply a repetition of the conflicts between the ontological elements found in the doctrine of God, and ask why the questions arising from these conflicts and the answer given them are not the same. Indeed, if the answer of God as being-itself can give finitude "the courage to be," why should one need the Christ? The answer to these questions lies in the distinction Tillich draws between *essential* finitude and *existential* finitude.

In the last chapter we spoke of man's situation in finitude and how it is threatened by non-being so that the ontological elements (freedom, destiny, etc.) come into conflict. This conflict was seen as a potential threat to man's being which he overcomes by the "ontological" courage to be, which courage, whether man knows it or not, is based upon the power of God's being. One could say that the creature as creature is threatened by non-being, but is saved from it by God as the creator. But all this takes place on the level of essential finite being. It describes the situation of created being as such, of finite being before the Fall. The situation of existential finite being—fallen, sinful man—parallels the above situation, but is quite different.

This becomes understandable if we consider the relation of finitude to death. Death is natural to essential finitude, to creation as such. Immortality comes as grace which, however, does not remove the necessity of dying. This necessity causes anxiety even in essential manhood (as in Jesus' anxiety over his death), but it is not tragic, because it does not mean the separation of man from God. But if we consider existential finitude, fallen man, we find that while death is still natural, sin gives a "sting" to it. The anxiety about non-being found in essential finitude becomes a horror of death in existential finitude. In the situation of estranged being, man has turned his back on the ground of his being and thus too on the possibility of the courage-to-be-in-spite-of-non-being-and-death. Moreover, his horror is increased by his recognition of his own guilt in this situation, for it came about through the actualization of his freedom even if universally destined. This means that the conflicts which appear in the onto-logical elements and categories of essential finitude have quite a different effect from the disruption of those same elements and categories in existential finitude. Existential man, in the radicality of his estranged being, cannot ask for the courage to be what he is, but must ask for new being. And the only answer which can be given him is the New Being in Christ.[5]

To continue our report: The structure of evil destroys the structure of being expressed in the ontological elements; a similar effect may be observed in the categories. In the state of estrangement "the categories control existence and produce a double reaction toward them—resistance and despair."[(68)] Having turned away from God and his time, eternity, man resists time by trying to prolong it, fill it, and continue it endlessly. But transitoriness defeats him and the result is despair. In the same way, having lost a sense of God's omnipresence, man experiences space as spatial contingency—he does not belong anywhere. And in spite of all his attempts to create his own place, he remains a "pilgrim on earth"—homeless and despairing.

THE QUESTION OF NEW BEING

Attempts at Self-Salvation

Man, by his very existence, is estranged from God and from his own essential being and "in spite of the power of his finite freedom, he is unable to achieve reunion with God."[(79)] Man cannot save himself, because the unity of freedom and destiny means "that no act within the context of existential estrangement can overcome existential estrangement. Destiny keeps freedom in bondage without eliminating it."[(78)]

But in spite of this limitation, man continues to seek salvation on his own. Religious legalism has been the most important way taken by man's attempts at self-salvation. The law is a divine gift, for it shows man's essential nature, but it becomes a tempta-

---

[5] This distinction between essential finitude and existential finitude was not made explicit in the first volume of Tillich's system nor in *The Courage To Be*, which appeared in the same period. In the latter book, Tillich mixed man's essential anxiety about non-being with existential man's despair, doubt, and meaninglessness and answered them both by the assertion of the courage to be found in "God above the God of theism." This unfortunately led many critics to believe that Tillich had replaced Christology with a deistic soteriology. That impression may be corrected by the distinction made here.

tion and a curse when man, blind to his estrangement, thinks that he can actually keep it and attain what he has lost. Another way of self-salvation is asceticism, which, while valid enough as self-restriction, is useless and dangerous when it tries "to force the reunion with the infinite by conscious acts of self-negation."[82] For the objects of concupiscence are not destroyed but only repressed to appear in some other, more destructive, way. Similarly, mysticism becomes an attempt at self-salvation when sensitivity to the presence of the divine in experience is replaced by self-imposed bodily and mental exercises by which a union with God is sought. "A real union of the mystic with God is never reached."[83] Other ways of self-salvation are found in Catholic sacramentalism and Protestant dogmatism. In the first case that which is given to man is distorted into the performance of ritual to induce the divine presence; and in the second, "faith as the state of being grasped [is reduced to] the belief in doctrine."[85]

All of these ways fail because man is trapped in estrangement, but at the same time they all presuppose a revelatory "breakthrough." "The question of salvation can be asked only if salvation is already at work . . . The quest for the New Being presupposes the presence of the New Being . . ."[80] This is consistent with what Tillich has called the "theological circle" and with the a priori which we have noted in his system as such. Man's situation in estrangement and his attempts at self-salvation both point to the necessity and to the possibility of his quest for the New Being.

This concludes the analysis of the existential human situation and the question which arises from it. We have found that "to exist" means to "stand out" of that kind of non-being which is mere potentiality. It means to leave potential or essential being by actualizing one's freedom. Therefore, existence implies the fall from essential being and is a universal and tragic quality of creaturely being. It means for man his separation and estrangement from his own essential being and from God as being-itself. This is the human situation. Man's actualization of his potentialities is, on the one hand, a matter of necessity (in the sense of destiny), for unless he chooses to actualize himself, he cannot *be* man. But, on the other hand, man's self-actualization is a matter of freedom; he chooses to do so and is therefore guilty of the separation from his own essential manhood and his estrangement from God. This responsibility points to man's sin, which is always an expression of his turning away from God and toward himself. This turning away results in the appearance of "evil" which destroys the very structure of man's being and drives him to despair.

Faced with this situation, man attempts to regain his lost unity with God and his essential manhood. But his attempts fail because he cannot but act within the context of his estranged being, where every free act is bound to the tragic destiny of the Fall. Man then has no recourse but to ask for a new being which can re-establish his lost unity with God and his essential self. This question is the question of the Christ, for the Christ is the one who brings the New Being and by bringing it restores man to his essential unity with God.

THE DOCTRINE OF CHRIST—HIS BEING

Tillich always refers to "Jesus as the Christ." This is no accident of terminology but exactly reflects the whole direction of his thought. He rejects the name "Jesus Christ" because it tends to unite two elements which he believes should be kept apart, "the fact which is called 'Jesus of Nazareth' and the reception of this fact by those who received him as the Christ."[97] Thus we begin with two propositions regarding the Christ: the one is that Jesus is the "anointed one" who *received* the office of the Christ, who *became* the Christ. And the other is that the event of Jesus as the Christ contains two interdependent elements, the fact of Jesus and his reception by men as the Christ. "The receptive side of the Christian event is as important as the factual side."[99] The decisive importance of these two propositions will become clear as our report proceeds.

The Historical and Biblical Witness to Jesus as the Christ

This double nature of the Christ event, the fact and its reception, determines Tillich's attitude toward historical-biblical criticism. He accepts absolutely the legitimacy of the application of historical research to the Bible and he finds valuable contributions for theology in the historical evaluation of various parts of Scripture and the analysis of christological symbols. But he rejects as a failure the attempted reconstruction of "the historical Jesus." "The historical Jesus, namely, the Jesus behind the symbols of his reception as the Christ, not only did not appear but receded farther and farther with every step."[102] This failure was not the result of inadequacies in the historical method as such; rather, it reflected the very nature of the case itself. In order to sketch a historical "life of Jesus," it is necessary to separate within the biblical reports those elements which express the subjective reception of Jesus as the Christ from those elements which are available to neutral scientific observation and can be established as historical fact. But, Tillich argues, Jesus as the Christ as a historical event is precisely the unity of these two factors. Therefore, the attempt of historical criticism was bound to fail. If either the fact or reception side of this event is isolated, one is no longer dealing with the object of Christian faith.

The failure of the quest for historical Jesus has led many contemporary critics to concentrate on the words of Jesus, for these at least are used to reconstruct the "teachings" of Jesus, or his ethics. Jesus is reduced "to the level of the Old Testament."[106] Tillich finds a "more profound" use of Jesus' words in the attempt of Rudolf Bultmann to reconstruct from them, not the teachings of Jesus, but his message that the Kingdom of God is at hand. Thus it is not moral precepts with which one is faced, but the demand for a decision and acceptance of the paradox of the Cross of the Christ. But this attempt also must be rejected, because "it does not show how the requirement of deciding for the Kingdom of God can be fulfilled. The situation of having to decide remains one of being under the law."[106] These historical treatments cannot show how it is possible to keep Jesus' commandments or decide for his Kingdom, because they have dealt with his acts or words, rather than his being. But, Tillich argues, it is his being, the New Being, which must be the primary object of theological concern.

This negative judgment on the search for the historical Jesus must not be construed as calling into question the factual element of the event "Jesus as the Christ." For, while ". . . faith cannot even guarantee the name 'Jesus' in respect to him who was the Christ. . . . [it] does guarantee the factual transformation of reality in that personal life which the New Testament expresses in its picture of Jesus as the Christ."[107] Tillich is willing to accept the possibility that Jesus of Nazareth never lived. He is willing to admit that historical criticism might be able to do away with every historical fact in the New Testament. But two things cannot be touched by historical criticism. They are the "essence" of the Christian faith and are guaranteed by it. The first is, as stated above, the fact of the reality of the New Being. "Faith can guarantee only its own foundation, namely, . . . that reality which has created the faith. This reality is the New Being, who conquers existential estrangement and thereby makes faith possible."[114] Faith guarantees itself. Historical criticism cannot question the validity of such "immediate awareness."

The other fact which faith can guarantee is that the New Being appeared in a concrete, personal life.[6] Criticism may call into question any and all specific traits of the biblical picture of this life. But it cannot deny that it is exactly this picture which has power to transform lives. The fact that this picture of a concrete life actually does mediate the power of the New Being proves at least "that there is an *analogia imaginis* . . . between the picture and the actual personal life from which it has arisen."[114-115] This "picture analogy" is, like the analogy of being, not a way given to man whereby he may "naturally" or empirically know the Christ, but a way through which he may speak about the one who makes himself known through that picture. Thus there is no way "behind" the biblical picture of the Christ. Man can never know or speak of the divine except through symbols, and

---

[6] Tillich's insistence upon the "personal" character of the New Being is based on his view of man as a microcosmos. All of the potentialities of being are completely actual only in a personal life. Thus, if the New Being is to conquer the estrangement of actuality or existence, it must do it as a person. In *Biblical Religion and the Search for Ultimate Reality*, *op. cit.*, pp. 75 ff., Tillich turns the problem around and shows the universal and ontological character of the personal life of Jesus as the Christ.

the given symbols of Scripture are self-authenticated by their power to mediate the New Being of the one whose picture they contain.

The New Testament is for Tillich the basic and original source for the knowledge of the New Being in Jesus as the Christ. An actual discussion of the critical and exegetical problems of New Testament Christology is not included in Tillich's systematic treatment. He confines himself to a few general observations which may be briefly mentioned: "All New Testament books are united . . . in the assertion that Jesus is the Christ."[117] Against Harnack, Tillich contends that there is no substantial difference between the message of the Christ given in the Gospels and the Letters. Within the Gospels, the synoptic tradition does vary from the Johannine in the former's emphasis on the participation of Jesus in the negativities of existence, and the latter's emphasis on the victory of Christ over existence. But these differences are not exclusive and do not create "a systematic problem." The New Testament is united, Tillich maintains, in showing three things about Jesus as the Christ: ". . . first and decisively, as the undisrupted unity of . . . his being with God; second, as the serenity and majesty of him who preserves this unity against . . . estranged existence; and third, self-surrendering love . . . taking the existential self-destruction upon himself."[138]

Tillich's view of the biblical witness to the Christ reflects directly his proposition that the event "Jesus as the Christ" is a combination of fact and reception. God's act and man's response are equally important for the reality and meaning of the Christ. Thus there is an aspect of this event which may be scientifically and objectively analyzed, and a part open only for faith. Here, as in Tillich's method of theology, there is a "correlation" between the act of God and the act of man.

The New Being in Jesus as the Christ

We must now ask in what way Christ's being is New Being and answers the question of finite existence. "New Being is essential being under the conditions of existence, conquering the gap between essence and existence.''[118-119] The New Being is new in two respects: "It is new in contrast to the merely potential character of essential being; and it is new over against the estranged character of existential being.''[119] Jesus as the Christ is the New Being because he brings to an end the old being. He is the end of the law, that is, the judgment of existence by essential being, because in him existence and essential being are united. He is the end of existence, insofar as it is expressed in estrangement, conflict, and self-destruction. He is the end of history, that is, the aim or *telos* of history.

We have seen that Tillich's main criticism of the attempt to find the "historical Jesus" is that it inevitably separates Jesus' being as the Christ from his words or deeds. This separation is impossible in the description of the Christ himself. "Jesus as the Christ is the bearer of the New Being in the totality of his being, not in any special expressions of it. . . . his being has the quality of the New Being beyond the split of essential and existential being.''[121] This means that the particular aspects of Jesus' life must always be subordinated to and interpreted by his being. This is clearly seen in the expression of his being through his words. The very fact that he is called "the Word" indicates that his words as such are not important but rather his being which they express. Similarly, the deeds of Jesus must not be construed as a new law, as in the tradition of the *imitatio Christi*, but must be seen as an expression of his peculiar being, in which we may participate, but which we cannot imitate. Nor should the suffering of Jesus be considered apart from or alongside of his being. The importance of the Cross has led many theologians to make this mistake. Thus for Anselm the Cross was an *opus supererogatorium* which itself accomplishes redemption and which, although efficacious because of the divinity of the Christ, was not seen as an essential part and expression of his being. But "the Cross is not something additional which can be separated from the appearance of the eternal God-Manhood . . . it is an inescapable implication of this appearance.''[123-124]

Although the particulars of Jesus' life do not offer deductive proof of his being as the New Being, they do bear witness to and confirm him as such. At every point his life contradicts the life of existential estrangement. There are "no traces of estrangement between him and God and consequently between him and himself and between him and his world (in its essential nature)."[126] There are no traces of unbelief: even in his death he cries to the God who has forsaken him. There are no traces of *hubris* or self-elevation, for he requires that an acceptance of himself as the Christ be accompanied by an acceptance of his violent death. He resists the sin of concupiscence when he rejects the unlimited desire for food, knowledge, and power in the temptations in the wilderness. He was sinless and he was good. But, Tillich warns, neither Christ's sinlessness nor his goodness may be interpreted as a special ethical quality. His goodness and sinlessness are ways of speaking of the being of Christ—which was the New Being overcoming the estrangement of existence.

If the Christ was really the New Being, then how, it is asked, could he have been tempted as are men living under the power of the old being? Was the obedience of Christ a matter of chance? This would seem to be so if his temptations were real; he could have, and therefore might have, succumbed. But this seems impossible in the light of the New Testament's interest in his fulfillment of his destiny. On the other hand, if his victory over temptation was a matter of destiny or determination, how can his temptation be said to be real? In answer, Tillich again points to the polarity of freedom and destiny. Jesus' resistance to temptation is an act "of decision by himself and [a result] of a divine destiny. Beyond this unity we cannot go, either in the case of Jesus or in the case of man universally."[130] Jesus' temptation expresses his finitude. "As a finite being, he is subject to the contingency of everything that is not by itself but is 'thrown' into existence."[131] The marks of his finitude are many: he has to die, and is anxious about it; he lacks a definite place and is homeless; he must suffer bodily, social, and mental insecurity; he is lonely, and like all men finds it impossible to penetrate into the center of anyone else. We find in him uncertainty in judgment, risk, and error. Moreover, he participates in what Tillich calls "the tragic element of existence." This means that

Jesus as the Christ, being subject to finite existence, is also subject to the ambiguity between good and evil in it. This is especially evident in his relation with Judas. Tillich argues that since the New Testament clearly shows that Jesus knew what Judas was about, Judas could not have betrayed him "without the will of Jesus."[133] Jesus, therefore, "participates" in the guilt of Judas. Jesus as the Christ was subject to the conditions of existential estrangement, but he was not defeated by them; rather, he conquered them by bringing them into his unbroken unity with God.

The Christological Dogma

Tillich asks two questions of the christological formulas of Nicaea and Chalcedon: Did they succeed in protecting the Christian message from distortion, and did the tools they used provide "a conceptually clear expression of the meaning of the message?"[141] He feels that the first question can be answered "fairly positively," but the question of the adequacy of the conceptual tools he holds to be unambiguously answered in the negative. However, Tillich does not agree with Harnack's thesis that the inadequacy lay in an "intellectualizing" of the faith by the use of Greek philosophy. The failure lay rather in the fact that the creedal formulations were built by "an accumulation of powerful paradoxa" and were unable to give Christology "a constructive interpretation, although this was just the reason for the original introduction of the philosophical concepts."[141-142]

The problem of the early church, says Tillich, was how to *think* the concept of unity of God and man in Jesus as the Christ. If his human nature was slighted, his total participation and effectiveness in human existence would be threatened. And if his divine nature was not expressed, the totality of his victory would be in doubt. This question arose first in the debate over the relation of the Logos to the Father. The Christ was identified with the power of the Logos, and so, if the Logos were thought equal with the Father, the distinction between the Father and the Son seemed lost. This was the position of the Sabellian heresy. But a more serious danger seemed to lie in the Arian belief that the Logos (and therefore also the Christ) was a creature, for a mere creature would not be able to save creation. Thus, the term *homo-ousios*,[7] which means that the Christ is of "equal essence" with God, was offered by Athanasius. The victory of Athanasius at Nicaea assured the divinity of Christ in the creed, and it saved Christianity "from a relapse to a cult of half-gods. It rejected interpretations of Jesus as the Christ which would have deprived him of his power to create the New Being."[(144)] But it did this at the expense of the "Jesus character" of Christ. His humanity became threatened. Tillich blames this tendency on popular and monastic piety which did not want a paradox, but a miracle. "They wanted a God, walking on earth . . ."[(144)] and were "fanatically" against the participation of Christ in man's existential predicament. But this tendency was defeated at Chalcedon by men like Leo of Rome who emphasized the historical-dynamic character of the New Being in Christ. Thus, "In the two great decisions of the early church, both the Christ-character and the Jesus-character of the event of Jesus as the Christ were preserved. And this happened in spite of the very inadequate conceptual tools."[(145)]

We must now consider Tillich's "constructive" correction of the church's dogma. He asserts that the motive behind all Christology is soteriological. The church wanted somehow to correlate the "greatness" of its salvation with "great" statements describing him who brought it. But their concept of what was "great" as applied to the Christ was in error. A "high" Christology was thought to emphasize his divinity. Against this, Tillich maintains that only a "low" Christology which takes seriously Christ's humanity is adequate for the salvation which he brings and is therefore the truly "high" and great Christology.

Tillich's main criticism and correction centers on the word "nature" as used in the creedal formulas; "when applied to man, it is ambiguous; when applied to God, it is wrong."[(142)]

---

[7] Tillich's dissatisfaction with this word is to be found also in the very important preparatory study which he made for this volume. See Paul Tillich, "A Reinterpretation of the Doctrine of the Incarnation," *Church Quarterly Review*, Vol. CXLVII, No. 294 (Jan.-Mar., 1949), pp. 133-148 (catalogued amusingly enough in the bibliography of *The Theology of Paul Tillich, op. cit.*, p. 362, as "A Misinterpretation of the Doctrine of Incarnation").

Man's "nature" can mean either his essential or existential nature, either his character as created or estranged. And obviously, it is the second meaning which is applied when we speak of such men as ourselves. But if the term "human nature" is applied to Jesus as the Christ, only the first meaning may be used. For his humanity is never outside the unity of essential being with God. He has human nature in the existential sense only as a potentiality—which he refuses to actualize. Therefore Tillich suggests dropping the term "human nature" when speaking of the Christ. What about the divine God-nature of Christ? This, too, must be rejected because God has no "nature," that is, something to which he conforms in order to be who he is. God is beyond essence and existence. He is who he is. At best one could say that his nature is what he makes himself in his eternal creativity. But such a nature is not available to human analysis. "There is no divine nature which could be abstracted from his eternal creativity."[147] In any case, the term "divine nature" cannot be applied to Christ; for the Christ, unlike God, "is not beyond essence and existence."[148] He was a person, born into and subject to existence.

In the place of asserting the unity of divine and human natures in Christ, Tillich prefers the assertion that in him "the eternal unity of God and man has become historical reality."[148] He is the "re-established unity between God and man."[148] The concept "the divine nature" in him is replaced by the concept "eternal God-man-unity." This way of expressing the matter, Tillich argues, replaces a static essence with a dynamic relationship. And instead of "human nature," we must speak of the Christ as "essential man."[8] "It is essential man who represents

---

[8] "To essential man belongs the unity of his finiteness with his infinity, and it is precisely this unity which I have called God-manhood" (Tillich, "A Reinterpretation of the Doctrine of the Incarnation," *op. cit.*, p. 143). Tillich himself calls our attention to the similarity between his interpretation of Christ as "essential man" and Schleiermacher's description of Jesus as the *Urbild* (original image) of what man essentially is. The difference, he maintains, is that, while Schleiermacher's *Urbild* represents the idealistic transcendence of true humanity over existence, his "New Being" participates in existence. But Schleiermacher too could speak of Jesus (the *Urbild*) entering "into the corporate life of sinfulness" (Friedrich Schleiermacher, *The Christian Faith*; Edinburgh: T. & T. Clark, 1928, p. 381).

not only man to man but God to man; for essential man . . . represents the original image of God embodied in man."[94] Tillich sees that "abstract definitions of the nature of this unity are . . . impossible."[148] However, he believes that two concepts are given in the New Testament which point toward a correct interpretation of it. The first is "adoption," which is already seen in his phrase "Jesus as the Christ," and the second is "incarnation." The concept of adoption is necessary, Tillich maintains, because if the eternal unity of God and man is actualized in existence, it can be so only through an act of finite freedom. God chooses to "adopt" the man Jesus as the Christ, and Jesus chooses to accept his adoption through obedience. However, this free choice is not contingent—it is destined; and this unity actualized in Jesus as the Christ is not finite—it is eternal. Therefore, it is also necessary to speak of the incarnation. But if this word is used (and Tillich is doubtful about its usefulness), it must be kept clear that it is an expression of the eternal character of the relationship found in this man. It seeks to "express the paradox that he who transcends the universe appears in it and under its conditions."[149]

Tillich's sharp rejection of the traditional use of the word "incarnation" is one of the most striking characteristics of his Christology. "Who is the subject of Incarnation? If the answer is 'God,' one often continues by saying that 'God has become man' . . . But the assertion that 'God has become man' is . . . a nonsensical statement."[94][9] It is nonsensical because it cannot mean what it says. God cannot become something else; he cannot cease to be God. And Tillich thinks that this is what is said if one says that "God has become man." The main danger that Tillich sees is that incarnation will be interpreted in terms of a mythological transmutation! "If the *egeneto* in the Johannine sentence, *Logos sarx egeneto*, the 'Word became flesh,' is pressed, we are in the midst of a mythology of metamorphosis.[10] . . . The

[9] And yet Tillich himself can say in the context of a discussion of biblical personalism, "God can become man, because man is person and because God is personal" (*Biblical Religion and the Search for Ultimate Reality*, op. cit., p. 38).

[10] George Tavard has rebuked Tillich on this point, saying, "We should

Incarnation of the Logos is not metamorphosis but his total manifestation in a personal life.''[149] '' 'Logos' is the principle of
the divine self-manifestation in God as well as in the universe, in
nature as well as in history.''[95] In other words, Tillich wishes
the concept of incarnation to be interpreted as the manifestation
of God ''in a personal life-process as a saving participant in the
human predicament,''[95] but he does not want it to be the symbol
which controls our understanding of the unity of the divine and
human in Jesus as the Christ.

In order to avoid what he believes to be the idea of transmutation inherent in the concept of incarnation, Tillich again turns
to the word ''adoption.'' It is in this concept that he finds the
best chance for a positive reconstruction of christological dogma.
''Adoption'' points to the element of freedom in the event Jesus
as the Christ, without which he cannot be said to have really
been a man who participated in the tragedy of human existence
and sin. If we are to understand Tillich's Christology, we must
remember that for him man is always a correlate in God's revelation of himself, so that no revelation takes place which is not
received by man, and it can only be received as such if it comes
to man ''in his own terms.'' This certainly means that in the
context of Tillich's systematic thought the revelation of God in
the event Jesus as the Christ must mirror this same correlation.
In this revelatory event, the place and activity of man must be
also independent and free. On the other hand, we have found in
Tillich's doctrine of God a God who is absolute and transcendent,
of whom men can speak only in symbols. If we speak of this God
as revealed in Christ, Tillich insists, this cannot mean that he
ceases to be absolute and transcendent. God's ''otherness'' can
be better protected if his relation to the Christ is seen as a
''choosing of,'' or a ''manifestation through,'' rather than a
''unity with.'' Tillich has said that ''the incarnational Christology was needed to explain the adoptionist Christology . . . [and]
incarnational Christology needs adoptionist Christology . . .''[149]

---

pay [the Church Fathers] the compliment of considering them too intelli-
gent to have tried to express a divine mystery 'in terms of a higher
chemistry' '' (Tavard, *op. cit.*, p. 169).

But we would be wide of the mark if we interpreted this as meaning that there is a balance at this point. Tillich has not said, nor will he say with the "incarnational" Christologies of Nicaea and Chalcedon, that Jesus Christ was "truly God and truly man." No, it is the adoptionist position to which he holds with greater consistency. God chose Jesus; Jesus became the Christ.[11]

THE DOCTRINE OF CHRIST—HIS WORK

We come now to the last step in the method of correlation, which is to show the way God's revelatory answer in Christ answers man's question and fulfills his quest. We pass from anthropology and Christology to soteriology, because the final answer to man's search for New Being is his salvation.

The saving work of Jesus as the Christ was accomplished by his total participation in man's existential estrangement and his victory over that estrangement. "The subjection to existence is expressed in the symbol of the 'Cross of Christ'; the conquest of existence is expressed in the symbol of the 'Resurrection of the Christ.' "[152-153] Tillich calls the Cross and the Resurrection "symbols" or "myths," and we must recall once again that for him, neither symbol nor myth means "untrue." Myths are to be judged only "on the basis of their power to express what they are supposed to express, namely . . . the New Being in Jesus as the Christ."[152]

The Cross and the Resurrection

The Cross was not an isolated event. While it is certainly the most powerful symbol of the subjection of the Christ to the conditions of existence, there are many other reports in the New Testament which "corroborate" that one event. There is the description of the Christ who gave up his divine form and became a servant (Philippians 2); there are the stories surrounding his birth, his poverty, the flight into Egypt, the threats against his life; there are the many descriptions of his low estate, lone-

---

[11] Gustave Weigel has called Tillich "Adoptionist" and "Nestorian." It is interesting that Tillich praised Weigel's article as "the best analysis of my thought I have ever seen" (Weigel, *op. cit.*, p. 185).

liness, and suffering. And finally there is the climax in Geth-
semane, his death and burial. All of these are part of the same
story. "They are important in their power to show the subjection
of him who is the bearer of the New Being to the destructive
structures of the old being."[159] The meaning of the Cross is
that the divine self-manifestation came among men, subjected
itself to the conditions of existential estrangement, and therefore
could conquer them in the power of the New Being.

Tillich rightly sees that the Cross and the Resurrection cannot
be separated; they are interdependent. "The Cross of the Christ
is the Cross of the one who has conquered the death of existential
estrangement."[153] And this means that Cross and Resurrection
are both reality and symbol. "In both cases something happened
within existence."[153] But the difference is that while the Cross
took place in "the full light of historical observation, the stories
of the Resurrection spread a veil of deep mystery over the
event."[153] But this difference is not exclusive. Both combine
the factual and the mythical. The Cross is a fact which is given
mythical, that is, universal, significance. The Resurrection is a
myth somehow related to a fact which was experienced by the
disciples of Jesus.

There is no doubt, Tillich states, that the idea of resurrection
came to the church by way of mythological polytheism and
Jewish apocalyptic literature. The symbol is not original with
the New Testament; it was there to be used. But this does not
mitigate the fact that the church was born out of the certainty
of the Resurrection. "A real experience made it possible for the
disciples to apply the known symbol of resurrection to Jesus . . .
it was a combination of event and symbol."[154] Tillich is sure
that there is a factual element in the story of the Resurrection.
But no historical elaboration of this element can have anything
but probability. Here, as in the discussion of the historical Jesus,
faith is its own guarantor. "It is the certainty of one's own
victory over the death of existential estrangement which creates
the certainty of the Resurrection . . ."[155]

There are three interpretations of the Resurrection which
Tillich feels are inadequate. The first is the "primitive" but

"most beautifully expressed" theory of the physical raising of Jesus' body, but which is inadequate because it is a rationalization of a divine act and leads to "absurd" questions of physics and chemistry. The second is the "spiritual" interpretation, which speaks of the presence of Jesus' soul among his disciples; but this interpretation is really based on the presupposition of the immortality of the human soul—and is, therefore, false. The third attempt is a psychological one, which states that the Christ was present mentally to his followers. This interpretation is given some weight by the experience of Paul, "if we exclude the physical interpretation,"[(156)] but it is inadequate because it misses the reality of the event.

Tillich's own interpretation of the Resurrection, which, he is careful to say, can only be considered a theory, is what he calls the "restitution" of the Christ. The Resurrection was not meant to overcome the natural death of one individual man, Tillich argues, and therefore cannot be understood in terms of the revival of an individual man. What is overcome in the Resurrection is the *disappearance* of him who brought the New Being. We remember that the conquest of transitoriness was one of the requirements of the New Being—man must be saved from the threat of finite time. Thus, if Jesus was really gone, "passed away," how could he have been the New Being? The tension created by this situation in the minds of the disciples was resolved in the unique experience we call the Resurrection. "In an ecstatic experience the concrete picture of Jesus of Nazareth became indissolubly united with the reality of the New Being."[(157)] The power of the New Being had not left them, although Jesus had. Thus Jesus "returned" when the disciples perceived his unity with what had remained. This was no bodily return, but a spiritual presence. Tillich's concept blends the Resurrection, Pentecost, and the Ascension into one event. "The concrete individual life of the man Jesus of Nazareth is raised above transitoriness into the eternal presence of God as Spirit. . . . This is the event."[(157)][12] This event happened to some of his followers

---

[12] Easter, then, does not concern ". . . the historical demonstration that once a man, Jesus of Nazareth, rose from the grave" (Paul Tillich, "Ostern," *Hannoverscher Kurier*, No. 179, April 17, 1927, p. 1).

"in the hours of his execution; then to many others; then to Paul; then to all those who in every period experience his living presence here and now."[157] Tillich thus holds an immanent view of the Resurrection as the confirmation of faith in Jesus as the Christ by the presence of the Holy Spirit.

We cannot fail to note the lack of exegesis in Tillich's approach to the Resurrection. He does not mention the various accounts and traditions found in the Bible, but confines himself to the barest allusion to the spiritual character of 1 Corinthians 15, dismissing any "literal" interpretation of the rather physical language Paul uses in the first part of that chapter. We will treat this problem of interpretation below.

The Doctrine of the Atonement

"The doctrine of atonement is the description of the effect of the New Being in Jesus as the Christ on those who are grasped by it . . ."[170] It thus has two sides, which correspond to the divine act and human reaction to it. Accordingly, there are two types of the doctrine of atonement which reflect this twofold character of God's saving act. The first is the objective type, represented by Origen, which stresses the deliberation and action of God in accomplishing man's salvation, without the necessity of any human reaction. But, objects Tillich, there can be no salvation for man outside of his experience and acceptance of it; therefore this view must be rejected. On the other side there is the position of Abelard, which stresses the subjective element in the atonement. In this view salvation is accomplished through man's response of love to the love of Christ, and God is seen as a God of love and not wrath. From a purely psychological standpoint, Tillich holds this view as inadequate, because it forfeits God's justice without which man has no security as to his forgiveness and acceptance. Finally, there is the mediating view of Anselm, in which it is God's action which saves men, but which does so through the satisfaction of his justice in the innocent and substitutionary suffering of the Christ. Tillich finds here the danger that a Mediator or Redeemer will be understood as a "third reality" beside man and God, a half-god, who is needed by God to unite the divine and human spheres and to carry out the demands of reconciliation. This would imply that it is God, and not man, who needs to be reconciled.

In order to achieve a balancing of God's objective action and man's subjective reaction, Tillich offers six principles which should operate in the further development of the doctrine of the atonement. (1) It must first be remembered "that the atoning processes are created by God and God alone . . . the Christ . . . mediates the reconciling act of God . . ."[174] (2) There can be no conflict between God's love and his justice. (3) Atonement does not mean a denial of man's sin or of the radical nature of his estrangement. (4) Atonement means God's participation in man's estrangement. "The element of non-being which is eternally conquered in the divine life. . . . is the suffering that God takes upon himself."[175] (5) We see in the Cross the divine participation in man's estrangement. However, "the Cross is not the cause but the effective manifestation of God's taking the consequences of human guilt upon himself."[176] (6) When man participates in (accepts?) the New Being in Jesus as the Christ, he also participates in the atoning act of God. The atonement is God's saving act in Christ, but in Tillich's thought this act is not effective alone. It requires on the part of man "participation in the divine participation, accepting it and being transformed by it."[176]

The Doctrine of Salvation

"Salvation" means "healing" (*salvus*). It points to that which reunites what is estranged and overcomes the split between man and God. "Salvation is reclaiming from the old and transferring into New Being."[166]

We come now to a very difficult point in Tillich's soteriology. We remember that in his doctrine of revelation he asserted that where there is revelation, there is salvation—which is certainly true. But a question arose when we learned that this revelation was to be found in nature and history as well as in the Word of God. This problem now has a direct effect upon his doctrine of salvation. Tillich quite rightly begins by saying that Christianity "does not separate salvation through the Christ from the processes of salvation . . . which occur throughout all history.''[166] But then he goes on to say that it would be ''wrong to deny that revelatory events occur anywhere besides the appearance of Jesus as the Christ.''[166] Tillich means here that there is a line of revelatory and saving events which leads up to and proceeds from the center of revelation and salvation found in Jesus as the Christ. This line is broadened into a universal presence of the saving power of the New Being, without which ''the self-destructive structures of existence'' would plunge ''mankind into complete annihilation.''[167] If salvation were contingent upon an encounter with Jesus as the Christ, then, Tillich argues, only a few men would be saved—an ''absurd and demonic idea'' which theologies of universalism have tried to avoid. The concept of healing delivers theology from this dilemma. All men are somewhat saved by the power of the New Being, or else they would have no being; and no man is totally saved, or else he would no longer be a finite being under the conditions of existence. It ''cannot be that there is no saving power apart from [Jesus as the Christ] . . .''[168]

This understanding of salvation forces us back upon Tillich's Christology. To be sure, it is the power of the New Being in every age and in every man which affords healing of any kind. And this New Being is manifest in Jesus as the Christ. But he is evidently not identical with it, in Tillich's thought: ''. . . the New Being in Jesus as the Christ . . . is the ultimate criterion of every healing and saving process.''[168] But Tillich is not ready to say that he *is* that healing and salvation.

In conclusion we must briefly note Tillich's interpretation of the threefold character of salvation. Salvation must first be considered as new birth or regeneration. This refers to the objective action of God in establishing the new state of things which is the unity of finite existence with himself. It is the objective fact or reality which draws men to itself. The second characteristic of salvation is justification, which must be placed after regeneration because it presupposes faith on the part of man. But it must not be forgotten, Tillich insists, that faith is not a human act; it is being grasped by the divine Spirit. Therefore,

Melanchthon was wrong when he put the reception of the Spirit after man's act of faith. Justification means literally "making just," and the paradoxical point is that God makes those just who are not just and accepts those who are not acceptable. But this acceptance must not be isolated from the subjective side of justification, namely, man's acceptance of it. The call to faith, which is well and powerfully expressed in Tillich's theology and sermons, is to accept the fact that you are accepted. This entails a recognition on man's part of his unacceptability, which is possible only in the power of the New Being in Jesus as the Christ. Tillich strongly insists that the *articulus stantis et cadentis ecclesiae* indicated in the phrase "justification by grace through faith" must be kept clear. "The cause is God alone (by grace), but the faith that one is accepted is the channel through which grace is mediated to man (through faith)."(179) And finally, salvation is transformation, or, in traditional language, sanctification. Actually, regeneration and justification are one, regeneration pointing to reunion, and justification to the paradoxical character of reunion. Sanctification is distinguished from these two as "a process is distinguished from the event in which it is initiated. . . . [It] is the process in which the power of the New Being transforms personality and community, inside and outside the church."(179-180) But this process belongs to the work of the Spirit in history and therefore will be elaborated in the two concluding parts of Tillich's system, "Life and the Spirit" and "History and the Kingdom of God."

SUMMARY AND ANALYSIS

Extreme caution must be used in the analysis of this part of Tillich's theology, lest, in a too hasty or absolute rejection of what is certainly a heterodox presentation of the doctrine of Christ, one misses the very real contributions to be found here as well as the deeper problems involved. To object that Tillich is "too philosophical," or "too impersonal," or that he expresses the concrete symbols of the New Testament in abstract terms is to criticize him from the outside and fails utterly to penetrate to the substance of his thought. Such philosophical, impersonal, and non-biblical symbols are to be judged—as Tillich himself has said—only on the basis of their ability to express the reality of the New Being in Jesus the Christ. And this ability depends much more on the use of such words than any inherent meaning they may have. Therefore, our approach to his whole system, and to this part in particular, must be one of seeking understanding, appreciation, and only then friendly criticism.

If we have understood Tillich correctly, there is much here with which we can agree and enthusiastically second. For must we not support him against philosophical essentialism and theological humanism and agree that man is in a state of radical estrangement from his essential self and from God? And certainly we must follow his insistence that this fall of man into sin and evil is nothing less than his turning away from God and toward himself. Neither can we doubt that this turning from God creates and constitutes a structure of evil which corrupts the life of man and from which he cannot extricate himself. Thus when Tillich describes man's need for an absolutely new being, we cannot but agree.

New Being is certainly found in Christ who constitutes a return to the original unity between God and man. Moreover, Tillich has rightly pointed out that the anticipation of the New Being is itself already a work of the New Being. How else can we explain the prophetic hope for "new heavens and a new earth" (Isa. 65:17) or for the "new covenant" (Jer. 31:31) than as a gift of the Spirit of him who is himself the New Being? We cannot overlook the fact that Tillich finds in the event of Jesus, the Christ, as witnessed and presented by the New Testament, the manifestation of the New Being for the salvation of men. And he is true to the nature of that biblical witness when he holds that it is not empirically verifiable or available to historical criticism as such, but authenticates itself by the faith created through it. In this same line we should underline and support Tillich's assertion that Jesus is the Christ, not because of what he did or said, but because his being is the New Being. This must always be emphasized against both liberal and fundamentalistic tendencies to discover the character or "prove" the divinity and authority of Jesus through the data of the scriptural accounts of his life. Tillich's understanding of the being of Jesus the Christ is problematic. But we can nonetheless support his attempt to improve on the creedal formulations of the early church.[13] These are not sacrosanct, and their re-evaluation and reinterpretation is a perennial task of theology. His dissatisfaction with the "two natures" of Christ, as discussed at Nicaea and Chalcedon, is understandable, and his denomination of Christ as the "eternal God-man-unity" is not at all a bad substitute. But here interpretation plays an all-important role!

Tillich's translation of salvation as "healing" is certainly not out of place insofar as Jesus' own ministry to the sick was a sign of his saving power. And Tillich is right in maintaining the centrality of the Cross in the story of this salvation as an expression of God's participation in man's situation which, together with its correlate, the Resurrection, is the place of his victory over that situation. No less do we agree with Tillich's conviction that the central and primary thing is grace, that "the atoning processes are created by God and God alone."[173]

The points of agreement we have listed (to which others could certainly be added) represent the aim and purpose of Tillich's system and assure it its own place in the whole body of Christian theology. We therefore find it impossible to agree with Nels F. S. Ferré that Tillich is "the most dangerous theological leader alive,"[14] nor can we count as serious the warning of R. Allen Killen: "There is a real danger . . . that some of his successors may find some other religion just as compatible with his ontology while rejecting the Christ whom he represents."[15] We cannot but

---

[13] For this reason we must take exception to one aspect of George Tavard's otherwise excellent and important book *Paul Tillich and the Christian Message*. Insofar as his analysis and critique of Tillich's Christology assumes that "The norm of Christology cannot be the new insights that theologians may reach; it must always be the consistent interpretation of Jesus the Christ that has developed in the Church along the lines set by the orthodox Fathers . . ." (*op. cit.*, p. 2), he obscures the valid criticisms and new insights which he himself reaches. We may sympathize with the necessities of the *nihil obstat* and *imprimatur* laid upon Catholic theology, but in no case can we allow tradition to replace the Word of God as the only norm for theology.

[14] Quoted in *Time*, Vol. LXXIII, No. 11 (March 16, 1959), p. 51.

[15] Killen, *op. cit.*, p. 265.

believe that Tillich deserves a better reading than this. There is
no suggestion here of an *interpretatio in bonam partem*, but only
the insistence that the uniqueness of Tillich's language and the
highly problematic character of many of his concepts not blind
the reader to the positive and constructive effort of his theology
to interpret for men the meaning of Christ and his salvation.
Unless this is seen, Tillich will be criticized on peripheral issues
and the central problem and danger of his (and not only his!)
theology will be passed by.

This problem and danger, to put the matter simply, is the lack
of a consistent focus on the revelation of God in Jesus Christ.
In the doctrines of man and Christ which we have reviewed, there
is the danger that man will be seen apart from who he is revealed
to be in Christ and that God's revelation and salvation will be
found in some other way or at some other place than in Jesus
Christ. Christian theology bases its knowledge of God entirely on
his self-revelation in Jesus Christ. Thus it cannot speak of God
apart from what he has revealed himself to be in Jesus Christ.
And because this revelation took place in and through a *man*,
Christian theology finds in Jesus, the Christ, not only the revelation of God, but also the revelation of what man was, is, and shall
be. It is therefore equally impossible to approach either God or
man apart from this revelation.

Such a centeredness, concentration, and consistency of focus is
only valid if the revelation of Jesus Christ actually demands it.
Tillich's position, if we have understood him correctly, is this:
Jesus is the Christ because his contemporaries recognized in him
the manifestation of the divine Logos, the eternal principle of
God's self-revelation called the New Being. The Logos or New
Being transcends the event of Jesus, the Christ, although it is
manifest in him. This conception Tillich finds expressed in the
first chapter of the Gospel of John where "the mythological
element is reduced to a great extent by the categories Logos,
Life and Light," the Logos being "a divine principle in which
the mythological implications of pre-existence have been overcome . . ."[16] Thus Tillich maintains that John not only allows,

---

[16] Tillich, "A Reinterpretation of the Doctrine of the Incarnation," *op.
cit.*, p. 135.

but directs, our attention from Jesus to this divine "principle."[17]

Is John really concerned with a principle called "Logos"?
What the author had in mind when he used the word is not
known, and even whether he was consciously using a philosophical concept is an open question. What is known is that John had
no interest in developing any meaning for this term itself, for
"Logos" does not appear in the same context again in his
Gospel.

Thus we find in John no "higher principle," name, or concept than Jesus Christ. The first sentence of his Gospel does
not point up and away from Jesus, but down the page and into
the story of his life which it contains. The categories of Logos,
life, and light have no meaning for John apart from Jesus Christ,
nor do they point to any divine activity beyond or beside him.
Here we find no prologue in which a divine and transcendent
drama sets the stage for the human event about to be unfolded.
Rather we are given an overture which outlines and rehearses
the various facets of the single theme in the work itself. That
theme is Jesus Christ, the only Son of God, who, because God
makes him known, is called the Word of God, and who, because
he is "in the bosom of the Father," is said to be "in the beginning" and "with God," and who therefore—in this sense—is
God. It is difficult to understand how Tillich can find in the
Gospel of John any transcendent and eternal principle of the

---

[17] "*En arche en o logos, kai o logos en pros ton theon kai theos en o
logos.*" "The word was original, which is to say that it was with God,
which is to say that it *was* God in that it shares a mode of being with
God." More than this or less than this John is not trying to say. "Logos"
as it appears in verse 1 has no content. It has been called "a stop-gap"
(Karl Barth, *Church Dogmatics*, Vol. II, Part 2, *op. cit.*, p. 96), a word,
meaningless in itself, which will receive meaning later. It is like the *x* of
an equation, "whose value we can know only when the equation has been
solved" (p. 97). The equation is solved in verse 2, where the Logos is
definitely identified as *outos*, the same *outos* as appears in verse 15 (note
in both cases the construction *outos en*). The subject of this section of
John 1:1-18 is the same as in the following account of John's baptism of
Jesus; it is the same *outos*; it is the one named in the climax of verse 17,
". . . grace and truth came through Jesus Christ. No one has ever seen
God; the only Son, who is in the bosom of the Father, he has made him
known." This certainly demands the conclusion that John is not here
writing about the Logos, but about Jesus Christ. He certainly "had no intention of honoring Jesus by investing him with the title of Logos"
(*ibid.*, p. 97).

New Being in terms of which Jesus is accepted as the Christ and over against which he is judged. The New Testament is consistent in its sharp and clear focusing on the person of Jesus Christ. Its authors did not, and we dare not, look elsewhere, because there is nowhere else to look. Where else could they look if "the Word [who was God] became flesh," if in Jesus Christ God is present to man and man is present to God?

This insight is important for the problem of the incarnation. If we say that in Jesus Christ we see the unity of God and man, we certainly mean that in him the divine majesty, dignity, power, and love is present to men. In him we see the glory of God's gracious election, but also the terrible nature of his rejection. In Jesus Christ, God's ways and works, his purposes and its fulfillment, are manifest in such a way that if man looks inward upon himself or outward upon nature, backward into the past, or forward into the future, downward at his estrangement or upward at some concept of essential being—and seeks there the revelation of God—this can be nothing less than a turning away from God's revelation as it in fact has appeared. In Jesus Christ we see God and for this very reason our gaze may not wander. But in him we also see man. In him one appears who is flesh of our flesh and bone of our bone, truly God, but also truly man. But we cannot make any sense out of this manhood unless we see that it is *God's* manhood that is revealed there. If the event of Jesus Christ meant that God became our type of man, then we would surely be in the "absurd" and "impossible" situation which Tillich has described as transmutation and metamorphosis. But the manhood of Jesus is the humanity of *God*. The deity of God is not self-confined, but has room for and includes humanity. From the beginning, God has included within himself humanity in Jesus Christ, being free to turn toward man in love and fellowship without prejudice to his divinity. If Jesus was divine, this can only mean that God is human. Now of course we mean that God includes within himself the man who is not separated from him. We may even call this humanity "essential manhood" if we mean that Jesus Christ represents the original unity between man and God which has been completely lost to man and that he represents the destined reuniting of our manhood with God. He is the original and ultimate image of man. He is the reality, norm, and standard of humanity. As such, he represents God's will, purpose, and decision regarding man, so that it is possible to speak of true manhood only in the light of that Man.

It is certainly true that essential man is united with God and that existential man is estranged from him. But has Tillich seen exactly and exclusively who this essential man is? Has he seen that just because we are in a situation of estrangement, this essential manhood can in no sense be ours except in the negative sense that it is not ours, that it is lost? But God has not lost this essentiality. He has kept it from the beginning within his own life, and it has pleased God in the fullness of time to reveal to man not only divinity but also this humanity in Jesus Christ. How then can we speak of an "adoption" of Jesus by a divine principle called the New Being? Is there really a need to speak of him thus so as not to violate either his divinity or humanity? God is Spirit, to be sure, but does this mean that he is not capable of the flesh? Is he not free to be open toward man and include his creatureliness within himself? Is this not exactly what we see in Jesus Christ? Is it really the case that if "God becomes man," he becomes something other than who he by nature, already, in the beginning, was?[18]

If God has revealed himself in both his deity and his humanity in Jesus Christ so that there is nowhere to look for his ways and works except in him, serious questions arise concerning Tillich's view of the Cross and the Resurrection. He sees that the Cross is both an event in which the subjection of Christ to the estrangement of finitude is shown, and a symbol of the whole revelatory self-giving and sacrifice of God for men. But does he see that it is only in that life and in that event that God's gracious turning to man, as well as his dying for man, is seen? Is it not his

---

[18] George Tavard agrees that by "two natures" the church does not mean two different natures, but two aspects of the same nature, that is, God's manhood and ours. God includes the concrete and particular. The movement is not from one kind of being to another, but it is a movement of the concrete and human life of God above history into history. (See *Paul Tillich and the Christian Message, op. cit.,* pp. 168 ff.)

thesis that the New Being as an eternal principle of salvation somehow exists apart from, even though "completely expressed in," the Cross of Jesus?[19] The New Testament is quite specific in insisting that in Jesus Christ the whole work of God is to be seen. The Resurrection shows that it was exactly this man who was victorious over the powers of sin and death, and that whatever the nature of this event, it may not be separated from him. But do we not see just this separation in Tillich's "restitution theory"? Jesus did not rise from the dead, but after his death his Spirit witnessed to the reality of the New Being in him. Is there not here a darkening of him whom the New Testament illumines? He stands in the shadow, and our attention is directed elsewhere. Concerning his being we were asked to look before him to a transcendent principle of salvation, and now concerning his work of salvation we are asked to look after him to the presence of the Spirit. In neither case are we required to look only at him and see in him the presence of God in the midst of man's sin and death and his victory over it.

Tillich maintains the necessity of his reformulation of the doctrine of the Resurrection as a guard against the absurdities of a "physical" theory. But who, in affirming the creedal assertion that "the third day he rose again from the dead . . ." really has hold of a physical, historical, or natural concept with which his mind can construct a discernible object of faith? The New Testament itself does not offer this kind of object, and so it is not strange that our reaction to its testimony should entail the same elements of mystery, doubt, hiddenness, and even contradiction found there. But this should not prejudice the fact or

[19] From the beginning of his career Tillich has given his readers reason to think so. In a debate between himself and Karl Barth in 1923, Tillich could speak of "a history of revelation which is hidden in history and which has found its complete expression in Christ" (Paul Tillich, "Kritisches und positives Paradox: eine Auseinandersetzung mit Karl Barth und Friedrich Gogarten," *Theologische Blätter*, Vol. II, Nov., 1923). Barth answered Tillich with the assertion that Jesus Christ presents us with "a special happening, which is revealed only by God, and which may be apprehended only as we are apprehended by it. Both the event and the knowledge of it are an occurrence between persons, a communication, a 'given' in the strongest sense of the word" (Karl Barth, "Von der Paradoxie des 'positiven Paradoxes': Antworten und Fragen an Paul Tillich," *Theologische Blätter*, Dec., 1923, p. 292).

significance of the New Testament witness to the Resurrection
of Jesus Christ. For whatever we may think about the matter, or
the apostolic writers may have thought about the matter, it is
obvious what they said about it. And what they said, with rare
unanimity, was that Jesus, the Christ, who was crucified, dead,
and buried, rose from the grave. Therefore as much as we may
agree as to the necessity of recognizing a symbolic element in the
story, we must question Tillich's interpretation of 1 Corinthians
15, in which he finds support for his theory of "restitution."[20]

It would be unwise to suggest what form thought should take
when it encounters the mysterious, hidden, and strange event of
the Resurrection. It obviously is not "historical" in any scientific sense of that word. It obviously is not available to empirical
analysis. Therefore all of our speaking about this event must
reflect a definite reserve; we must not even abstract the word
"physical" from the New Testament narrative, for the term
"physical Resurrection," asserted or denied, carries with it
scientific elements alien to the account we are given. This, however, does not mitigate the fact that in the New Testament itself,
the Resurrection is seen as an event concerning Jesus of Nazareth

---

[20] In the first place we must ask whether it is not highly questionable
procedure in a discussion of the nature of the Resurrection to appeal
exegetically to only one of many passages which apply. Tillich maintains
that 1 Corinthians 15 is the "oldest source" for the Resurrection; this
distinction probably should go to 1 Thessalonians 4:14. Moreover, it is
obvious that Paul's knowledge of this event is based on the same body of
tradition expressed in the Gospels, for his accounts do not vary essentially
from theirs. Would it not therefore seem incumbent upon Tillich's argument that he deal also with the Gospel accounts and show in what way
their description of Christ's Resurrection is symbolic of his restitution
through the Spirit or else show why they are not to be considered authori-
tative at this point?
Turning to 1 Corinthians itself, where Tillich claims special support for
his theory of restitution, we do find such passages as "flesh and blood
cannot inherit the kingdom of God" (vs. 50), and "It is sown a physical
body, it is raised a spiritual body" (vs. 44). But insofar as Paul speaks of
the bodily nature of that spiritual Resurrection, it is hard to see how he
either denies a physical or asserts a purely spiritual interpretation. Much
more to the point are Paul's comments on Jesus' Resurrection in the first
part of the chapter. ". . . he was buried, . . . he was raised on the third
day . . .'' (vs. 4), and then "he appeared to Cephas, then to the twelve.
. . . Last of all . . . to me" (vss. 5-8). It has been suggested that Paul's
identification of his conversion experience with the Resurrection demonstrates the "spiritual" character of the latter. Paul, of course, meant it
to do just the opposite. Nowhere does he identify his experience with

which took place in time and space and not in the minds of the
disciples or through the presence of the Spirit. It was a real and
actual appearance of the Crucified three days after he died.
Tillich is right when he says that we are able to believe in the
risen Christ only because he is present in and through his Spirit.
But the Spirit witnesses to the Word of God and the stark and
inexplicable event there presented. Therefore we must listen to
that Word, and let it speak to us as it will, with no prejudice as
to what is or is not possible. We may not know what to make of
it or just what to believe about it. But we are not required to
make anything of it or to believe this or that about it. It is only
required that we listen. It is only required that we be willing to
hear of the stone rolled away and the empty tomb, of the coming
of Mary and the others, of the strange trans-spatial presence
and the stranger wounded flesh that was seen and touched. It is
only required that we let the Gospels tell their story, a story
based on a man who really lived and an event which really
happened and which, now as then, is the basis of our faith and
the power of our salvation.

If the Resurrection story is not heard as the story of Jesus

Pentecost; everywhere he connects it with the risen Christ. This was the
basis of his claim to apostleship, and it therefore had to be qualitatively
different from the sending of the Spirit to the whole church. He goes on:
". . . if Christ is . . . raised from the dead . . . if Christ has not been
raised, then our preaching is in vain . . . God . . . raised Christ . . . If
Christ has not been raised . . . But in fact Christ has been raised . . ." (!)
(vss. 12-20). Again and again he drives home this fact! Christ is raised
from the dead! How can this possibly be interpreted as any kind of denial
of his bodily Resurrection? It is clear that in the Gospels, and in Paul's
letters as well, the Resurrection was considered as a real and actual fact
and event in which the crucified Jesus was brought back from the dead.
Their description of that event, being so mysterious and hidden in character, certainly prohibits our going beyond the assertion of that fact to
physiological or biological calculations—which Tillich rightly calls "absurd." But their insistence upon the fact of the event and Jesus' place
in it also prohibits any denial of its physical character. Nor are we
allowed to "spiritualize" this event. The New Testament isolates Easter
from Pentecost for this very reason. The Resurrection did not create faith
within the church; the word "faith" (*pistos*) does not appear in any of
the accounts. The Resurrection was not an idea which either grew in the
minds of the disciples or was ready at hand to be used under the stimula-
tion of the Spirit. It was a fact which they had experienced and upon
which their faith, later granted by the Spirit, was built. Nowhere in the
New Testament is the risen Christ confused with the presence of his Spirit.

Christ, if whatever doubts or problems there may be do not converge on him, if all our attention is not centered there, how can our ultimate concern be anchored in a concrete reality, as Tillich says it must? How will our salvation be seen but as the general truth that God's being overcomes the power of non-being? Tillich is quite specific in saying that such salvation is possible apart from Christ. But where and how are we to know of it? Is it not the whole point of the New Testament that we may and must look only here, to Jesus Christ, for such a manifestation of the power of the New Being? What else can it be but a turning away from this revelation if we seek another before, after, or alongside of him?

We began our discussion of this part of Tillich's theology with the doctrine of Christ because we believe that this is where all theology should begin—with this gracious Word which has been spoken to man. But if the fact that God was present to man in Jesus Christ is kept clear, and if he remains the focus, concentration, and interest of theology, then we can and we must also speak of man. The human situation is certainly the other side of the theological task, and there is no doubt that it must be understood if the church's message is to be relevant. It is the great strength of Tillich's work that he has given this necessity such powerful expression. But in the final analysis, we must speak of man because we have spoken of God in Christ, who was man. He was the real, the original, the "essential," and only true man. Thus we can speak of man only as we see who and what he is in Jesus Christ.

Tillich's whole method and aim in writing theology is to correlate man's situation with the revelatory answer of God. This is quite right. The Word of God speaks to man as he is and where he is. But the whole question hangs on the definition of this man and his situation. Tillich's approach might be described in the following way: God is the creator and sustainer of the universe; therefore, both man and nature are created as good. But there is the reality of sin and evil in human life. How can these two aspects of humanity be explained or reconciled? From this understanding of the problem, Tillich then proceeds to describe man in terms of the dialectic of freedom and destiny, essence and existence, and the creation and the Fall. But is this the right question with which to start? Can theology begin with the problem of theodicy, that is, how can God permit evil? Can this question be interpreted as anything but a refusal to see that God in fact does *not* permit sin and evil, that he does not allow it, that he has done something very explicitly about it? We can agree with Tillich's assertion that man is created as essentially good, as essentially united with God. And we certainly must agree with him that man in his existential condition has turned away from this goodness and this unity to stand upon himself and that it is this act which causes man to exist in a state of estrangement and a structure of destruction. But can we at all agree with the correlate which Tillich sees to this truth, namely, that this is man's destiny? For what is man's destiny except to be reconciled and reunited with God? How can we speak of man's fall from grace except in the context of God's lifting him up again in grace? How can we speak of a universal destiny which does not include the aim and purpose of God, which is the salvation of men? In short, how can we speak of man apart from who he is in Christ?

And if man's true situation and destiny is seen in his reunion with God in Jesus Christ, how can we agree with Tillich that man's turning away from his true being and destiny is an act of freedom? What else can this falling away from God be but an act in which man delivers himself over to the slavery of his own will? Tillich says that man uses his freedom to lose his freedom, but what sort of free act can it be that denies and makes freedom impossible? It has always been one of Tillich's major interests to protect the freedom and the integrity of man against every kind of heteronomous authority. But what sort of freedom is man left if left to himself? Is there any oppression to equal man's own authority over himself, or slavery to equal his own self-imposed will? How else can we express man's turning away from God and his own essential nature than as a radical denial and abdication of freedom? Who is the free man? Only that man who is united with God; only that man who is obedient to and lives for God; only that man we see in Christ! Therefore, if we analyze man apart from who he is in Christ or if his humanity is judged by any norm other than the humanity there revealed, we are no longer analyzing a real man, but one who forfeits his humanity in ever new attempts to play the slave. But this charade will be exposed; this too must be said. In the final analysis man's attempts to enslave himself will not succeed, because God does not and will not allow it. Man tries it, but his destiny is that his attempt will fail. Man is not free to turn away from God, nor is the universe free to fall from the unity of essence to the estrangement of existence. The so-called reality of sin can only be considered the most unreal and impossible of situations, which cannot stand and which itself is destined to fall. Thus there is no coincidental equality between created goodness and actual evil, for this evil is only a burden of falsehood and untruth, of self-deception and prideful imagining that man has laid upon himself, but which God has determined from the beginning to take away and has taken away in Jesus Christ.

What relevance do these considerations have for the rest of Tillich's theology? We noted that in his doctrines of revelation and God, Tillich sought through the concepts of the *analogia entis*, "depth of reason," and *imago Dei* to reserve for man and nature an integrity and possibility which he does not believe is present in a theology which maintains that outside of Jesus Christ there is no capacity or possibility for a knowledge of God, salvation, or true manhood. But what is the result of Tillich's view? Is it not that finally man is left to his own freedom and therefore loses it; that the universe is caught up in a tragic destiny which separates it from God? Does it not finally lead to a confusion of the Fall with creation so that we may no longer say in any unambiguous way that what God has created is good? What kind of a positive view of man and the world is it that leaves them both hanging on the horns of a dilemma called the polarity of freedom and destiny? How much more hopeful and how much more positive would be an approach to man and his world in terms of the divine grace and acceptance given them in Jesus Christ from the very beginning!

We have said that we are under no obligation to reject Tillich's definition of theology as "apologetic," or his method of correlation. Theology may begin with man and his situation, but it must be very clear just who this man is. The man who is the proper object of theological analysis, whose situation and questions are answered by the revelation of God, is the man addressed by God in Jesus Christ. He is the man elected, the man to whom mercy has been given, the man called, sanctified, and glorified in Jesus Christ. Is this the man addressed and analyzed in Tillich's apologetic theology? If the man who asks for God is the man who has already been found by God, how can we draw a distinction between apologetic and kerygmatic theology? How can we approach this searching man and his question as if he had not already been found and his question answered? How can we speak of the possibility of this man's question controlling the form of his answer when his question itself was only made possible through the answer and the very specific form in which it came to him?

These are the questions which must be asked of Paul Tillich's theology. They are all dependent upon the single truth that in Jesus Christ, God has fully revealed both his deity and his humanity in such a way that we can speak neither of the knowledge of God nor of man apart from him. But the questions asked above are neither refutations nor dismissals. Still less do they seek to detract from the depth and seriousness of Tillich's theology or to call into question the definite and positive contributions which he has made. The problem of such a report as ours is that the limitation of time and space are such that we can only attempt to lay before the reader Tillich's systematic theology and some of the major problems found there. But we do this in the confidence that these problems will not obscure what Tillich himself says, even in this abbreviated and condensed presentation, and that he will draw a warm response and appreciation from the reader as he has from the reporter. The problems we have raised, however, should suggest a possible corrective to Tillich's formulations. If his concept of the being of Christ in terms of the "eternal God-man-unity" were seen not as the unity of God with our essential manhood, but with his own humanity, and if this were developed as a real a priori for his whole system, then we believe that he could better accomplish the task which he has set. Of course such a developed a priori would radically change the structure of his system, but if it were allowed to do so, his intention to expound the meaning of Jesus Christ for men would be served.

VI

LIFE AND THE SPIRIT

In all life processes an essential and an existential element, created goodness and estrangement, are merged in such a way that neither one nor the other is exclusively effective. . . . this is the root of its ambiguity. . . . The quest for unambiguous life is for a life which has reached that toward which it transcends itself.[(107)][1]

The Spiritual Presence, elevating man through faith and love to the transcendant unity of unambiguous life, creates the New Being above the gap between essence and existence and consequently above the ambiguities of life.[(138-139)]

We have seen that for Paul Tillich the threat of non-being drives man to the question of the ground of being. This is the question of God. In the last chapter we found that man's situation of estrangement leads him to ask after that which can reunite him with his own essential nature and the ground of being. This is the question of the New Being which has appeared in Jesus as the Christ. We now turn to the third person of the Trinity, the divine Spirit. Tillich's approach to this doctrine again follows his "method of correlation" in which he first analyzes the life of man to discover the nature of the questions for which the divine Spirit is given as the answer. This situation he describes in terms of the ambiguities of life in all dimensions. Tillich then proceeds to discuss the divine Spirit as presented in revelation and finally shows the application of the Spirit to the ambiguities of life in raising man to transcendent unity with God, to unambiguous life.

This part of Tillich's *Systematic Theology* is certainly the most complex and intricate of his whole work; not only does he develop

---

[1] Numbers in parentheses in this chapter refer to page numbers in Paul Tillich's *Systematic Theology*, Vol. III (Chicago: The University of Chicago Press, 1963).

here the doctrines of the Spirit and the church and outline his view of ethics, but he also attempts to analyze "life" and the dialectical tensions within it. Tillich's perceptive and analytical mind ranges over such broad and diverse fields as art, technology, politics, medicine, and music, and into even such specialized areas as magic, nuclear physics, psychiatry, and semantics. We cannot of course reproduce the many and infinitely detailed patterns which Tillich has woven into the fabric of this volume. But we have sought to indicate the most important subjects and through them the basic outline of his thought, and to elucidate those concepts which clearly indicate the purpose and meaning of the whole. The subject matter and details of this chapter are new, but the fundamental philosophical and theological assertions here applied will be found consistent extensions of those in the previous parts of the system.

LIFE AND ITS AMBIGUITIES

The Multidimensional Unity of Life

By "life" Tillich means something different from either essence or existence. "Essence," in the classical tradition and in this system, is defined as that which makes a thing what it is. For man, his essential nature is his original created nature; it is his unity with the ground of his being in God. Tillich has called it a state of innocence or potentiality. "Existence," on the other hand, is the word that Tillich has used to describe man's fallen state, his estrangement from God. Essence points to created goodness. Existence points to sin and separation, for both men and nature. But actual life is a mixture of essence and existence. For in spite of their existential estrangement, trees remain trees and man remains man. They do not lose their essential nature. The reason for this actual continuance of being in spite of the existential threat of non-being was seen in the doctrine of God to be his sustaining creativity in which the power of his being overcomes non-being and gives to man the ontological courage to be. This was seen also in the doctrine of Christ as the universal healing and saving power of the New Being, without which all men would fall victim to the structure of destruction in which they live. Thus, life is a mixture of essence and existence, estrangment and salvation, and this mixture makes life "ambiguous."

"Life" defined as this mixture of essence and existence is universal, and applies to all things, for all things share equally in this definition. Life, therefore, is a unity. Tillich is opposed to the Thomistic description of life in terms of levels, that is, the distinction of degrees of life, beginning with the inorganic and ascending to the divine life itself. Such a view tends to isolate the different forms of life and ultimately leads to a dualism expressed in supernaturalistic interferences in the human level. Tillich prefers the term "dimension" for the various forms of life, for, to use a geometric simile, it has the advantage of expressing the crossing of lines in one area of space (life) without interference or contradiction. Thus the term "dimension," while expressing distinction, also includes the idea of unity. It is of course fundamental to Tillich's system that all things find their unity in being. We have seen in the first part of his system, "Reason and Revelation," that Tillich asserted the unity of reason expressed in its universal structure which he calls the *logos*. This formed a kind of rational bridge between God and man which makes revelation possible. Similarly, in the second part of the system, "Being and God," man's consciousness of his own being and its essential unity with God as the ground of being enabled man to ask the question of God. And it was this same unity from which man is estranged in existence, but from which he cannot be entirely cut off, which is expressed in the New Being. It is only natural that this motif should continue in this part of the system which deals with the presence of the divine Spirit with man.

Life is a unity, but it does contain different dimensions. Among these Tillich distinguishes the inorganic, including the realms of the macro- and micro-cosmic, and the organic dimension in which are found the plant, animal, human, and most significantly the spiritual, realm. The establishment of the dimension of "spirit" as a part of the organic dimension is necessary at this juncture, for, "Without knowing what spirit is, one cannot know what Spirit is."[22][2] The dimension of spirit includes those cognitive and moral functions of life in which the personal center sees itself in relation to the world and acts upon its world. Human "spirit" is then the "unity of power and meaning."[22] With this definition Tillich combines the Hebrew and Indo-Germanic understanding of spirit as the breath or power of life and the Western philosophical conception of spirit as mind or intellect. Neither definition alone suffices. While the spiritual power of animation never operates outside the universal structure of reason, spirit is more than reason; it includes passion, eros, and imagination. Spirit is the unity of power and meaning, manifesting itself in the free and creative encounter of the personal center with its environment. This self-world relationship which is the spiritual dimension of man is the source of the functions of life, and we shall see that it is within these functions that we find both the ambiguities of life and the answer to those ambiguities in the presence of the divine Spirit. But it is only within the dimension of the spirit of man that this quest can be raised and the answer be given.

Actual Life and Its Ambiguities

Having established the unity of life and the dimension of the spirit as that dimension in which life actualizes itself, Tillich turns to the analysis of life and its functions. In each of the three functions of life analyzed below, it will be seen that it is in the realm of the spirit that the decisive actualization of life takes place for man and that it is also in this realm that the ambiguities of life, which raise the question of the divine Spirit, are most clearly seen.

The first function of life under consideration is that of self-integration. In this function self-identity is established, drawn into alteration, and then re-established. This is the basic, "dialectical" function of life. We have discussed this function already

---

[2] The reader must take care throughout this chapter to distinguish between the lower and upper case *s* in reference to man's *s*pirit and God's *S*pirit.

in Chapter IV under the ontological polarities of individualization and participation. ''Centeredness'' is a universal principle which applies equally to the realm of the inorganic and the organic. Everything that is has a center, an indivisible point, which cannot be violated as long as the thing has being, as long as it *is*. The space around this point constitutes its area of participation. Where there is no participation, there is no life. For instance, where there is health, there is a balance between the participation of the organism in its environment and its resting in its own center. Disease can be caused either by the inability of the organism to return to its self-identity (infectious diseases), or by its resting upon itself to such an extent (avoiding the dangers of participation in terms of food, exercise, etc.) that it falls victim to decay and disintegration. In all dimensions of life, there must be movement out of the center toward participation and a return to the center and self-integration.

If we now look for self-integration under the particular dimension of the spirit we find it in the moral act, because it is there that man constitutes his personal self. The only thing which limits and, therefore, also establishes man's centeredness, is another self, and this ego-thou relationship creates the ''oughtness'' of the moral imperative. Therefore, under the dimension of the spirit, the self-integrating function of life is the function of morality. The self-integration of one's personal center takes place over against another personal center rather than an environment. If there is to be real participation, the one person must acknowledge the other as a person. For Tillich, this relationship is the basis for morality, its description is ethics, and its character is love (*agape*). ''. . . it is *agape* which gives concreteness to the categorical imperative, centeredness to the person and the foundation of the life of the spirit.''[46]

But in actual life this very ''law of love'' as the basis for the moral imperative brings with it ambiguities. For if under the conditions of existence, individuality becomes separation, it is nevertheless true that participation holds the danger of loss of self. Thus the concept of love does not offer any simple answer to moral questions, for ''How is participation in the center of the other self related to participation in or rejection of his particular characteristics?"[46] Furthermore, in relation to the contents of the moral law, ambiguities arise because law is abstract and therefore unable to meet every concrete situation. To fulfill its norm (the law of love), the special contents of law must often be disobeyed. The law claims universality but is historically conditioned. And insofar as "law" is needed, it expresses our estrangement and so, while it may motivate men to do the good, it also drives to resistance. "It produces hostility against God, man, and one's self."[49] Therefore, the moral law in actual life cannot overcome the split between essence and existence, between self and world, or between man and God. "The experience of this situation leads to the quest for a morality which fulfils the law by transcending it, that is, *agape* given to man as reuniting and integrating reality, as new being and not as law."[50] The ambiguity of man's moral life drives him to ask for the Spirit of love.

The second function of life which Tillich examines is culture, which includes self-production or growth. Here we find the same tension between life going out from and returning to its center, but expressed in terms of the second polarity of being, dynamics and form. We have seen that the basis of the moral law, the relation of love, presupposes the separation and estrangement of personal centers and so at the same time expresses the ambiguities of morality. This same tension and ambiguity is found in the cultural function, because the productive act of the spirit is resisted by encountered reality. "This conflict is based on the estrangement between subject and object, an estrangement which is, at the same time, a condition for culture as the whole of creative, receiving, or transforming acts."[64] Without the split between subject and object we could not speak of production whereby the subject acts upon and changes the object. On the other hand, it is this very separation which makes man's productivity meaningless and destructive both to the subject and to the object. It will suffice if we mention only the principal examples of this ambiguity.

Language is the first and basic productive function of culture. It is present in all other functions whether cognitive or aesthetic,

technical or political. Its functions of communication and deno-
tation reflect the basic self-world structure of man's life. It shows
that while man is separated from the objects of his experience,
he also belongs to them. This constitutes the basic ambiguity of
language, for the "act of grasping objects by the mind, on
which language is based, opens up a gap between the object
grasped and the meaning created by the word."[69] The *cognitive act* follows from language; it grasps the ontological structure of reality and seeks to bridge the gap between subject and
object. The result of successful cognition in these terms is
"truth." However, "the ambiguities of the cognitive act . . . are
rooted in the split between subject and object. This split is the
precondition of all knowledge and, at the same time, the negative
power in all knowledge."[70] *Personal growth* as a cultural function means that each individual tries to attain his essential humanity. But he is separated under the conditions of existence
from his essential nature and is, therefore, in the position of
trying to determine himself in the power of that which he does
not have. For instance, "in order to will the good, the will itself
must be good. Self-determination must make it good, which is to
say that the good will must create the good will . . . in an endless
regression."[75] This same ambiguity is seen in the cultural function of *communal transformation*. The social group does not have
a responsible center; nonetheless it strives toward justice in the
same way that the individual strives for humanity. Justice
demands that the group be inclusive, but the maintenance of the
group's identity demands that it be exclusive. Justice demands
equality, but because social dynamics implies competition, inequality is inevitable.

We have described the functions of culture and their ambiguities. In each case the ambiguities they present are based upon
the radical subject-object split incumbent upon man's existential
estrangement. This situation is inevitable and cannot be overcome in life. To overcome it, life must transcend the split between
essence and existence and between subject and object. It must
return to the essential unity of being. And this unity is a gift of
the divine Spirit.

Thus we come to the third and final function of life, the *self-*

transcendent or the *religious function*. Life driving beyond itself is called "sublime" and is related to the ontological polarity of freedom and destiny. The life that can transcend itself is free, even if never separated from its destiny, for in transcendence is found the unity of freedom and destiny. But life in transcendence tends either to annihilate itself in the act of transcending itself, or in the anxiety of that possibility "rests in itself" and resists transcendence. This is the basic ambiguity of transcendence. Life remains "profane," i.e., "before the temple," or "outside the holy."

Religion is "the self-transcendence of life under the dimension of spirit."[95] As such it should not be considered a separate function of life but a quality of the two previous functions of morality and culture. For essentially both morality and culture have within themselves the quality of transcendence; morality has the unconditional moral imperative, and culture has the ultimate *telos* of the production of meaning which points beyond itself. However, the ambiguities noted above mean that in actual life morality and culture lose their transcendent function, and thus religion as a separate function does in fact arise. But religion as self-transcendence is itself ambiguous because "something is transcended and at the same time not transcended."[97-98] There must be something concrete, otherwise nothing would be there to transcend, but at the same time this something should not be "there" anymore but negated in the act of being transcended. This, says Tillich, is the situation of all religions in history. Religion cannot escape the ambiguity of transcendence. It remains profane. And because religion "claims to be the answer to the ambiguities of life in all other dimensions . . . it falls into even profounder . . . ambiguities. Religion is the highest expression of the greatness and dignity of life; in it the greatness of life becomes holiness. Yet religion is also the most radical refutation of the greatness and dignity of life; in it the great becomes most profanized . . ."[98]

The basic ambiguity of religion is expressed in the tension between the divine and the demonic. The demonic appears when something finite is raised to infinite value. The Greek hero suffers tragedy because he approaches the sphere of the divine, but he is not necessarily demonic. The tragic is the "inner" ambiguity of human greatness; the hero touches the divine sphere, but does not aspire to be like it. When such a movement is conscious, the demonic appears. The tragic is blind; the demonic is split. The split in the demonic is the reaction of other parts of the centered personality to the raising of one part to infinite meaning and value. This happens in religion when certain moral and cultural forms which serve as mediums of revelation claim ultimate significance for themselves. "These forms participate in the holy to which they point, but they are not the holy itself. The claim to be the holy itself makes them demonic."[104]

Thus, the human situation is such that even in its function of self-transcendence and religion, the ambiguities of life are manifest. Man attempts to transcend his estrangement and reunite with his own essential being and with God. But he cannot do it. He is thus driven to ask for that which can bring about such transcendent unity. This is the quest for the divine Spirit. With these considerations Tillich has established the problem out of which the questions of man arise and the form in which the revelatory answer will be given. The analysis of life and its ambiguities establishes the question of unambiguous life, and the description of the spirit as a dimension of life establishes the context and form of the answer.

We have seen that the ambiguities of life result from the separation and mixture of essential and existential elements in life. This was seen directly in the function of religion where man in existence reaches for essential unity, but cannot attain it; and it was seen indirectly in the functions of morality and culture where ambiguities arose from the split between subject and object. Man attempts to relate himself to, and produce, the good, but he cannot because he is in a state of estrangement from himself and others. Therefore, religion with its ambiguities is not the answer to the quest for unambiguous life. But it is the place where the question is asked, and it is the place where the answer is received. The function of religion furnishes three main symbols for the answer of unambiguous life: Spirit of God, Kingdom of God, and eternal life. The latter two symbols constitute the fifth and last part of Tillich's *Systematic Theology* and will be covered in the next chapter. We are concerned now with the first, the symbol of the Spirit of God.

"The Divine Spirit is 'God present.' The Spirit of God is not a separated being."[107] Therefore, Tillich prefers the symbol "Spiritual Presence." "It is directly correlated to the ambiguities of life under the dimension of spirit although, because of the multidimensional unity of life, it refers indirectly to all realms."[107-108] We now turn to the second section of this part of the system for an analysis of that which gives the answer to man's question, the Spiritual Presence itself.

THE SPIRITUAL PRESENCE

The Spiritual Presence and the Spirit of Man

As we have seen throughout this study, in Tillich's method of correlation it is the function of philosophical analysis not only to establish the problems and the questions of man, but also to indicate the form of the theological answer. Thus the description of human spirit as a dimension of life and as the unity of power and meaning determines the form of Tillich's description of the divine Spirit.

"The Spiritual Presence" is Tillich's way of saying that the divine Spirit is "in" the spirit of man. He means that man's spirit is driven out of itself into successful transcendence; it is grasped by something unconditional and ultimate which delivers it from the ambiguities of life noted above. This situation is called by Tillich "ecstasy." Ecstasy does not destroy the rational structure or the personal center of the individual while driving it out of itself, but it does change life, making it unambiguous. On the other hand the human spirit is not able to "force" the divine Spirit upon itself. Man cannot lift himself above the ambiguities of his life. The divine Spirit and human spirit are united, but must not become confused. The Spiritual Presence is often confused with chaos and irrationalism, and this confusion is the root of psychological reductionist attempts to suppress it. Tillich resists such attempts to "explain away" the Spirit by arguing for his doctrine of the multidimensional unity of life. This concept of unity among all the dimensions of life allows him to say that it is exactly through the dynamics of the psychological self that the Spirit brings meaning-bearing power. Yet, there are such subjective phenomena as intoxication and other forms of self-losing excitement which destroy rationality and the personal self. Therefore, the question arises: How are we to distinguish between Spirit-given ecstasy and self-destructive excitement? "The criterion . . . is the manifestation of creativity in the former and the lack of it in the latter. The use of this criterion is not without risk, but it is the only valid criterion the church can employ in 'judging the Spirit.' "(120)3

The Spiritual Presence is manifested to man through the word and the sacraments, which correspond to the subjective and objective elements of life. They represent "the primordial phenomenon that reality is communicated either by the silent presence of the object as object or by the vocal self-expression of a subject to a subject."(120) This means that the sacrament is "older" than the word because it contains the word, or rational conception, before it is vocally expressed. Sacraments fall into three groups: the *largest* group which includes everything through which the Spiritual Presence is experienced; a *narrower* group which reflects the experience of the Spiritual Community (which includes, but is not identical with, the church); and a *narrowest* group in which are found the "great" sacraments through which the Spiritual Community actualizes itself. Tillich's interpretation of the sacraments is based upon what he calls "Protestant principle and Catholic substance." With this formula he seeks to place himself in agreement with the Reformers' attack upon the Roman Catholic doctrine of *opus operatum* which distorted the sacraments into non-personal acts of magical technique. But at the

---

3 "Beloved, do not believe every spirit, but test the spirits to see whether they are of God . . . By this you know the Spirit of God: every spirit which confesses that Jesus Christ has come in the flesh is of God, and every spirit which does not confess Jesus is not of God" (1 John 4:1-3). Even allowing for the problem of interpreting what "Jesus Christ . . . come in the flesh" means, the biblical point appears to be quite different from Tillich's.

same time he denies the Protestant tendency to reduce the sacraments to intellectualism or moralism. The Catholic substance which Tillich wishes to preserve is the concept of the sacraments as symbols rather than signs. We have noted in several places above that Tillich views symbols as "intrinsically" related to what they express (one could say ontologically related). This means that sacraments have "inherent" qualities which make them adequate and irreplaceable for their sacramental function.[4] The criteria for judging and evaluating sacraments are that they must express the basis of the Spiritual Community in the New Being of Jesus as the Christ and be subject to the revelatory experience of the Spiritual Community through which the central revelation of the New Being has been expressed. Here as elsewhere in Tillich's thought, Jesus as the Christ and revelation as such are kept separate.

The word is the other medium of the Spiritual Presence. Tillich's doctrine of the "Word of God" has already been covered in Chapter III. Here we may simply repeat the thesis we found there, that " 'Word of God' is a term which qualifies human words as media of the Spiritual Presence."[124] This means that there are an infinite number of words which can become the Word of God. But there is a twofold limitation on this infinite expansion. First, a word must be a word for somebody; there is no Word of God unless it is received as such. The second limitation is that the biblical words must be seen to "constitute the ultimate touchstone for what can and cannot become the Word of God for someone. Nothing is the Word of God if it contradicts the faith and love which are the work of the Spirit and which constitute the New Being as it is manifest in Jesus as the Christ."[125]

An interesting part of Tillich's discussion of the Spiritual Presence in the "Word of God" is the problem of the "inner word." The spiritualists (e.g., Anabaptists) voiced a protest

---

[4] It should be mentioned that this view of the sacraments, while developed in much more detail in "Nature and Sacrament" in *The Protestant Era* (*op. cit.*, pp. 94 ff.), is a definite advance over that treatment insofar as there Tillich could develop a whole view of sacramentalism apart from an expressed view of the Spiritual Presence.

against the authority of the Pope on the one hand and the authority of Scripture on the other. Tillich agrees with these aims and even goes so far as to say that "the present system is essentially, but indirectly, influenced by the Spirit-movements, both through their impact on Western culture in general (including such theologians as Schleiermacher) and through their criticism of the established forms of religious life and thought."[126] But to this sympathy of aim Tillich adds the warning that the term "inner word" is misleading. If it is truly "inner," then the hearer listens only to himself. Where there is real communication, the word one hears within must come from without. Yet, Tillich immediately goes on to say, "If God were not also in man so that man could ask for God, God's speaking to man could not be perceived by man. The categories 'inner' and 'outer' lose their meaning in the relation of God and man."[127]

The Spiritual Presence solves the ambiguities of life by creating transcendent union. This transcendent union "appears within the human spirit as the ecstatic movement which from one point of view is called 'faith,' from another, 'love.' "[129] Faith and love form the "content" of the manifestation of the Spiritual Presence. As elsewhere in Tillich's system, faith is here defined formally as the state of being grasped by an ultimate concern. Thus, in a formal sense, everyone has faith, for everyone is concerned ultimately about something. But the material definition of faith is "the state of being grasped by the New Being as it is manifest in Jesus as the Christ."[131] Yet for Tillich the formal definition seems the more basic. "Faith as the state of being opened by the Spiritual Presence to the transcendent unity of unambiguous life is a description which is universally valid despite its particular, Christian background."[131] But this universal validity of "faith" in Tillich's thought should not obscure the fact that for him faith is the result of divine and not human activity. Faith is not an act of man's will, intellect, feeling. It is being grasped. "This implies and confirms the basic theological truth that in relation to God everything is by God."[133]

Love is the other mark of the Spiritual Presence; "love is the state of being taken by the Spiritual Presence into the transcendent unity of unambiguous life."[134] As we noted in Chapter IV, Tillich wishes to free the word "love" from a purely emotional interpretation. In the sense in which it is used here, "love" means "reunion"; it is *agape*, and it is characterized by God's unambiguous love for his creatures. This love is only possible for man within the union given by the Spiritual Presence.

The Spiritual Presence in Historical Mankind

The preceding section discussed the manifestation of the divine Spirit in the human spirit. "We must now determine the place in historical mankind in which the New Being as the creation of the Spiritual Presence is manifest."[139] When the Spiritual Presence appears in human life, it brings unambiguous life, but it brings it fragmentarily. The love which man may experience under the impact of the Spiritual Presence is unambiguous, but it is partial, unfulfilled. As a broken statue can express unambiguously the ideal of the sculptor, so the partial fulfillment of life by the Spirit points unambiguously to man's essential unity with God. This "makes it possible for us to give full affirmation and full commitment to the manifestations of the Spiritual Presence while remaining aware of the fact that in the very acts of affirmation and commitment the ambiguity of life reappears."[140] This fragmentary character of the transcendent unity given by the Spirit is a most important aspect of life as we shall see below. It is a direct correlate of Tillich's idea of the partial character of salvation (or healing) which we encountered in the last chapter.

But where and to whom does the Spirit come? Here again we are given an answer similar to the description of the universal presence of the New Being found in Chapter V. "Mankind is never left alone. The Spiritual Presence acts upon it in every moment and breaks into it in some great moments, which are the historical *kairoi*."[140] Since "mankind is never left alone," there is a common experience of the Spiritual Presence in all religions. This implies a common denominator among all religions not found in phenomenological comparisons, but in the identity of the dimension of the spirit in every being which has language. On this basis one may affirm the Spiritual Presence in the various religions.

The question thus arises: What is the special and specific relation of the Spirit to Christ? Tillich maintains that it was only in Jesus as the Christ that the divine Spirit was present without distortion. "In him the New Being appeared as the criterion of all Spiritual experiences in past and future. Though subject to individual and social conditions his human spirit was entirely grasped by the Spiritual Presence . . ."[144] The relation of the divine Spirit to the Christ as developed in this very short section is entirely consistent with Tillich's earlier christological assertions. We find the same adoptionism, the same revolt against the God-man idea. "Jesus was grasped by the Spirit at the moment of his baptism. This event confirmed him as the elected 'Son of God.' "[144] The divine Spirit found a "vessel in which to pour itself . . ."[144-145] That Jesus was grasped by the Spiritual Presence is seen from his manifestation of the marks of the Spirit which we have noted above, namely, faith and love. Tillich notes the rarity of any mention of Jesus' faith in the Bible, but insists that denial of faith in Jesus is an example of a "crypto-Monophysitic" movement in the church to deprive him of his full humanity. Insofar as faith is "being grasped," Jesus must certainly be said to have had it. Moreover, Tillich argues that Jesus, as all men, experienced both faith and love fragmentarily, if unambiguously.

Tillich's pneumatology carries two important connotations for his doctrine of Christ. First, "it is not the spirit of the man Jesus of Nazareth that makes him the Christ, but . . . it is the Spiritual Presence . . . This insight stands guard against a Jesus-theology which makes the man Jesus the object of Christian faith. . . . The other implication . . . is that . . . Jesus, the Christ, is the keystone in the arch of Spiritual manifestations in history."[146-147] Tillich is here clearly reversing the *processio* of the Spirit from the Father and the Son expressed in the Western version of the Nicaean Creed. This he explains by saying, "In the divine economy, the Spirit follows the Son, but in essence, the Son *is* the

Spirit."[148] Tillich holds that when the Eastern Church "asserted that the Spirit proceeds from the Father alone, [it] left open the possibility of a direct theocentric mysticism (of course, a 'baptized mysticism')."[149] The Son is the Spirit. Thus the Spiritual Presence cannot be differently manifest "before" or "after" the event of Jesus as the Christ. ". . . the divine Spirit . . . of Jesus as the Christ . . . is the criterion to which every Spiritual claim must submit."[152]

We have seen that the Spiritual Presence appears universally, that is, in all religions, including the Old Testament; and it appears in its central manifestation in Jesus as the Christ. Now we must see that it appears also in the Spiritual Community or the church. We remember that Tillich stated in his Christology that the Christ is not the Christ unless he is received as such. This implies the necessity of a place where he could be received and this place is the Spiritual Community. The Spiritual Community is unambiguous; it is New Being, created by the Spiritual Presence. But it is fragmentary, for it appears under the conditions of finitude.

Tillich speaks of the Spiritual Community as "latent" and "manifest."[5] And we must note immediately that this duality does not correspond to the "invisible" and "visible" church of Calvin, but rather to the general and universal as opposed to the specific and Christian manifestations of the Spiritual Presence. The latent and manifest stages of the Spiritual Community correspond to a "before" and "after" relation to the event of Jesus as the Christ. Specifically this "before" and "after" refers to each person's existential encounter with him. The latent church manifests the impact of the Spiritual Presence, but without its ultimate criterion in Jesus as the Christ. Tillich offers as examples of the "latent church" various religions and philosophies—humanism, Israel, Islam, mythology, etc. The church is the Spiritual Community in its manifest stage, and the individual churches are judged against the characterization of the

[5] See also Paul Tillich, "Die Doppelgestalt der Kirche," *Neuwerk*, Vol. XIII (Oct.-Nov., 1931), pp. 239-243, for a more detailed analysis of these terms.

Spiritual Community as found at Pentecost, which includes
ecstasy, faith, love, unity, and universality.

Wherever the Spiritual Community appears, it unites the
functions of life under the dimension of the spirit. Essentially the
functions of morality, culture, and religion are one, but we have
seen that they are separated under the conditions of existence.
The Spiritual Presence unites these functions in the Spiritual
Community unambiguously, but fragmentarily. Thus the divine
Spirit heals the break between essence and existence; it reunites
the estranged and creates unambiguous life fragmentarily above
the ambiguities of life.

THE DIVINE SPIRIT AND THE AMBIGUITIES OF LIFE

Tillich has given a description of ambiguities of life, and he
has given the revelatory answer that the divine Spirit solves
those ambiguities. It is now left to describe the work of the
divine Spirit in raising life to transcendent unity above its ambiguities in the three functions of life which correspond to
religion, culture, and morality.

The Spirit and Religion

The Spiritual Community is the essence of the visible church
and in this way is equivalent to the invisible church. Thus we
may say that the ambiguities of life are conquered in life through
the church. But we may not lose sight of the fact that the churches
contain the paradox "that they participate, on the one hand,
in the ambiguities of life in general and of the religious life in
particular and, on the other hand, in the unambiguous life
of the Spiritual Community."[165] Tillich wishes to steer a course
between a view of the churches as mere sociological institutions
and the Roman Catholic view of a church whose history is holy
history. In terms of both the members and the institution, the
churches are "holy" because of the holiness of their foundation,
but not in themselves.

The church is where the struggle against the ambiguities of a
religion takes place under the impact of the Spirit. But again,
the victory of the Spirit is fragmentary. ". . . the ambiguities

of religion are not eliminated but are conquered in principle. . . .
The ambiguities of the religious life are conquered . . . their
self-destructive force is broken.''(172-173) We have seen above
that in the religious function, faith and love always remain
ambiguous. But in the churches they are experienced unambiguously, but fragmentarily, under the impact of the Spirit. The
early church had the *fides quae creditur* upon which its creedal
foundation was built. But the whole history of the church since
then has shown that such a faith is no longer active in its members. Skepticism has weakened the conscious base of belief of
the church. How then can we say that the church is the Spiritual
Community where faith is experienced unambiguously? The
answer to this situation, says Tillich, is that the faith of the
members and the churches is not dependent upon their individual decision, but is rather based upon the Spiritual Presence in
it, grasping it and its members. In the same way, love in the
churches, *agape*, exists because of the foundation it has in Jesus
as the Christ. Yet it is made ambiguous by the existential conflicts within and between the churches and their members. Unambiguous love is experienced when under the impact of the Spiritual Presence the churches fight against disunity and division.
Love is unity, and under the power of the Spirit, the church and
its members are united with their essential being. This happens
unambiguously, but fragmentarily.

At this point in his development, Tillich's aim is to develop a
doctrine of the church built on the description of its relation to
the divine Spirit. But according to Tillich's phenomenological
approach, to describe the church, he must describe the functions
of the churches, which he distinguishes as the constitutive, the
expanding, and the constructing. All of these functions ''participate in the paradox of the churches. They are all performed in
the name of the Spiritual Community; yet they are also performed by sociological groups. . . . [But] their aim is to conquer
these ambiguities in the power of the Spiritual Presence.''(183)
The constitutive function of the churches expresses the reception
and mediation of their message and this implies the necessity of
both tradition and reformation. In the Spiritual Community

these are in tension but not in conflict. The expanding function of the churches includes missionary, educational, and apologetic activity. The problem is thus raised as to how to adopt the message of the church to culture and yet maintain its integrity. Tillich's point in this regard is that under the impact of the Spirit we need not fear culture, but can "speak through" it. The constructing function of the churches receives detailed analysis because it uses all the cultural functions of life. And here again Tillich brings forward the argument which appears so often throughout his system, that the use of cultural forms is unavoidable because we have to use language, voiced or unvoiced, and language is a cultural product. There is, therefore, no "diastasis" between the cultural and the religious sphere.

If we now ask about the churches' relation to the world, Tillich requires that we first remember that the churches are sociological entities in paradoxical relation to their essence in the Spiritual Community. This means that they act on and receive from other social agencies. Tillich lists three ways in which this happens: silent interpenetration, which might be called the "priestly" function of the churches; critical judgment, which might be called the prophetic function; and political establishment, which is the kingly function. In fulfilling these functions the churches must maintain their character as the Spiritual Community. But the churches are not separated from the world, for "the world which is opposed by the church is not simply not-church but has in itself elements of the Spiritual Community in its latency which work toward a theonomous culture."[(216)]

We turn now from the churches as institutions to the individual member. "The Spiritual Community is the Community of Spiritual personalities. . . . As the Spiritual Community is the dynamic essence of the churches, so is the Spiritual Personality the dynamic essence of every active member of a church."[(217)] Tillich notes that the problem of whether the church precedes the members or the members precede the church has created an objective and a subjective interpretation of the church. Infant baptism, for instance, is a product of the objective type which emphasizes the church over the individual. "It rightly points to

the fact that there is no moment in the life of a person when the
state of Spiritual maturity can be fixed with certainty. . . .
faith . . . is a reality which precedes the ever becoming, ever
changing . . . acts of personal faith.''[217-218] The subjective type
of church is correct in seeing the necessity of conversion, for there
must be a conscious turning away from estrangement and an
affirmation of the New Being. But, ''Conversion can have the
character of a transition from the latent stage of the Spiritual
Community to its manifest stage. This is the real structure of
conversion; it implies that repentance is not completely new and
that neither is faith.''[220]

The word ''experience'' accurately describes the participation of the individual church member in the New Being, because
there ''must be some kind of participation in what I believe and
therefore a kind of certainty which prevents an infinite regression of the type represented by the statement 'I believe that I
believe that I believe, and so on.' ''[221] As we saw in the last
chapter, the individual experiences the New Being as creation
(regeneration), paradox (justification), and process (sanctification). Tillich reverses the ''order of salvation'' of the Reformers
by placing regeneration before justification, because he feels that
this order makes more clear the fact that the beginning principle
of salvation is the acceptance of man by God in giving him New
Being. It also avoids the Lutheran error of making a work out
of faith by underlining the primacy of grace. Justification then
comes after regeneration. It is the basic and first principle of
Protestantism ''that, in relation to God, God alone can act and
that no human claim . . . or . . . 'work,' can reunite us with
him.''[224] This means for Tillich that Luther's formula must be
removed completely and replaced with ''Justification by grace
through faith.''[224] Justification, which Tillich prefers to call
acceptance, ''is manifest through the picture of Jesus the Crucified. God's acceptance of the unacceptable . . . appear[s] in a
unique, definite, and transforming way in him. It appears in him,
but it is not caused by him. The cause is God and God alone.''[226]

Sanctification is the experience of the New Being as ''process.''
Luther and Calvin agreed that the sanctifying process of the

Christian life requires law as an instrument by which man's essential nature is revealed. The law exposes man's existential nature and thus drives him to seek reunion. Apart from this negative function, Calvin also saw the law as a positive guide for the Christian life, while Luther looked for such guidance more in the free working of the divine Spirit. The Evangelical Radicals followed Calvin's idea of the law as the discipline of the Christian life toward sanctification, but lost his sense of the paradox of that process. They saw life then as perfectionistic, moralistic, and needing proof of election in good works. Lutheranism, on the other hand, tended to view the Christian life as a series of ups and downs of ecstasy and anxiety. In reaction to the uncertainty and lack of moral discipline resulting from that view, the Pietist movements arose. Tillich wishes to avoid these contradictions which he finds in Reformation theology by formulating a doctrine of sanctification which describes a process of increasing consciousness of the work of the divine Spirit. This means there should be in the believer an "increasing awareness" of the ambiguities of life and the demonic, and of the unambiguous Spiritual Presence in the self. There should be "increasing freedom" from the law as unity with one's essential nature grows. There should be "increasing relatedness" to others and to oneself made possible by the transcendent unity of the Spiritual Presence above the existential split between subject and object. And these all mean that there should be "increasing transcendence" which accompanies the experience of the Spiritual Presence.

We have examined the function of religion in its relation to the Spiritual Presence and have found that in every case it obtains that toward which it reaches only when the divine Spirit elevates man above the ambiguities and limitations of his existence. This means that religion as a function of the human spirit is conquered and overcome by the divine Spirit.

The Spirit and Culture

In existence, culture and religion are separated, but under the impact of the Spiritual Presence they are united. This allows Tillich to say certain things not possible before about the relation between the two. It must be seen that the secular is open to the Spiritual Presence apart from the mediation of the church. This happens when the Spirit speaks through men and groups prophetically outside the church, which creates a convergence of the holy and the secular. This constitutes the "latent" church. "The secular is driven toward union with the holy, a union which actually is a reunion because the holy and the secular belong to each other."[248] They belong to each other because, for instance, the holy needs and uses the secular language and cognition for the expression of its belief. Thus we may say "that religion is the substance of culture and culture the form of religion."[248] The presence of the Spirit in culture creates what Tillich calls "theonomy," which is "the directedness of the self-creation of life under the dimension of the Spirit toward the ultimate in being and meaning."[249] Theonomous culture expresses ultimacy and consecration; it affirms productivity and does not contradict the rational structure of the world nor suppress human freedom in it.

Theonomous culture implies that the split between subject and object has been overcome. We saw this split most clearly in the cultural functions of language and cognition, although, being the result of existential estrangement, it is the fundamental cause of all the ambiguities of life. Mysticism attempts to answer the subject-object split in cognition by achieving a state of mind where "the universe of discourse" disappears. Subject and object are swallowed in ecstatic unity. But mysticism fails because the experiencing self, the subject, remains aware of this "disappearance." Some forms of love attempt to overcome this split by the submersion of the lover into the personal center of the loved. But complete identification never takes place; if it did, the person of the lover would itself be destroyed. Only the Spirit, by creating theonomy, by directing life toward the transcendent unity of all being, can bridge the gap between subject and object. It overcomes the subject-object split in language by elevating language to symbols. "The word which bears the Spirit does not grip an object opposite to the speaking subject, but it witnesses to the sublimity of life beyond subject and object."[253-254] And this of course has special significance for Tillich's doctrine of the Word. The "Word of God is the Spirit-determined human word. As such it is not bound to a particular revelatory event, Christian or non-Christian; ... It appears wherever the Spiritual Presence imposes itself . . ."[254]

The Spirit overcomes the subject-object split by bringing the subject to a sublime transcendence in which it participates in the unity of being beyond subject and object. This solution applies to the other ambiguities of culture. The Spirit overcomes the subject-object split of cognition by raising the particular to the eternal where true "wholeness" is found which includes both the subject and the object. (This, says Tillich, does not deny the possibility of cognition within the subject-object scheme, but gives it a direction, a "Spirit-determined wisdom.") The subject-object split within each person is demonstrated when the self as subject tries to determine the self as object in the power of that which it does not have, namely, essential unity. Under the impact of the Spirit, the self as subject and as object is united in the unity of the Spiritual Presence. In the realm of communal relations the ambiguity of inclusiveness and exclusiveness is overcome by the Spiritual Presence, as it creates ever larger unities so that the idea of community becomes universal. In the same way the ambiguity of equality and inequality is overcome by giving to all an ultimate equality which places existential inequality under judgment. These examples suffice to show that theonomous culture under the impact of the Spiritual Presence heals the ambiguities of culture—even if fragmentarily.

The Spirit and Morality

The Spiritual Presence also creates a theonomous morality. In this discussion, Tillich denies the possibility of independent theological ethics. If the theologian speaks of morality and the moral imperative, he does so as a "philosophical ethicist." This is so because ethics as such has to do with "the nature of the moral function and judges the changing contents in the light of this analysis."[267] Theological assertions, says Tillich, do not apply to arguments about the nature of the moral imperative.

The Spiritual Presence makes itself felt outside the realm of the church and theology, and it does this by creating theonomous ethics in which "the religious substance—the experience of an ultimate concern—is consciously expressed through the process of free arguing and not through an attempt to determine it."[268] In other words, ethics, because of the changing nature of its contents, must be the task of philosophy and not theology, for there is a danger in theology that revelatory authority will be given to ethical analysis. "Intentional theonomy is heteronomy and must be rejected by ethical research. Actual theonomy is autonomous ethics under the Spiritual Presence."[268] Philosophy, being free (autonomous) and objective in its analyses, may, if grasped by the Spiritual Presence, become theonomous ethics.[6]

At the beginning of this chapter we spoke of the basic moral ambiguity of sacrifice. In the act of sacrificing oneself by participating in another there is the danger of losing oneself. Moreover, in every moral act the law of excluded possibility operates, which means that every good choice includes the exclusion of other goods. But under the Spiritual Presence the "ambiguity of sacrifice" is overcome because the personal center is united with the universal center where it is safe. Thus the question is answered

---

[6] This radical denial of theological ethics in favor of philosophical ethics seems to mark a definite movement in Tillich's thought away from an earlier position. In 1935 he could inaccurately criticize Barth's "refusal to recognize a theological ethics . . ." (Paul Tillich, "What Is Wrong with the 'Dialectic' Theology?" *The Journal of Religion*, Vol. XV, April, 1935, p. 144). Again, in *Systematic Theology*, Vol. I, his point was that ethics cannot be isolated as a theological discipline, but must be implicit in all parts of systematic theology. But it was not separated from theology. In answer to criticism on this point by George F. Thomas, he could even say: ". . . the ever changing problems of ethical existence are . . . much needed. . . . In this work theological ethics and theological apologetics receive an independent function" (*The Theology of Paul Tillich*, op. cit., p. 344). But then in *Love, Power, and Justice*, op. cit., he moves toward a philosophical and explicitly Kantian view of ethics as requiring an ontological rather than a strictly theological basis. ". . . the law given by God is man's essential nature, put against him as law. . . . Every valid ethical commandment is an expression of man's essential relation to himself, to others and to the universe. This alone makes it obligatory and its denial self-destructive" (op. cit., pp. 76-77). Then as now Tillich wished to avoid a "heteronomous" understanding of "the moral commandments as expressions of a divine will, which is sovereign and without criteria" (p. 76). He is fearful of the destruction which he believes follows "the submission of one's personality centre to a strange will . . ." (*ibid.*).

as to how much or how little of life one can afford to take. For "where there is Spirit, the actual manifests the potential and the potential determines the actual."[269] This also means the removal of "the ambiguous and tragic character of the sacrifice of life possibilities . . ."[271] Another ambiguity of morality was seen in its nature as law, insofar as "law" implies "oughtness." Tillich argues that the basis of the moral law is *agape*, but one cannot command: "Thou shalt love . . ." Therefore morality is not law, but it is reality; it is not an "ought," but a matter of being. As long as law is seen in terms of obedience, says Tillich, it is ambiguous. But if we see it as love, the law is grace working in man. "The many forms of ethics without Spiritual Presence . . . cannot show the power of motivation . . . Love can do it, but love is not a matter of man's will. It is a creation of the Spiritual Presence. It is grace."[274-275]

We have now seen how the divine Spirit, present in the Spiritual Community, creates theonomous culture and morality and thereby fulfills the quest of man for unambiguous life. In actual life this fulfillment is fragmentary, but it elevates all of life by directing it to its essential unity with God. Wherever life comes under the impact of the Spirit, it is healed. "Healing," we remember, is Tillich's word for "salvation" and forms a link between the final fulfillment of the Kingdom of God and the limited presence of the Spirit. Yet there remains the fact of sin and death. Healing in all its forms remains fragmentary. This "leads us to the question of the Eternal Life as symbolized by the Kingdom of God. Only universal healing is total healing—salvation beyond ambiguities and fragments."[282]

SUMMARY AND ANALYSIS

For Paul Tillich, life is a unity which does not contain levels, but dimensions. The spiritual dimension of life is the unity of power and meaning; it is that which controls man's encounter with his world and as such is the source of the functions of life. It is the place where the ambiguities of life are encountered and also where the answer to those ambiguities is found—in the divine Spirit.

Life is a mixture of essence and existence; it is therefore ambiguous. Life is ambiguous because it attempts to express its essential nature, but cannot because it is in the situation of existential estrangement. This estrangement is most clearly seen in the split between subject and object, between man and his world. In the moral function of life, for instance, man as subject finds it impossible to unite in love with his neighbor as object, for participation carries with it the danger of loss of self-identity and individuality. In the cultural function of life the result of the subject-object split is seen in the inability of language and cognition to overcome the gap between the knower and the known. And it is seen in communal relations where the group as subject must reject the individual as object in order to maintain its own identity. In the religious function of life, man as subject is unable to unite with God as object, and in his attempt to do so he runs the risk of the demonic, which is the confusion of finite objectivity with an infinite subject. Life is ambiguous. In all its functions the gap between essence and existence, and between subject and object, prohibits life from reaching that for which it grasps. Therefore, life asks for that which can lift it above that gap in transcendent union and thus bring about unambiguous life. This is the quest for the divine Spirit.

The divine Spirit is "God present." It is effective in all dimensions of life, but is only apprehended in the human spirit. The Spiritual Presence occurs in all of history and in all religions fragmentarily. It is mediated to men through the sacraments and the Word of God, which are broadly interpreted as any thing or word through which the Spirit comes. But the Spirit is not confined to the Christian revelation. Yet it was manifest without distortion only in Jesus as the Christ. The Spirit also appears in the Spiritual Community. This community may be distinguished in its latent and manifest form, by which Tillich means "before" and "after" the personal experience of the Christ as the criterion of the Spiritual Presence. The Spiritual Community is latent universally and is manifest in the church.

The Spirit answers the question of life by lifting it to transcendent unity above its ambiguities. The Spirit appears in the church constituting the Spiritual Community (invisible church) within it. The ambiguities of religion are conquered wherever and whenever the Spirit saves the finite from demonic self-elevation by elevating it through grace to transcendent unity. The Spiritual Presence overcomes the subject-object split which causes the ambiguities of culture by creating theonomous culture. It elevates language to symbols, and the knower to the unity of being which includes the known. And the Spirit overcomes the ambiguities of morality by uniting the personal center of man with the universal center of being-itself in order that man may participate in other beings without loss of self. Thus the Spirit creates the possibility of that love which is the end and answer to law.

The question of man's life, expressed in its ambiguities, is answered by the Spirit who heals life by elevating it to transcendent union where estrangement between essence and existence is overcome. It does this really and in power, but fragmentarily. All of life is not healed, but its ambiguities are all conquered in principle in the power of the divine Spirit.

There can be no doubt that the actual life of man is ambiguous and that this ambiguity is the result of estrangement. And there can be no doubt that life is changed and healed by the presence of the Holy Spirit, who as the Counselor (*parakletos*) answers the deepest questions of men (John 16:7) and who as the Spirit of truth (*pneumates aletheias*) leads them into all truth (John 16:13). Moreover, Tillich's approach to the doctrine of the Spirit is valid insofar as the Spirit is certainly analogous to the human spirit as the subjective possibility of the reception of revelation. Tillich rightly sees the Spirit as the Redeemer, whose work is eschatological in nature, pointing to ultimate fulfillment. In all this we are in agreement.

But a question arises as to *who* this Spirit is. Tillich says that he is "God present," and that is true enough. But then the question inevitably follows: Who is this God who is present? The whole matter comes to rest again at this point: If the Spirit is really "God present," and if God is who he reveals himself

to be in Jesus Christ, then where else can or need we seek the
identity of the Spirit than in Jesus Christ? Tillich maintains
that the Spirit (like the Logos and the New Being) exists *apart*
from Jesus, even if manifest in him without distortion. But what
can such an assertion mean but a denial of his divinity and a
turning away from the revelation of God and the Spirit found
in him? This was the issue at stake in the original debate over
filioque. Tillich places himself on the side of the Eastern Church
which sought the origin of the Spirit in God alone; his reasoning
is that the oneness of God is threatened by asserting the Spirit's
dependence upon the Son. "Monotheism" may well be served by
such reasoning, but is the unity and oneness of "God"? For who
is this God who is one, and how can we speak even of his oneness
except he reveal himself as such, and where else has he revealed
himself except in Jesus Christ?

If God the Father is not seen as he who reveals himself in
himself as God the Son through his presence as God the Spirit,
how can we speak at all of the Trinity? The concept of the
Trinity as it appears in Tillich's theology seems to come in one
place from the movement of religion from a universal to a concrete idea of the divine which results in actual trinities in various
religions (see Chapter IV). In another place it is argued that
the dialectical movement of life from the individual self toward
participation and a return to the self must be applied to God if
God is life, and that this movement is symbolized in the Trinity.
In still another place God as God is said to represent power, the
creative meaning of which is found in the Logos; and the actualization of both power and meaning is found in the Spirit. Such
considerations are for Tillich "trinitarian principles" which are
the products of human observation, reason, and intuition and
as such are presuppositions for the Christian doctrine of the
Trinity.[7] But if such principles actually do become presuppositions for the doctrine of the Trinity, so that one may speak of
three modes of God apart from their revelation in Jesus Christ,
then has not the danger always present in such *vestigia trinitatis*
become a reality, and reason taken the place of revelation? Of

---

[7] *Systematic Theology*, Vol. I, pp. 250 ff.

course it is not possible to speak of God apart from the words
and concepts of our own creaturely existence. But is it not quite
another and more dangerous thing if we allow such words and
concepts to form "presuppositions" of our understanding of
God's life as it is revealed to us in Jesus Christ by the Holy
Spirit?

If the divine Spirit is not seen as the Spirit of Jesus Christ,
if he does not always direct our attention to the grace of God in
him, how are we to understand his redemptive and sanctifying
work in the lives of men? It is one of the great strengths of
Tillich's presentation that morality and ethics are seen to be
matters of the gracious presence of the Spirit. He has rightly seen
that ethics has to do with grace and not law, that it is established
by God's love which creates the possibility of man's love in
response.[8] But what is the specific nature of this love? Is this
spiritual gift for Tillich really something we do not already have?
Tillich holds that the Spirit raises man to ecstatic and transcendent unity with God above the ambiguities of life, whereby man is
allowed to realize the essential unity of his nature. Thus there is
no command from the "outside" of man, but only the "inner"
command of his own essential being. But does not such a formulation of man's own potentiality for the good place us directly in
the Catholic frame of reference?[9] When Tillich says that "the
law given by God is man's essential nature . . . [it] is not strange
to man . . . it is natural law,"[10] is he not stating exactly the
basis of Roman Catholic moral philosophy and theology?

Tillich's view is that autonomous, philosophical ethics alone is
free to decide in an unprejudiced manner about the changing
forms and bases of the moral imperative and that it alone is
used by the Spirit in the creation of theonomous morality in a

[8] In this respect we certainly must set aside the criticism of George
Tavard which is based on the supposition that "there is no true ethics of
love that is not, first, an ethics of law. . . . In the realm of ethics, obedience can only be to objective standards, that is, to laws" (op. cit.,
pp. 157-158).

[9] We may strongly suspect so, because in this matter Tavard is in agreement with Tillich, stating that his ethics "already exists . . . in Catholic
theology." He sees a direct parallel between Tillich's view of natural law
and Catholic teaching (op. cit., pp. 158-159).

[10] Love, Power, and Justice, op. cit., p. 76.

given society. But does this view take seriously the fact that the basic question of the good is no longer open?[11] What else can the good be except the will of God, and what is this will except that men should believe in Jesus Christ by whom they are being saved? Tillich has certainly seen that the good is love because love is reunion with God. But has he seen that this good is established once for all in Jesus Christ so that he who would know the good, or do it, must only know Christ and do what he commands, namely, to accept *this* as good for man himself? There is of course more to be said; there are applications and implications to be recognized, and perhaps philosophical ethics may aid in this task, but must we not keep very clear that the basis for all ethics is the proclamation of the good grace of God in Jesus Christ?

As we have indicated above, the root of Tillich's rejection of theological ethics is his belief that it entails a "command" of God which is forced upon man simply because God is the stronger. But is this at all the case? What does such a command have to do with God's command? His command does not come because he is the stronger, but because he made himself the weaker! If we say that God commands, we can only mean that his commandment is one of grace. We mean that its form and content is his purpose and will for man revealed in Jesus Christ; we mean that his commandment is his love and acceptance of men which permits them to love him and accept each other. To be sure this is a command, a demand, a determination on God's part that we shall hear and accept his grace. But it is a command which, far from destroying man's personal center, integrity, and freedom, establishes it. For what freedom or integrity has man if left to his own determination? We cannot but think that if the Spirit which Tillich sees as the basis of morality and ethics were seen as

---

[11] In his long-awaited and important book, Paul Lehmann writes that "Christian ethics is *not* chiefly concerned with the *Good* but with 'what, as a believer in Jesus Christ and as a member of his church, I am to do'" (*Ethics in a Christian Context*, New York: Harper & Row, Publishers, 1963, p. 272). Furthermore, if the concern of ethics is a theological matter, so is the question of ethical behavior, for it involves "men in the doing of what God is doing in the world to make and to keep human life human" (*ibid.*, p. 284). Lehmann argues convincingly that philosophical ethics finally proves inadequate because it can neither overcome nor explain "the gap between the ethical claim and the ethical act" (*ibid.*, p. 280).

the Spirit of Jesus Christ in whom the command of God takes this gracious and saving form, there could be no thought of the oppressiveness of theological ethics which finds in him the loving claim of God.

This view of the Spirit is crucial for the doctrine of the church. Tillich has rightly seen that the holiness of the church and its members is not dependent upon any quality or characteristic of their own, but solely upon the presence of the Spirit which creates the Spiritual Community. But if the Spirit which establishes and guides the church is not seen to be the Spirit of God in Christ, then is there not the greatest danger that the church, looking "before" him in its "latent" stage or "after" him in its "manifest" stage and finding (as we believe) nothing there upon which to base itself, will turn back to itself and become its own foundation and authority? Do we not see exactly this self-constitution in the "latent" Jewish Church and the "manifest" Catholic Church? Do we not see this inevitable tendency in Tillich's view of word and sacrament? For if the sacraments are inherently sacramental and if the Word of God in its "final" form is *any* human word, then will not those sacraments and words take an importance and authority in and of themselves? Is not the Word which the church must hear, proclaim, and serve none other than Christ, himself the Word of God? Is it not this Word and no other to which the Spirit leads the church and by which he builds it?

But we neither need nor ought to end on this interrogatory note. In the six years between the publication of this last volume of Tillich's system and the second on Christology, many commentators maintained that Tillich's theology was "closed" and that one could expect nothing new from it.[12] But this is not the case. Tillich is, of course, the systematic theologian par excellence, and many of the problems we have noted are simply the result of a consistent extension of basic concepts which appeared at the very first. Yet may we not perceive here a happy movement of emphasis from the correlation between the acts of God and man so strongly stressed in the first volume toward the

12 Cf. Hopper, *op. cit.*, pp. 36-43.

primacy of God's act of grace itself? Surely the increasing reference to *sola gratia* in such statements as ". . . in relation to God everything is by God"[133] is a sign of such a movement. And while many counter statements could be cited and while Tillich certainly would not repudiate his concept of correlation, this increasing emphasis on grace may perhaps be taken as the context in which he now wishes his earlier work to be interpreted. This emphasis which we spoke of before as a "hidden a priori" makes us wish all the more that the actual place and identity of this grace which is found in Jesus Christ could find a clearer and less ambivalent expression in Tillich's system, for if it did, we cannot but believe that his underlying purpose and intention would better be served.

VII

HISTORY
AND THE KINGDOM OF GOD

There is no history without factual occurrences, and there is no history without the reception and interpretation of factual occurrences by historical consciousness.[(302)1] *. . . In the Christian vocational consciousness, history is affirmed in such a way that the problems implied in the ambiguities of life under the dimension of history are answered through the symbol "Kingdom of God."*[(349-350)] *. . . everything that is participates in the striving toward the inner aim of history . . .*[(350)]

The demonic forces [in history] are not destroyed, but they cannot prevent the aim of history, which is reunion with the divine ground of being and meaning.[(373)]

INTRODUCTION

The subjects of history and the Kingdom of God not only bring us to the end of Tillich's *Systematic Theology*, but also mark a return to the major concern of his earliest work. Beginning with Schelling's history of religion (*Religionsgeschichte*)[2] and continuing into the political upheavals of Germany in the 1920's, historical-political problems claimed Tillich's first attention. This interest grew even sharper after his departure from Germany in 1933 and found expression in his many articles and addresses dealing with World War II and the problems of German reconstruction.[3] In recent years Tillich has occupied himself with a

[1] Numbers in parentheses in this chapter refer to page numbers in Tillich's *Systematic Theology*, Vol. III.

[2] Tillich's doctoral dissertation was entitled: "Die religionsgeschichtliche Konstruktion in Schellings positiver Philosophie, ihre Voraussetzungen und Prinzipien" (Breslau: Fleischmann, 1910).

[3] See especially "Storms of Our Times," an address delivered by Tillich in 1942 and published in *The Protestant Era, op. cit.*, pp. 237 ff.; "Spiritual Problems of Postwar Reconstruction," *ibid.*, pp. 261 ff.; and "History as the Problem of Our Period," in *The Review of Religion*, Vol. III, No. 3 (March, 1939), pp. 255-264.

variety of political questions and the formulation of a philosophy of history, which we now have before us.

Tillich's aim is to develop a Protestant philosophy of history which allows man to "stand in nature, taking upon [himself its] inevitable reality; not to flee from it, either into the world of ideal forms or into the related world of super-nature, but to make decisions in concrete reality."[4] This means that his view of history, unlike that of Hegel, requires the acceptance of man's radical estrangement from his essential self and God. There can be no solution within history for the dialectic of history. At the same time Tillich, in agreement with Schelling, believes that history is a process in which the divine enters history by human acts of freedom and love, and thereby overcomes man's estrangement and gives to history ultimate and eternal meaning. Thus Tillich is concerned to show two things: that history does not contain within itself its own *telos* and meaning, but that it is never without the presence of such. This of course is a direct extension of his ontology, in which finite reality is estranged, but never separated, from the ground of being. And just as we have seen this essential connection between man and God expressed as the universal *logos* in relation to revelation, as the unity of being in relation to the doctrine of God, and as the New Being in relation to Christology, so here we find the concept of "*kairos*" expressing the presence of the Kingdom of God in history. In classical Greek, "*kairos*" means "the right time" for a particular action. It was used in the New Testament in the sense of "fulfilled time," which was the time of the appearance of the Christ. For Tillich, Jesus as the Christ is the center of history because through him the power of God and his Kingdom, which is the aim of history, become real for man. The Christ event is therefore the basic *kairos*. But "*kairoi*" appear also in other moments in history (just as do revelation and the New Being). Such general *kairoi* may be interpreted as those times in which the eternal breaks into human history, judging and transforming it. This concept became normative for Tillich's under-

[4] Paul Tillich, *The Interpretation of History*, Part II, tr. Elsa Talmey (New York: Charles Scribner's Sons, 1936), pp. 134-135.

standing of the history of Europe following the First World War, and his interpretation of that era in terms of *kairos* was his particular contribution to the Religious-Socialist movement.[5]

These introductory remarks may serve as a frame and point of reference for the detailed and at times highly abstract exposition of his philosophy of history and its relation to the Kingdom of God which Tillich presents in this last part of his system. This chapter is actually an extension of Chapter VI ("Life and the Spirit") because history, being a product of man's interpretation of his relation to the world, is a dimension of life and is actualized only in the realm of the spirit. But it is given a separate part in *Systematic Theology* because "history" embraces all the dimensions and ambiguities of life, and "Kingdom of God" embraces and expresses the fulfillment of salvation.

The method and outline of this part of Tillich's system is consistent with all the others. First, man's situation in history is presented, and this means that the nature and structure of history must be established. Secondly, the question of the meaning of history is raised by a discussion of the ambiguities of man's historical existence. The answer to this question is found in the Kingdom of God, which is first defined and described in itself and in relation to the world and then given as the answer to human history in terms of fulfillment and eternal life.

THE NATURE AND STRUCTURE OF HISTORY

A Definition of History

That "history" includes a subjective as well as an objective element is seen in the Greek word *historia*, which primarily means inquiry, information, and report, and only secondarily the

[5] The largest and most thorough presentation of Tillich's thought in this area is to be found in his *Die sozialistische Entscheidung* (Potsdam: Alfred Protte, 1933). In this book Tillich's position as a "quietistic" socialist emerges ("Expectation is the symbol of socialism," p. 131) in opposition to both Communism and National Socialism. Tillich frankly admits that his "participation in the Religious-Socialist movement underlies this part of *Systematic Theology*" (p. 490). In another place he says that "the *kairos*-doctrine was conceived in a situation in which it was necessary to find a way between socialist utopianism and Lutheran transcendentalism" (*The Theology of Paul Tillich*, op. cit., p. 345).

event reported. And this means that while interpretation does not precede the event temporally, it does precede it "historically" in the sense of transforming mere happenings into historical events.[6]

The interpretation of events which constitutes history always takes place in the context of a "historical consciousness" or "tradition." A tradition is a collection of events recollected in terms of their special significance for a special group. In epics, sagas, and legends, such recollection takes place in a highly symbolical way. But even the modern historian who attempts to demythologize history cannot escape the traditional and symbolic in his own work, for his choice of historical objects is dependent upon his own participation in a group with its special traditions and memories. "There is no history without factual occurrences, and there is no history without the reception and interpretation of factual occurrences by historical consciousness."[(302)] This situation does not deny the necessity of strictness, accuracy, and honesty in historical research, but it does mean that the historian must acknowledge that in the very act of applying his methods, his own historical consciousness is effective. Historical consciousness implies an a priori understanding of the meaning of life and indeed is controlled by that understanding. In this regard Tillich admits that his own concept of history and all the historical passages in this part of his system are unconsciously under the effective impact of Christian symbolism.

A "historical event" has a subjective-objective structure, which makes it a peculiarly human phenomenon. For in the first place, historical events show intention and purpose. "Processes in which no purpose is intended are not historical."[(303)] Secondly, historical events are products of man's freedom, resulting from his intention and purpose. ". . . no historical situation determines any other historical situation completely."[(303)]

6 This subjective element in history may be seen as the basis for Tillich's assertion that historical criticism and faith as such are not in conflict. Both interpret the meaning of events, and when this happens from the point of view of man's ultimate concern, "historical truth [is transferred] into the dimension of the truth of faith" (Dynamics of Faith, op. cit., p. 86).

Thirdly, because historical events are products of freedom, they produce the "new." And fourthly, historical events, in producing the new in value and meaning, produce events of unique significance, by which Tillich means that they ". . . represent essential human potentialities, they show these potentialities, actualized in a unique way . . ."[305] These characteristics imply a distinction between "natural" processes and human history. Neither in the development of the species of higher animals nor in the development of the astronomical universe can we find freedom or purpose which transcends the satisfaction of needs. Neither can we find in natural history unique significance or absolute meaning; that is reserved for the dimension of the human spirit which alone can experience the ultimate. ". . . the biological is not spirit. Therefore, history remains an anticipated, but unactualized, dimension in all realms except that of human history."[306]

"Man actualizes himself as a person in the encounter with other persons within a community."[308] Therefore human history is the history of a group. Such a group must be able to act in a centered way; it must be able to maintain itself from within and protect itself from without. A group fulfilling these requirements is a "state," by which Tillich means any corporate entity (families, tribes, cities, etc.), in which the conditions of centeredness have been fulfilled. The history-bearing group is not based primarily on force, although it necessarily uses force, but it is based on the feeling of belongingness of the individual members. This sense of belonging expressed in blood relations, language, and traditions is that upon which the group is founded and by which it is maintained. Groups are the bearers of history because they have a "vocational consciousness" which is the "aim toward which they strive and a destiny they try to fulfill."[310] Such vocational consciousness is different for each group in each era. For Rome it was the ideal of law, for France it is the leadership of intellectual culture, for Russia the Marxist prophecy, and for the United States the concept of new beginning and democracy. The group is the bearer of history in all realms, but basically, and inclusively, it expresses history through politics because politics is the constitutive function of the group. Even the Bible expresses its view of history in terms of a political state—the Kingdom of God. "The element of centeredness which characterizes the political realm makes it an adequate symbol for the ultimate aim of history."[(311)][7]

It might be asked if the drive toward unity and centeredness does not make mankind as a whole the bearer of history. To this Tillich answers that complete unity is not a possible goal in history, for even if a political unity were achieved, it would only "be the framework for a disunity that is the consequence of human freedom with its dynamic that surpasses everything given."[(311)] Nor can the individual be considered the bearer of history apart from the group. It is true that the group is a product of the social function of individuals, but the individual is the bearer of history only in relation to the group. "Biography is not history."[(312)] Individuals, if they represent the group, may bear and shape its history, "but as mere individuals they have no historical significance. History is the history of groups."[(312)]

We may summarize Tillich's definition of "history" in the following way: History is the interpretation of a fact or series of facts arising from free and purposeful acts of man in which he creates the new in terms of value and meaning. Such interpretation, and therefore history itself, takes place in the context and under the control of a particular group, or "state," and its "vocational" self-interpretation.[8]

The Categorical Structure of History

In Chapter IV we dealt with the ontological categories of time, space, causality, and substance in their relation to finitude

---

[7] See also Paul Tillich, "Die Staatslehre Augustins nach 'De Civitate Dei,'" *Theologische Blätter*, No. 4 (April, 1925), pp. 77-86. Against the Lutheran doctrine of the "two kingdoms," Tillich here underlines the symbolic function of the state. It represents the judgment under which the world stands vis-à-vis the Kingdom. In contrast, "The concrete dominion of the Kingdom of God is the church" (p. 84).

[8] Or, expressed a little differently, "History is the totality of remembered events, which are determined by free human activity and are important for the life of human groups" (Paul Tillich, "The Kingdom of God and History," *Oxford Conference Series*, Vol. III; New York: Willet-Clark, 1938, p. 108).

generally. In this last part of his system, Tillich applies them
to the dimensions of life under the inclusive dimension of history.

Time and Space: Time and space are interdependent propor-
tionately, so that when in one realm, for instance in the inorganic,
space is predominant, the category of time is less so. Nothing
unites either the various spaces or different moments in inorganic
matter. But in the dimension of the organic, this exclusiveness
is broken by participation and unity. A tree, for instance, is
composed of various elements, roots, leaves, etc., each with its
own space. But these spaces participate in each other and form
a unity. Similarly the times of these various elements are not
exclusive, but are united in the process of growth. In the dimension of animal life it is the "awareness" of time and space which
breaks the exclusiveness of both categories. In the functions of
memory and self-directed movement the animal is actually able
to enlarge both his time and his space. In the realm of human
life, which Tillich calls the dimension of the spirit, both time and
space are unlimited. But there remains the reality of the limitation imposed upon the spirit by the concrete situation. "The
spirit has a time [such as the 'time' of a painting] which cannot
be measured by physical time although it lies within the whole
of physical time."[317-318] Similarly, "the space of the creative
spirit unites an element of abstract unlimitedness with an element of concrete limitation."[318] The spirit may transcend a
given temporal and spatial environment, but it is always forced
to return to the concreteness of some space—be it a house, a city,
or a country—at some time.

History includes all dimensions of life, the inorganic as well
as the human, but in terms of time and space it points beyond
them. In the realm of history time is as predominant over space
as space is over time in the inorganic realm. Time in all the
dimensions shows an irreversible quality; it never goes backward; it always runs toward the new. But in this respect historical time shows a quality all its own. Because it is united with the
dimension of the spirit, historical time is creative and aims toward fulfillment. History "drives beyond all [other dimensions]
toward a fulfilment which is not relative and which does not need

another temporality for its fulfilment."[319] Thus the fulfillment of history is also the fulfillment of temporality under all other dimensions. What is true of time in the historical dimension is also true of space, for there can be no time without space. As in history the temporal quality of "after-each-other-ness" drives to a fulfillment, so the spatial quality of "beside-each-other-ness" drives to the fulfillment of space, to a "kingdom" which unites all spaces. In history these drives are raised to consciousness as a question. And, "The answer given in our context is 'Eternal Life.' "[320]

Causality and Substance: ". . . causality is the order of things according to which there is a conditioning precedent for everything. . . . The general character of substance is 'underlying identity,' that is, identity with respect to the changing accidents."[321] Under the dimension of the inorganic, cause and substance are exclusive. Cause is kept at a distance from its effect insofar as that relation is calculable and expressible in quantitative terms and mathematical equations. Furthermore, there is no relation between the substance, or identity, of one thing and another. Everything is "subject to the radical beside-each-other-ness of space in the inorganic realm."[322] In the dimensions of the organic and animal life, the categories of causality and substance again show unity by participation. Both cause and effect are united within the same organism even though the cause may be quantitatively measured. And the substance of a centered organ or animal is the same regardless of possible changes in the accidents of its parts. In the dimension of human life, or spirit, causality predominates over substance. Creations of the spirit are not substantially conditioned because a creation implies the "new." By "new" Tillich does not mean the next situation in the process of becoming but rather that which is underived, the product of freedom over against determination. "It is in this sense that we speak when we say that under the dimension of the spirit, general causality becomes causality creating the new."[324] Therefore it is also true that the dimension of the spirit is not bound to substance, but in creating the new it transcends substance and affects the character of the substance. "The spirit-determined, centered being, the person, is the source of creative causality; but the creation surpasses the substance out of which it comes—the person."[324]

Historical causality is future-directed and draws substance with it toward the new. Every creation of the human spirit, being tied to the past in some way, is in some way "old." Historical consciousness, however, looks toward the absolutely new, the "new creation," and it looks to the possibility of an absolutely transcendent and universal substance or situation. Thus all the categories, time, space, causality, and substance, under the dimension of history, point to that which cannot be achieved in the context of history, the Kingdom of God.

The Movement of History

History implies movement, movement toward the new. Thus history involves change, and the question arises whether these changes are the result of necessity or contingency. Tillich speaks of historical necessity as "trend" rather than immutable law, for history is never without change. Trends point to regularities in history which cannot be predicted in terms of scientific determinism. As there is necessity or trend in every historical situation, so there is contingency, which Tillich calls "chance." "Chances are occasions to change the determining power of a trend."[327] The fact of chance in the historical situation definitely denies all forms of historical determinism. The movement of history may be described in terms of action and reaction, growth and decay, and dialectics. These elements must be considered in any interpretation of history, but, Tillich warns, they must be seen in flexible structures within which history moves rather than a fixed framework determining history. The dialectical movement of all life has often been affirmed by Tillich and has even been applied to the divine life itself (in the doctrine of the Trinity). Historical dialectics take place "wherever life comes into conflict with itself and drives toward a new stage beyond the conflict . . ."[329] However, Tillich insists that if dialectics is made into a fixed law (e.g., Hegel), life is distorted into a mechanized scheme and the use of the term is no longer empirically justifiable. In the same way one must be careful in the use of names to indicate the movement of historical periods. If we speak of the Victorian, Renaissance, baroque, or feudal period, it must be remembered that "History moves in a periodic rhythm, but periods are periods only for those who can see them as such."[331]

History moves not only in terms of the ontological categories, but also in terms of the processes of life. These processes, which we saw in the last chapter to be self-integration, self-production, and self-transcendence, are united in the historical dimension as a movement toward a single aim. The self-integrating function of life drives historically toward "an unambiguous harmony" between groups and individuals expressed in power and justice. The self-producing function of life drives historically toward a really new creation. And the self-transcendent function of life moves in history "toward the universal, unambiguous fulfilment of the potentiality of being."[332] But history, like all of life, stands under the ambiguities of life, which means that the drive toward fulfillment is unfulfilled in history. History can ask the question, but it cannot give the answer of the Kingdom of God.

At the close of his description of history, Tillich raises the question as to whether or not the movement of history toward fulfillment may be called "progress." Progress has two meanings: on the one hand it can be called "a step beyond the given,"[333] and in this sense the whole movement of history is progressive. But on the other hand progress can mean "that history progressively approaches its ultimate aim . . ."[333] In this sense Tillich is most reticent to apply the word to the functions of life in history. For instance, there is no progress in the moral act; each individual makes his decision on his own. The ethical act itself is always new. The same is true of art. One may speak of progress within a certain stylistic tradition, but actually each work of art, like each tradition of style, stands alone and is not the result of progress. Progress in these areas may be quantitative, but cannot be qualitative. This is certainly true for humanity as such. There may be a quantitative increase in breadth, refinement, and depth in each succeeding generation, but the maturity and realized humanity of each person is quite independent of these cultural factors.

Theologically the question arises whether or not there is progress in religion. "Obviously there is no progress in the religious function as such. The state of ultimate concern admits no more of progress than of obsolescence or regression."[336] Neither is there progress from one religion to another or from one revelation to another. Revelation "is always what it is, . . . in this respect there is no more or less, no progress . . ."[337] The ultimate victory over the demonic has taken place in Jesus as the Christ. "According to Christianity this event is not the result of a progressive approximation, nor is it the actualization of another religious potentiality."[337-338] Thus it is not Christianity which is the basis for the prophetic breaking of the power of the demonic, "but the event by which Christianity is created and judged to the same extent as any other religion . . ."[338] Therefore, there is no possibility of a horizontal progress of religion.

We now turn from Tillich's description of history to his analysis of its ambiguities, for it is out of the ambiguities of history that the question of history arises which is answered by the Kingdom of God.

THE AMBIGUITIES OF HISTORY

"History, while running ahead toward its ultimate aim, . . . actualizes limited aims, and so doing it both achieves and defeats its ultimate aim."[339] This is the basis for all the ambiguities of history. As in the case of the ambiguities of life, the ambiguities of history may be distinguished in terms of the functions of self-integration, self-production, and self-transcendence. The historical ambiguity of man's self-integration is expressed in the formation of empire. Empires, says Tillich, are not simply products of man's will to power, but more especially express the vocational self-interpretation of a historical group (e.g., Roman law, Russian social justice, and American liberty). Such aims are not bad in themselves, but it is obvious that they have caused unspeakable suffering, and the loss of life and meaning. The ambiguity of history expressed in self-integration is not only seen in the external force of empirical inclusiveness, but also in the internal force of centeredness. When the group is in danger from without or within, its members are liable to totalitarian control, and therefore the ambiguity arises that while "the group is able to act historically because of its severe centralization, . . . it cannot use its power creatively because it has suppressed those creative potencies which drive into the future."[342] In the historical dimension the ambiguities of self-production are expressed in revolution and reaction. The basis of this ambiguity is the truth that "everything new in history keeps within itself elements of the old out of which it grows."[343] We see this in the fight between every young generation which rightly seeks to make its own place, but fails to appreciate the accomplishments of the old it sets aside, and every older generation which refuses to give place to new creativity.

The self-transcendent function of life becomes ambiguous when that which is finite is raised to infinite value and meaning. In the historical dimension this happens when either the old or the new claims ultimacy for itself. This claim "takes the form of the claim to have or to bring the ultimate toward which history runs."[344] By far the most direct and demonic form of this claim is found in religion, where theological totalitarianism has often resulted in physical as well as spiritual persecutions. The claim for historical ultimacy is often expressed in the idea of the "third" or final stage of history. With Augustine, this third stage was the age of the church. With Joachim de Fiore, and the Montanists before him, it was the immanent age of the Spirit (from which comes the present-day millennialist expectation of the thousand-year reign of Christ on earth). Such expectation is not confined to religion, but also finds secular expression in, for instance, "the age of reason" or "the classless society." Whenever a particular movement or a utopian expectation is absolutized in history, the inevitable result is either the loss of the self-transcendent function of life by identifying the historically finite with the ultimate (as in Roman Catholicism), or cynicism and despair over disappointed utopian hopes.

For Tillich the place of the individual in history is one subordinate to the political group, but the individual nevertheless constitutes the group and therefore has a significance in history. Within this personal sphere, profound ambiguities are to be found. If we accept democracy as the "best yet" guarantee of individual freedom, says Tillich, it must nonetheless be admitted that precisely in the democratic organization of life there are structures which violate this freedom. Techniques of representation reduce the individual's place in government. Public communication can create conformity which kills the freedom of creativity. Splits within the group can arise, result in chaos, and lead to dictatorship. These ambiguities lead to the abandonment of political responsibility, a sense of hopelessness, and resignation. Men see themselves victims of forces which they cannot influence. In this situation, says Tillich, the question arises to which all the previous analyses have led : "What is the significance of history for the meaning of existence universally ?"[348] To this question and its answer we now turn.

THE MEANING OF HISTORY

The Problem of Historical Interpretation

History may be interpreted in a negative (non-historical) or positive (historical) way. Tillich sees the negative approach in the "tragic" example of Greek thought. History in this view does not run toward a goal, but in a circle, back to its beginning. The glory of life here and now turns into tragedy because life proves to be short and miserable. "There is no hope, no expectation of an immanent or transcendent fulfilment of history."[357] Another form of the negative interpretation of history is found in the mysticism of Eastern thought of Vedanta-Hinduism, Taoism, and Buddhism. In these forms historical existence has no meaning in itself. They recognize the tragic quality of life, but show no way of dealing with it except through the mystical transcendence of life. Thus these religions reject the necessity of transforming historical existence; one is not to conquer life but to conquer one's involvement in reality. Still a third type of the non-historical interpretation of history is to be found in the modern preoccupation with technical time. The question of the aim, purpose, and meaning of history is viewed with indifference and one oscillates between unrealistic optimism or profound pessimism with catastrophic effect upon his historical consciousness and responsibility.

Positive views of history are no more adequate than negative views. Progressivism, for instance, is a real interpretation of history because it recognizes the fact that history is going somewhere. One may distinguish two forms of this view: that which sees infinite progress itself as a process without end and that which believes in a final stage of fulfillment. In the first case, progress becomes a universal law. But the calamities of our age have almost completely eradicated the power of this interpretation of history. In the second case we are confronted with utopianism. In this view, "present revolutionary action will bring about the final transformation of reality, that stage of history in which the *ou-tópos* (no-place) will become the universal place."[354] Utopian idealism is always disappointed and destroyed because it is basically idolatrous; it raises the conditioned (a particular historical situation) to ultimate significance.

A third type of positive historical interpretation is what Tillich calls "transcendent utopianism." According to this approach history is the place where the Christ has appeared to save men from sin and guilt and make them members of a heavenly realm after death. Tillich's main criticism of this view is that it is irrelevant. It is unable to see any relation between the justice of God's Kingdom and the justice of the world. It separates the salvation of the individual from the salvation of the world in general and the group in particular. Tillich argues that such transcendent utopianism makes the salvation of life ununderstandable, because, if social institutions—which are integral parts of life—cannot be saved, life cannot be saved. Furthermore, a salvation such as this, which allows the individual to enter the Kingdom of God only after death, effectively denies the New Testament teaching that the Kingdom of God is powerful in the world, transforming and saving it in the present.

We have seen at the beginning of this chapter that the subject-object character of history means that all history is interpreted history. In every historical narrative there is a subjective selection of theories, evaluations, and facts. Thus the question arises: How can there be valid interpretation of history if the study of history itself has this subjective character? Why should a Christian interpretation take precedence over others? The answer which Tillich gives is admittedly circular. It is the "vocational consciousness" of a particular group which opens up the true meaning of history. And if the question is asked: "Which group?", any answer would imply a prior commitment to a particular group and its vocational consciousness. Here again we have "an unavoidable consequence of the 'theological circle' within which systematic theology moves."[(349)] "In the Christian vocational consciousness, history is affirmed in such a way that the problems implied in the ambiguities of life under the dimension of history are answered through the symbol 'Kingdom of God.' "[(349-350)] Thus the Kingdom of God is the final and valid meaning of history.

The Kingdom of God as the Meaning of History

The Kingdom of God is the final meaning of history because it grants fulfillment to man in every area of his life. The Kingdom of God is political: This agrees with the predominance of the political realm in history and means not only that there is a realm where God rules, but more importantly, *that* he rules over history. The Kingdom of God is social: "In this way the Kingdom of God fulfils the utopian expectation of a realm of peace and justice while liberating them from their utopian character by the addition 'of God . . .' "[(358)] The Kingdom of God is personal: It gives eternal meaning to individuals. The fulfillment and unity toward which it runs does not destroy personality, but fulfills and unites it. And finally, the Kingdom of God is universal: It is not a kingdom of men alone; it includes all the dimensions of life, for, according to the multidimensional unity of life, the salvation of one dimension implies the salvation of all others.

The Kingdom of God is the most inclusive symbol for salva-

tion. It expresses historical salvation through the presence of
the Spirit, and it expresses transhistorical salvation through
eternal life. The Kingdom of God as both historical and transhistorical means that it is both immanent and transcendent to
the world. The prophets of Israel proclaimed a Kingdom identified with the history of the nation, but they nonetheless emphasized that it was *God* who would win Israel's battles and that it
was *God's* holy mountain that would be established. The disasters
which Israel and Judah experienced upset this balance. The
world was despaired of, and God's redemption was sought in a
super-historical event as described in the apocalyptic writings
of the postexilic period. This view, Tillich says, became decisive
for the New Testament. But the inner-historical element was not
entirely abandoned, for the New Testament viewed the final
judgment in terms of its own political situation. And most important, "The New Testament adds a new element to these
visions: the inner-historical appearance of Jesus as the Christ
and the foundation of the church in the midst of the ambiguities of history."[361] Therefore, taken as a whole, the biblical
presentation of the Kingdom of God offers a meaningful interpretation of history as both saved in the present and fulfilled in
the future. It now remains for us to follow Tillich's analysis of
how the Kingdom of God answers the questions of man's historical existence.

THE KINGDOM OF GOD

"The History of Salvation"

The Kingdom of God means salvation for human history and
therefore creates in history a special "history of salvation"
(*Heilsgeschichte*). The history of salvation is identical with the
history of revelation. "Where there is revelation there is salvation!"[362] This relationship was given already in Chapter III
under the discussion of revelation. And the same universalism
we found there is repeated here. ". . . by speaking of universal
(not 'general') revelation, we have spoken implicitly of universal salvation."[362] But this is not to say that the history of salva-

tion is identical with human history. Here Tillich clearly states that they are not the same and that the one cannot lead to the other. The ambiguities of life prohibit any identity of human history, its processes and progresses, with the saving event of God which stands over against them, judging and saving them. Nor is salvation identical with the history of religion or the history of the churches; both stand in the state of existential estrangement. How is the history of salvation manifest in human history? The answer is that saving history is ". . . a sequence of events in which saving power breaks into historical processes."[363] But if salvation breaks into history it must prepare history in order to be received and it must change history in manifesting its power. Therefore one can speak of salvation as a part of universal history, for "it can be identified in terms of measured time, historical causality, a definite space and a concrete situation."[363] It is manifest in history, but it is not a product of history; yet just because it does manifest itself in history, the salvation of the Kingdom of God should not be spoken of as "super-historical."

Christ and History

Christianity considers Jesus as the Christ the "center" of history. But this center does not mean a midpoint between an indefinite past and indefinite future nor does it indicate a midpoint in the cultural process. Rather, it "expresses a moment in history for which everything before and after is both preparation and reception. As such it is both criterion and source of the saving power in history."[364] Thus Tillich denies any relative evaluation of various revelations in history; every such manifestation is dependent upon and judged against the one event of Jesus as the Christ. Also denied is the concept of "progress" in such revelations; no revelations before or after this event can be considered qualitatively different from this event, but only valid or invalid in terms of it. But there is, says Tillich, a progressive element in the reception of revelation. "Mankind had to mature to a point in which the center of history could appear and be received as the center."[365] But this process of maturation is not restricted to the pre-Christian epoch. It is carried on in every age and in every person. The "central event" of Jesus as the Christ, while occurring only once, is actually repeated over again in his reception as the center of history and life. The "latent church" anticipates him as the central event; thus he is central not only in terms of all of history, but also in each moment of history, before and after the event of his reception. This, says Tillich, is the meaning of the Johannine concept of the "pre-existence" and transtemporality of the Christ.

The Concept of Kairos

The center of history is God's action in Jesus as the Christ. But this action took place at a moment when, through the process of maturity, history was able to receive this event. Such a moment is called in the Greek New Testament *kairos*, the "fulfillment of time." The original meaning of this word, the "right" or "proper time," must be contrasted with *chronos*, which simply means measured time. The Greeks used *kairos* to indicate any good occasion for any action. In the New Testament it is used to indicate the occasion of the coming of the Christ. Jesus speaks of his own time (*kairos*) of suffering and death, and both he and John the Baptist speak of the time of the fulfillment (*kairos*) of the Kingdom of God.

Just as the Christ becomes the center of history again and again whenever he is received as such, so *kairos* occurs again and again. ". . . the 'great *kairos*,' the appearance of the center of history, is again and again re-experienced through relative '*kairoi*,' in which the Kingdom of God manifests itself in a particular breakthrough."[370] These later (or earlier) fulfilled times find their criterion and power in the one great fulfillment of time. Therefore, all *kairoi* must be tested against the *kairos*. This is not to say that the spiritual manifestation of the Kingdom of God is not always the same, but it may not be recognized as such. Thus every true *kairos* must be judged against the "great *kairos*," the appearance of the New Being in Jesus as the Christ. Not every time is a time of fulfillment in which the power of the Kingdom of God in history may be seen. "*Kairoi*

are rare and the great *kairos* is unique, but together they determine the dynamics of history in its self-transcendence."[372] But
moments of *kairos* do come, and when they do the Kingdom of
God is revealed in history as the answer to history. In times
of *kairoi* the power of God may be revealed in terms of creation,
judgment, destruction, and promise, which, being interpreted, in
the light of the "great *kairos*" of Jesus as the Christ, reveal the
ultimate aim and victory of the Kingdom of God in history. To
be sure, the negative and ambiguous in history remain, "the
demonic forces are not destroyed, but they cannot prevent the
aim of history, which is reunion with the divine ground of being
and meaning."[373]

The Kingdom and the Church

We have seen that the churches represent the Spiritual Community. Now in terms of the more embracing dimension of history, Tillich can say that the churches are also embodiments of
the Kingdom of God. But even as representatives of this Kingdom, the churches are ambiguous. In terms of the holy, "they
reveal and hide."[375] But just as man, in spite of the ambiguities of life, cannot cease to be the bearer of the Spirit, so the
churches, in spite of the ambiguities of history, cannot resign
from representing the Kingdom of God. Tillich maintains that
they "cannot forfeit this function even if they exercise it in
contradiction to the Kingdom of God."[375] As representatives
of this Kingdom the churches share in the movement of history
toward its ultimate aim, when, under the power of the Spirit,
they fight against demonization and profanization in history.
They do not do this of themselves, but by the power of the
Kingdom and the reality of the New Being in their midst. This
power is manifested in the churches through their sacramental
function. This includes the "word," but much more, it includes
the consecration and symbolic participation of the whole universe of being in being-itself. "The sacramental consecration of
elements of all of life shows the presence of the ultimately sublime in everything and points to the unity of everything in its
creative ground and its final fulfilment."[377]

The "manifest" church is not the only agent that witnesses to the Kingdom. There is also the "latent" church which exists (both historically and existentially) before the event of Jesus as the Christ, and which expresses in a preparatory way the power of the Kingdom of God. Thus we see that the church as the manifestation of the Spiritual Community is not identical with churches which may actually be "latent" expressions of the Kingdom. The churches always have some form of the Spiritual Community within them. But, "where there are churches confessing their foundation in the Christ as the central manifestation of the Kingdom of God in history there the church is."[378] Thus, while we may say that the history of the true church is identical with the history of the Kingdom of God, yet the history of the churches is not. This history "is at no point identical with the Kingdom of God and at no point without manifestation of the Kingdom of God."[378] This ambiguous situation is seen in the fact that the life of the churches is confined to one section of mankind, and in the fact that church history has produced so many contradictory interpretations and profanizations of the central event upon which it is based. It is obvious in the light of this situation that church history is not sacred history or the history of salvation. Sacred and saving history is "hidden," if also revealed, in church history. But one thing can be said for the churches: They have within themselves the criterion of judging themselves (the witness to the New Being in Jesus as the Christ), and this no other historical group can claim. "The struggle of the Kingdom of God in history is, above all, this struggle within the life of its own representatives, the churches."[381] This struggle is always going on, and not without actual, if fragmentary, victories.

The Kingdom of God and the Ambiguities of History

We come now to that place in Tillich's system where he describes how the existential questions of historical man are answered by the revelation of the Kingdom of God. These questions have been described in terms of the ambiguities of the functions of life in history. The life function of self-integration, the drive toward centeredness, causes in the dimension of history what

Tillich has called the ambiguity of "empire," or "power." The group must assert itself by force, but the use of power can cause the group or nation to disintegrate and lose its identity. Again, the self-integration of a group necessitates control over its members, but this control may kill creativity and individuality in the very members who constitute the group. Thus the use of power in a historical group raises ambiguities which threaten the life of the group and renders its history meaningless. The Kingdom of God answers this ambiguity by expressing within history a divine power which does not make its object a mere object of control but allows it freedom within the structure of force. This power of the Kingdom may find expression in any political system which seeks "to resist the destructive implications of power."[(385)] This means that the churches must neither identify with nor seek to exercise control over particular political institutions, but must be willing to recognize the manifestation of the Kingdom of God wherever the ambiguities of power are overcome. Thus too the churches' attitude toward the use of power may not be one of simple rejection (as in pacifism), or absolute acceptance (as in militarism). Rather, the churches must judge every use of power in war and peace against the norm of the divine use of power which integrates life in the context of freedom. "In so far as the centering and liberating elements in a structure of political power are balanced, the Kingdom of God in history has conquered fragmentarily the ambiguities of control."[(386)]

The function of life called self-production, or self-creativity, gives rise to historical ambiguities in the area of social growth between forces of revolution and forces of tradition. Without revolution there can be neither change nor growth; without tradition the institutions being changed lose their identity and are destroyed. The Kingdom of God reconciles this ambiguity whenever the mutual "unfairness" of both tradition and revolution are overcome. Christian groups are wrong, says Tillich, in their historic anti-revolutionary attitude.[9] For the Kingdom of God may well appear in revolutionary form "where it can be dis-

---

[9] Tillich argues that Paul's admonition to civil obedience in Romans 13 was directed against eschatological enthusiasts, and not toward secular revolutionaries.

cerned that revolution is being built into tradition in such a way that . . . a creative solution in the direction of the ultimate aim of history is found.''[389]

The historical ambiguities of the self-transcendent function of life are caused by the confusion of fragmentary manifestations of the Kingdom of God with that Kingdom itself. One expects ultimate solutions from finite institutions, and an alternation between utopianism and cynicism results. Impossible hopes for finite existence inevitably end in cynical despair. This ambiguous situation is found in the churches in the conflict between the sacramental emphasis on man's future salvation and the prophetic preoccupation with social transformation. This conflict may be overcome by the Kingdom of God ''if a sacramental church takes the principle of social transformation into its aim or if an activistic church . . . [emphasizes] the vertical line of salvation over against the horizontal line of historical activity.''[391]

The Kingdom of God is the answer to the ambiguities of life, to the question of man's historical existence. The answers given thus far occur within history, and through the medium of finite institutions. Thus they are only fragmentary and partial. The final answer of history, however, is not fragmentary and does not occur within history, but at the end of history, in eternity. Thus we turn to the conclusion of Tillich's system, which is his description of the victory of the Kingdom of God over history, that is, eternal life.

The Kingdom of God and Eternal Life

There are those who maintain that no description of eternal life is possible, because of its mysterious and transcendent character. Tillich rejects this view, for ''we stand *now* in face of the eternal, but we do so looking ahead toward the end of history . . .''[396] Thus it is both possible and necessary for theology to describe the significance of the Kingdom of God and eternal life for the present history of man.[10] This does not mean, how-

---

[10] ''. . . man, in the Christian view, comes from the eternal and goes to the eternal; and he can experience the eternal in every moment of time

ever, that one may overlook the symbolic nature of this description, as do popular imagination and theological supernaturalism. Tillich's approach to the description of eternal life is based on the "assertion . . . that the ever present end of history elevates the positive content of history into eternity at the same time that it excludes the negative from participation in it."[397] Thus, that which is positive in history (love, creativity, etc.) can be used as adequate symbols for the end and fulfillment of history.

When we say that the negative is excluded from participation in the eternal, we have described the content of eternity in terms of what is called the "last" or "final" judgment. Positively, it must be said that nothing in creation is lost, but if it is not lost it must be liberated from those expressions of non-being which fight against creation. This liberation is judgment against negativity. The negative (e.g., illness, death, falsehood, destruction, and every kind of evil) has the appearance of a positive force in life. But it is revealed in eternity, in the presence of being-itself, as having no real ontological standing, and thus it is excluded. "Nothing that is, in so far as it is, can be excluded from eternity; but it can be excluded in so far as it is mixed with non-being and not yet liberated from it."[399] The positive in existence is raised to eternal life and is thus freed to participate unambiguously in essential being. Tillich is careful to point out that this "essentialization" of finite being does not simply mean a return to an original state of essentiality. Such a Platonic view would mean the denial of really new, positive, or creative acts in history. Tillich's position is that the products of history can add ontologically to essentiality. Thus "participation in the eternal life depends on a creative synthesis of a being's essential nature with what it has made of it in its temporal existence."[401]

The assertion that eternal life includes the positive and excludes the negative of finite existence implies a lack of movement, a static state, which seems untrue to life. For life must include the negative as that against which it actualizes itself.

. . . eternal life is *life* . . . the eternal now" (Paul Tillich, "The Immortality of Man," *Pastoral Psychology*, Vol. VIII, No. 75, June, 1957, pp. 23, 24).

How then can we speak of eternal *life* if this negative element is missing? The answer, says Tillich, is that while the negative, the power of non-being, is conquered, exposed, and excluded from eternal life and the Kingdom of God, it is nonetheless conquered, exposed, and excluded *within* that realm. Eternal life is not without the negative, or it would not be "life." As we noted early in this book, one of the elements of Schelling's philosophy which Tillich has accepted is the concept of the "becoming" of God. God could not be described in Scripture or popular piety as a "living" God if he were not in a state of becoming, that is, in constant movement away from and back to himself (as in the Trinity), or constantly involved in a victorious movement over non-being. "The Divine Life is the eternal conquest of the negative. . . . Eternal blessedness is not a state of immovable perfection. . . . But the Divine Life is blessedness through fight and victory."[405] This means for man that his participation in eternal life does not eliminate the dynamics of his life; negativity is present, present as that which is overcome.

In eternity, true being—essential being—is raised into unity with being-itself. This is what Tillich calls "universal essentialization," and this doctrine brings him into conflict with traditional views of salvation and damnation. On the one hand Tillich rejects the notion of a mechanistic universal salvation. Origen's doctrine of *apokatastasis panton* (the restitution of all things) does not take seriously enough God's judgment and wrath against every negative thing. On the other hand, Tillich vigorously denies the traditional belief in eternal damnation. "Absolute judgments over finite beings . . . are impossible, because they make the finite infinite."[407] Tillich's position is that the evil in every life is rejected and that which is positive is saved and raised to eternal blessedness. All men are mixtures of good and evil, being and non-being. No person is unambiguously good or bad, accepted or rejected. It is possible to speak of individual salvation and rejection, if individualism is not reduced to personalism so that we speak of the acceptance or rejection of this or that person. The individual is more than personal, he is united with the whole universe of being and in that unity is raised to eternal life.

The question naturally arises: What kind of life is eternal life? Tillich does not object to the word "immortality" if it is used as a symbol of man's awareness of his own finitude, which awareness also indicates his potential infinitude. But if by immortality is meant "a continuation of the temporal life of an individual after death without a body,"[409] then, says Tillich, "it must be radically rejected . . . for participation in eternity is not 'life hereafter.' Neither is it a natural quality of the human soul. It is rather the creative act of God . . ."[410] The phrase "immortality of the soul" can only be used if it is clear that the soul is "spirit," which includes the body, and that individual life does not simply continue, but is transformed and raised to transcendent unity beyond temporality. Thus the "resurrection of the body" seems to Tillich a more adequate symbol for eternal life. The term "body" saves theology from the anti-Christian dualism of Eastern, Platonic, and Neo-Platonic thought and asserts the goodness of God's creation and the fact that no being, physical or spiritual, is excluded from reunion with him. But one must beware of literalistic distortions of the phrase "resurrection of the body." Paul spoke of a "spiritual body" and so avoided the absurdity of materialistic interpretations of resurrection. The total life of man, both physical and spiritual, is raised, but it is raised only as it is transformed. "A Spiritual body then is a body which expresses the Spiritually transformed total personality of man."[412][11]

If the total person is raised to eternal life, so must his unique individuality be. Tillich maintains that we must affirm the individual in eternal life, for without a personal center it is impossible to speak even of participation. And yet the individual which is maintained is not the same, but, as in the case of bodily resurrection, he is transformed. This transformation is analogous to that of the New Being in which out of death God creates not another being or reality, but the same, renewed and changed.

[11] The fact that Tillich can discuss the resurrection of the body without reference to the Resurrection of Christ as either norm or criterion is the result of his belief that resurrection is a useful concept independent of Christology. It "is partly the cause, partly the result, of the belief in the Resurrection of the Christ" (Paul Tillich, "Symbols of Eternal Life," The Harvard Divinity Bulletin, Vol. XXVI, No. 3, April, 1962, p. 7).

"The Kingdom of God includes all dimensions of being. The whole personality participates in Eternal Life."[412-413] More than this cannot be said without crossing the border from concept into the realm of poetic imagination.

If everything that is is rooted in the eternal ground of being, how can we speak of a judgment against any being? How can there be such a thing as "eternal death"? Tillich admits that what he calls "universal essentialization" implies the final and universal unity of all being with God. But at the same time he is not willing to abandon the seriousness of God's judgment and the danger of negativity to life. Both of these views can be maintained if it is seen, first, that eternal death does not mean the raising of non-being to eternity. If we are to avoid dualism, non-being cannot be given ultimate significance—even negatively. Eternal death means "death 'away' from eternity, a failure to reach eternity, being left to the transitoriness of temporality."[415] The reality of this threat is a universal experience and cannot be overcome by the ontological certainty that being-itself must be victorious over every power of non-being and evil. It is only possible to hold both views if they are not mutually exclusive. Tillich seeks to reconcile the seriousness of man's negativity with the universal and final power of God over that negativity by arguing that eternity does not exclude temporality, change, or development. It allows for the possibility of human development and the victory over non-being *within* eternal life.

Eternity contains movement, change, and development. This means that a particular relation between our time and eternity is presupposed. When Augustine abandoned the Platonic view of circular time for a view of time as a straight line, moving from creation to the Kingdom of God, he expressed the Christian belief that time has a purpose and direction. But this linear interpretation of time did not make clear the fact that time not only goes from beginning to end, but also comes from and returns to the eternal. Tillich proposes that we view eternity as a straight line above human history, and our time as "a curve which comes from above, moves down as well as ahead, reaches the deepest point which is the . . . 'existential now,' and returns . . . to that from which it came, going ahead as well as going up."[420] This view allows for progression, for the curve runs in a forward as well as upward direction toward eternity.

God is eternal, and thus we identify him with that realm from which and toward which our history runs. And if we say that we are taken up into eternity, we must say at the same time that we are taken up into a life *in* God. This is what Tillich calls "eschatological pan-en-theism."[421] But what does it mean to be "in" God? How can we be in him and yet maintain the "otherness" without which there is no individuality? The answer, says Tillich, lies in a threefold use of the preposition "in" which is consistent with the ontological presuppositions upon which the whole of *Systematic Theology* is built. One is first of all "in" God as dependent upon his creative origin. This is very much like Aristotle's concept of the essences which exist "in" the mind of the deity. One is also "in" God as dependent ontologically at every moment on the ground of being which supports and sustains our being. And one is "in" God as ultimate fulfillment, which is the return to essential being, which being God is. This threefold "in-ness" points to the basic and necessary movement of life away from potentiality toward actualization and return to essential being. Our life and individuality cannot be apart from an identity with God at any moment, and thus to be "in" God as final fulfillment in no way mitigates the reality of our being, but makes that reality possible.

The point is that man is only what he is in God. The reader cannot fail to notice that, as Tillich readily admits, this description of man in the light of God brings into his theological system a radical reversal of approach. While Tillich argues that we would not be able to make such a description without the symbols given above in answer to the questions of human existence, yet this assertion at the end of his work brings into question anew the whole method of correlation because it is a radical reversal of it. "Although most considerations given within the theological circle deal with man and his world in their relation to God, our final consideration points in the opposite direction and speaks of God in his relation to man and his world."[422]

SUMMARY AND ANALYSIS

"History" for Tillich is not simply everything that has happened in the past, but rather it is the interpretation of purposeful acts of men in terms of the self-consciousness or "vocational" self-interpretation of their group. History by its very nature has the character of meaning and purpose. Historical time not only goes forward, but drives toward a fulfillment. In the same way, space, causality, and substance under the dimension of history point beyond themselves toward that which is universal and unconditional. History moves toward a goal, but it does not grow progressively nearer its goal. Although history does not and cannot achieve its ultimate end within itself, it nevertheless does achieve limited ends. It is the inevitable confusion between these two ends which is the basic cause of the ambiguity of history. These ambiguities may be seen in all functions of life. The self-integrating function of life moves toward universal participation but manages only to create empires and with them all types of oppression. This same ambiguity of history is seen in its self-productive function which aims at the new, but cannot escape the old and therefore falls into revolution and reaction. And it is seen in self-transcendence, when, in the hope and expectation of fulfillment, man does not look beyond himself, and therefore confuses his own period with the *parousia* and his own time with eternity. These ambiguities of history can only be solved by the real and final fulfillment of history in the Kingdom of God.

The Kingdom of God can be the answer to the ambiguities of history because it has appeared as the center of history in Jesus as the Christ. This center reappears as the criterion and source of history's fulfillment whenever and wherever the Christ is received as such. The Kingdom of God in history manifests itself in moments of *kairoi* in which the providence of God guides creation toward unity with himself. When the Kingdom of God appears in history it overcomes the ambiguities of history by reconciling the conflicts within the functions of man's life. For instance, the ambiguity of self-integration is overcome by the power of God which alone is able to use force in the context of true freedom. The Kingdom of God may appear through a political system, a revolution, a church, or an individual, and whenever it does appear it heals the conflicts of history—but it heals them only fragmentarily. For the ultimate and final answer to history is not found in history, but at the end of history. This answer is the salvation of God, called by Tillich "universal essentialization," which means that all being, man included, is raised to unambiguous unity with the ground and power of being, and therein finds its fulfillment. And because nothing created is lost, neither man's body nor his spirit, the most adequate symbol for the final answer to history is "resurrection." We must again emphasize our agreement with and acceptance of the greater part of Tillich's presentation of this last part of his system. His philosophy of history is convincing; he avoids the dilemmas of both idealism and materialism because he views history as a "product" of human consciousness based upon fact. We think that Tillich is right when he says that history is the expression of man's own self-interpretation within a particular group, that it is an expression of man's "state," and that it moves toward ultimate fulfillment. We believe that he has accurately analyzed the ambiguities of life in general and the expression of those ambiguities in the particular and all-embracing dimension of history. And finally we agree with Tillich when he points to the Kingdom of God as the answer to these ambiguities and the real fulfillment of history.

But just because we are so much in agreement with these and other points, we find ourselves led in quite a different direction than that which Tillich has taken. For if history is really a product of man's own self-interpretation, if it is really a reflection of his "state," and if it contains insoluble ambiguities so that it cannot be said to contain its own answer, what else can this mean except that man and his history cannot possibly be the vantage point from which to view God's saving history and his Kingdom? What we are asking is whether Tillich's quite true, accurate, and perceptive analysis of history should not have been reason enough not to make it the basis and beginning point of a study of "saving history" or a correlate of the Kingdom of God.

The problem which faces us here is perhaps basically the problem of time. For the proposition that seems to support Tillich's whole discussion is that "time" is an element common to both God's saving history and man's finite history so that it is possible to speak of the one in terms of the other. But is it really true that man shares the reality of time with God? Time is a problematic category for Tillich. He has described it as "a past that is no more . . . a future that is not yet . . . a present which is nothing more than the moving boundary line between past and future."[12] On the other hand he has said that it is creative, direct, and irreversible.[13] But finally, time is real for Tillich because the present is real. In this he follows Heidegger except that, instead of the reality of the present being based on man's own existential affirmation and courage, it is based on an "ontological courage," by which is meant the self-evident fact that man *is* present and does not succumb to the threat of non-being because his present participates in the power of being-itself. Tillich affirms the present, and with it the reality and integrity of time, in spite of the fact that we are always losing our present in the "no more" of the past and the "not yet" of the future. On the other hand he sees that God's time is eternity, which he calls the transcendent unity of the disconnected moments of our time. This time transcends, but also includes, our time, there being an undisturbed ontological relation between the two. The question we must ask is this: If Tillich is right in the first instance, that time for man does have this negative, ambiguous, and transient character, can he be right in the second instance, that this time as a category of being can be applied equally to God and man? If he is right, and we believe that he is, that it is the power of God which grants time to man, a kind of time which overcomes the ambiguities of man's time and gives it real direction, does this not mean that man's time is broken, overpowered, and replaced by God's time? It may be objected that such a radical questioning of man's time renders inexplicable the fact of creation. It certainly must be said that man is created

12 *Systematic Theology*, Vol. I. p. 193.
13 *Ibid.*

with time, indeed, God's time (expressed symbolically in Genesis as God's "presence" in the Garden). But this is just what man lost in the Fall. His time is no more his own (he must work), his time is taken away from him and he becomes transient (he must die). In the same way he loses his space, the place where he can be present; he is ejected from his home and is destined to be swallowed at last by the only space left him, the ground. This situation has been exactly described and analyzed by Tillich in terms of the ambiguities of life. Man has no time, and the only time that he has is passing time, time he is always losing; his time is only that which slips through his fingers. Therefore man's history is nothing more than his self-interpretation in a hopeless situation. He sees well enough that this passing time of his leads irrevocably to the end, but in the vanity of his heart he imagines that through secular or religious exercises he can change this end into a fulfillment. But as Tillich has shown, this hope is always broken on the rock of death.

Is there any other time available to man, is there a history which is something more than his own self-contemplation, a history that points to a real fulfillment? There certainly is! But this positive, meaningful, directed, and fulfilled time is not simply another and happier side of time from which we have come and toward which we are moving. It can only be understood as a time which breaks into, overpowers, and replaces our passing time. Such a time is God's time; not the time we were originally given and lost, but a new, gracious, and saving time, a true *kairos*. The fact that this other, positive, and lasting time is offered and in fact has been given means that now we do have time; it means that the chronological quality of our existence is changed from a passing away to a going forward. Yet it is no longer *our* time that we have, but the time that God has given us. This is the time of grace, the time of salvation, the time of Jesus Christ. In the light of these distinctions we would ask three questions.

(1) Tillich agrees that the history of salvation is not to be confused with the history of man. But does not just this confusion take place when he says that man's reception of the event of salvation, the appearance of the Christ, is made possible by a

process of maturation out of which existential questions arise
which point to revelatory answers? Is not this mature consciousness of one's existential situation the same self-interpretation
which constitutes man's history? The basis of this assertion is
found in Tillich's doctrine of revelation where he says that man
has in the depths of his natural self-consciousness a knowledge
of his relation to being-itself. It is this "depth of reason" that
allows man to ask for and therefore receive revelation. But would
not such a process of consciousness itself be part of the history of
salvation? Is this again not a confusion of nature and revelation,
or at best man's essential, created being with the New Being?

(2) How can Jesus as the Christ be the center of the history
of salvation unless he himself constitutes that salvation, unless
he himself is the fulfillment of the time that God has given us?
And if he is this center, then how can we speak of any "preparation" for him in our time? That is to say, if he is not only the
criterion but also the source of every saving event, how can there
be either preparation before his reception, or fulfillment after
it, that is not directly dependent upon him?

(3) Tillich is certainly right in saying that Christ is the
"great" *kairos*. But can this mean that there are lesser *kairoi*?
Tillich himself has said that there is no "more or less" in respect
to revelation. Should not this mean that there is only the one
great *kairos*? To what can the distinction and particularity of
the various *kairoi* point except to the distinct and particular
reactions of men to the one *kairos*? If in faith we are really
en Christos, need we, indeed can we, speak of any other *kairos*
but the one found in him? In light of the discussion above can
we speak of our time as offering occasions in which "from time
to time" we may receive other *kairoi?* Is he not always the only
"time" we have?

It is of course true that these questions imply a consistent and
absolute concentration on Christ as the beginning and end of all
of God's ways and works. We cannot return to this major issue
of theology without noting again, in spite of the questions raised,
what seems to be a movement of Tillich's thought in this direction. For instance, how could the interpretation of Jesus as the

Christ found in the second volume of his system allow him to say that Christ is the center of God's saving history, not only as its criterion, but also as its "source"? Nor does this seem consistent with his previous view of the New Being as being apart from Jesus as the Christ. We only wish that this centrality had been applied also to the processes of history in which man is "prepared" to receive the Christ. Again, Tillich's philosophy of history is not only acceptable but certainly a valuable contribution to our understanding of human history and its interpretation. But just for this reason should it not have been rejected as a possible introduction to saving history; should it not have made it all the clearer that the task of theology is not to discover what the Kingdom of God means in terms of our history, but to proclaim what our history means in the light of the Kingdom of God?

VIII

REVIEW AND CONCLUSION

We have noted that Tillich begins with man, man in his relation to his world. The interpretation of the situation arising from that relation and the revelatory answer to it is the task of theology. Theology is thus "answering" theology; it is "apologetic." This means that the method of theology must be interpreted as a "correlation" of the philosophical description of man's situation with the revelatory answer to it. This method is valid, Tillich maintains, because it is impossible that God should answer questions which have not been asked; such an answer would be incomprehensible for man. But this does not mean that man's questions precede God's answer unconditionally. For even as man asks his questions, he does so in the light of answers already given. Man's analysis of his situation always takes place over against some concept, no matter how dim or abstract, of the ultimate in contrast to which his situation is seen and toward which he looks for an answer. This is what Tillich calls the theological circle; it is specifically expressed in the theologian's prior commitment to a particular manifestation of his ultimate concern on the basis of which he asks his questions. But this a priori of faith is not where Tillich's theology begins, and this is the decisive fact about his system. He even argues that it is necessary for the theologian to proceed "as if he had never heard" of this prior commitment. And when he does turn to the answer of revelation in the Bible, church history, and the history of religion and culture, the theologian finds it given in terms of, or in the form of, the question which preceded it.

Is such an approach to apologetic theology possible? We have said that it could be possible if the situation of man is really seen and the revelatory answer really heard. But because we have not found in Tillich's system an understanding of the fact that only in Jesus Christ can man and his situation be clearly seen, because in his analysis this meaning of human existence was actually suppressed, and because the content of revelation as found in Christ was not allowed to speak for itself, but was forced into the form of a question asked as if it had not already been answered, we have not been able to respond to the above question in the affirmative. In spite of the erudition and analytical skill with which Tillich has expounded the human situation and in spite of his serious concern for and dedication to the Christian message, our study of his *Systematic Theology* has only confirmed us in this view.

In the first part of his system, "Reason and Revelation," Tillich analyzes reason and shows how the questions arising from it are answered by revelation. Reason for Tillich is both the quality of the mind which is able to grasp and shape reality, and the *logos* structure of reality which may be grasped and shaped. It thus has a subject-object structure which, under the conditions of existence, appears as a conflict from which the questions of reason arise. The most important element of Tillich's discussion of reason is what he calls the "depth of reason," that is, the realization or "awareness" within man that the universe is a structured, rational whole, based upon the unity of being in being-itself. Man is aware that he is integrally related to this whole and to its base, God. Thus man can ask for revelation because he is aware of the ultimate in the depth of his reason.

Revelation, which is essentially mysterious and remains so, occurs when either nature or history becomes for someone "transparent" to the divine ground of all being. Some part of reality is used by the divine in such a way that through it the divine is manifest. This is the basis for Tillich's doctrine of symbolism. For Tillich, Jesus as the Christ is the "final" revelation of God. As such he is the norm and criterion for all other revelations because in him revelation is seen in a way that answers the questions of reason. In him that which is relative appears as the absolute, but is sacrificed to the absolute in order to achieve transcendent unity. This is "the sacrifice of Jesus to the Christ," or the transparency of the medium for that which is revealed. Two important questions arose in connection with Tillich's presentation. The first was whether or not his concept of revelation is at all understandable as "revelation" if it is based upon a natural capacity or awareness in man of the presence of the divine Logos within himself. And the second was how God can have really and finally revealed himself if, as Tillich says, the manifestation of revelation, namely, Jesus, was sacrificed to the ultimate and *hidden* element, namely, the Christ.

In Tillich's doctrine of God found in the second part of his system, the philosophical basis of his thought was elucidated as an ontological construction in which man as a being is related to God as the ground of being. Within this structure of being, its elements and its categories, there is a negative element, a "not yet" or a "no more," which Tillich calls "non-being." In man this negative element presents a threat expressed in the conflicts and tensions between the polar elements of being and the categories. But man continues to be, and he does so because, in spite of the threat of non-being, his being is supported and grounded in the power of being-itself. This Tillich has described as the "ontological courage to be." Again, it is man's awareness of this characteristic of his own being, that is, its foundation in being-itself, which allows him to ask after God. For God is the ground and power of being—he is being-itself. This means for Tillich that God transcends all human categories and yet includes them all. On the basis of this ontological description, Tillich attributes to God the traditional appellation of "creator," because of God's originating, sustaining, and directing creativity. God may also be described in terms of that power which overcomes the conflicts within man's finite being. Thus he is said to be eternal, omnipotent, and omnipresent. But finally, God is described by Tillich as love, because as the ground of being he desires the unity of all being in himself and thereby fulfills and saves all being.

Tillich's view of man as a dependent part of the being of God and his description of this God as the ground of being are no doubt both correct. But the question was and is whether man, because of this ontological relation, is able to *know* God as the ground of his being. Does God reveal himself as the ground and power of being apart from his self-revelation in Jesus Christ?

This problem becomes all the more critical in the third part of *Systematic Theology*, "Existence and the Christ." Here Tillich develops an interpretation of existential man in terms of a "fall" from essential being. By the Fall he means the free choice of man to actualize the potentialities of his being, to stand alone and apart from the ground of his being. But man is destined to make this decision because he would not be man unless he did so. The result of this choice is real life, but it is also estrangement. When man actualizes his own particularity as an individual subject, he becomes separated from every object; he becomes separated from God and from other men and from his own essential nature. In this situation man experiences the conflicts and tensions of both the elements and categories of being in such a way that his own being is threatened with destruction. Thus man can only ask for a New Being which can restore him to the unity and power of being.

This New Being is brought by the Christ, who was made manifest in the personal life of Jesus of Nazareth. Jesus, says Tillich, was the Christ because he was received as the Christ. This means that while the accounts of this reception in the New Testament are available to critical study, the reality of the event itself is not; it is a matter of faith. What can be verified is that the picture presented of Jesus as the Christ in Scripture has brought New Being to men, and is therefore self authenticating. The New Being, seen in Jesus, represents the eternal unity of God and man. The central and final revelation of this unity had to be manifest in a human life, because only by so appearing could salvation really be brought into the midst of men so that it could be apprehended by men. But the Christ, the New Being, was not and is not tied to the human life we call Jesus. It saves and heals in history apart from him. Tillich's position becomes clear when he claims that the Resurrection was not the raising of the man Jesus, but rather the appearance of the divine Spirit of the New Being which convinced men that the saving power of

God which they saw in Jesus, but which exists apart from him, continues in the world after his death.

It is especially this Christology of Tillich which has caused us to ask very seriously whether he has been able to describe accurately either the human situation or the revelation of God. As long as God remains obscure in his divinity or operates secretly throughout history in other ways and in other forms than in Jesus Christ, does he not remain a hidden rather than a revealed God? But if God has come and is revealed in the flesh, in Jesus of Nazareth, should we seek him beyond or behind that man? And if this man has brought salvation to men, must not that fact be decisive for our anthropology? We can no longer interpret man as one lost in estrangement, but must see him as one called and saved in Jesus Christ.

In the fourth part of his system, entitled "Life and the Spirit," Tillich rightly sees life as a unity in which there are no "levels" of ontological value, but only dimensions of kind. The dimension of the spirit, however, is of peculiar importance because it is here that man experiences the ambiguities of life and the overcoming of those ambiguities by the presence of the divine Spirit. Life is ambiguous because it is a mixture of essence and existence. This ambiguity is described by Tillich in terms of the split between subject and object, between man and his world, between man's essential nature and his existential nature, and between himself and God. For instance, in the cultural realm the split between subject and object causes the problem of cognition; we are always isolated from every object of our experience. In the moral realm this split is seen in the inability of one man to unite in love with another; and in the religious realm it is seen as man's inability to unite with God, to transcend his own situation of finitude toward the infinite. But the presence of the divine Spirit raises man in ecstatic moments to transcendent life above these ambiguities. The Spirit is "God present," and in his presence man is reunited with the ground of being, with other beings, and with his own essential being.

But because Tillich does not see this Spirit as the Spirit of Jesus Christ, this question is raised: If the Spirit points man to a moral imperative which is only an expression of man's own essential nature, or if the Spirit is seen to raise man to a unity which is in any case only the unity natural to man's being, then is there not the greatest danger that this Spirit will become confused with the spirit of man?

The persistent question of the place and character of Jesus Christ in Paul Tillich's theology and the relation of this problem to his interpretation of both man's situation and the revelation of God are found also in the last part of his system, "History and the Kingdom of God." History is seen by Tillich as man's interpretation of events in terms of his own self-consciousness and the "vocational" consciousness of his group. Ambiguities arise in history because man confuses the limited ends of his finite existence with the ultimate end of history. For example, the self-integrating function of life, which may be historically interpreted as empire-building, becomes oppressive and leads to disintegration because man views his empires as absolute and final ends. Therefore, man in history asks for an end and fulfillment which transcends the limited ends of existence. This is the question of the Kingdom of God.

Tillich maintains that the Kingdom of God is neither isolated from nor identical with the historical process. The Kingdom appears in history in special *kairoi*, all of which are based on the "great" *kairos* of Jesus as the Christ. In him the Kingdom of God is manifest in an anticipatory way, but nonetheless fully and in power. Thus Christ is said to be the center of history; before his coming he was anticipated in the "latent" church, and now he continues to be received in the "manifest" church. The Kingdom of God, which is the content of every revelation and is realized fragmentarily through the divine Spirit, finally means that all of being will become New Being, that it will be raised to eternal life, to unambiguous and complete unity with the ground and power of being.

In this final part of Tillich's system we are forced back to the original question, namely, is it possible to approach the revelation or the salvation of God from the point of view of our own situation? Specifically, can we abstract from our history anything at all about God's saving history, or proceed from our time to God's time which is eternity? Is it not absolutely necessary to see that the only time we have is the time God has for us in Jesus Christ, through whom history is given a real goal and promise of fulfillment?

THE PROBLEM OF THE KNOWLEDGE OF GOD

The central and all-embracing problem of the place and character of Jesus Christ in Paul Tillich's *Systematic Theology* is the reason we are not able, finally, to accept either his view of theology as apologetic or the method of correlation. For the apologetic requirement for an understanding of the human situation cannot be fulfilled except in the light of the final and decisive word spoken about man and to man in Jesus Christ; nor can the revelation of God be seen apart from the one event in which he did reveal himself, Jesus Christ. These assertions must be the standard against which every theology is judged.

But this leaves unanswered the question of *why* Tillich chose to pursue the theological task in this way. It is clear that Tillich is not blind to the problem we have discussed. The proposition that theology must begin with God and not man is expressed in various places throughout his system. We see it in his defense of the "theological circle" in which the theologian's prior commitment always appears in his analysis of the human situation. It appears in the a priori which we have noted in such statements as "God answers man's questions, and under the impact of God's answers man asks them."[1] Why, then, we may well ask, has Tillich chosen systematically to ignore this a priori and begun his theology with man? This question becomes all the more acute when we note that Tillich has accurately described man as being in a situation from which one would think he could not move toward the divine revelation. Furthermore, he has repeatedly emphasized what he calls "the Protestant principle," that is, that in relation to God all things are from God. He has even said that God as object is nonetheless always subject. His intention has been to regard the *analogia entis* in a way which avoids natu-

[1] *Systematic Theology*, Vol. I, p. 61.

ral theology, and he has insisted that the Spirit of God must not be confused with the spirit of man, or saving history with human history. In short, within the fabric of Tillich's presentation there is interwoven a thread of thought which runs counter to the whole, one which, by its emphasis on the divinity of God and the humanity of man and the impossibility of confusing the two or proceeding from the second to the first, stands out in contrast to the method and development of the system as such. We cannot but believe that these latter considerations point to the basic intention and purpose of Tillich's thought. Why, then, have they been placed in a system which begins where they indicate theology cannot begin and proceeds in a way which "the Protestant principle" would indicate theology may not proceed?

To answer this question it is necessary to see the problem as Tillich sees it. He has often described himself as standing "on the boundary line" between philosophy and theology or, perhaps better, as standing between the actual human situation as it is expressed in the various dimensions of man's life, and the theological situation which includes the Christian faith and its proclamation. He has placed himself on this boundary line (or perhaps found himself there) and from it seeks to interpret for the men of his day the message he receives from "the other side." In order to do this he must be understood, and in order to be understood, Tillich feels that he must use the idiom and the thought forms of the culture to which he wishes to express the truth of the gospel. This means that he must discover a common denominator between the Word of God and the word of man in order to make the one understandable to the other. This common denominator is "being." Ontology is therefore seen as the key to the problem of the interpretation of the Christian faith. To put the matter in another way: Tillich, following the German idealistic and Greek classical traditions, sees knowledge as a union of subject and object. The particularism of nominalism is rejected because it is not able to explain how one can grasp the object of knowledge either in terms of similarity or distinction. Without universals or essences, knowledge is empty phenomenology; things remain things unrelated to other things and therefore without meaning or value. Thus Tillich turns to the ontology of universal being and finds there the possibility of a noetic relation between God and man. Man as a knowing subject may grasp objects in the unity of being, and he may himself be grasped and known. For Tillich, of course, God is not an object of knowledge among other objects; he transcends the distinction between subject and object. Yet it must be admitted that systematically God is the "object" of theology and he is certainly approached as such by Tillich's methodology.

But we have seen that this approach denies the very foundation upon which Christian theology is built, that is, that man as such is separated from God and can only be reunited with him in the subjective act of God's revelation of himself in Jesus Christ. This foundation is undermined by the assumption that man is naturally "aware" of God as the ground and power of his being. If such an awareness is real, the presence of its object is real; for what purpose then is revelation? Is it only to add to man's knowledge, to give him more information about his relationship with God who is in any case seen as the ground and power of his being? What more could or need be said? Tillich admits the problem, but replies that unless this approach is accepted, there is no way in which man as subject can either receive or understand the object of revelation. Man as subject can only understand his object, God, on the basis of what he already knows, and what he already knows most basically is his own being and its dependency on being-itself. It is therefore in these terms, says Tillich, that theology must state its case.

Is there any other way to speak of the knowledge of God than a way which begins with man and his knowledge of himself?[2] We believe there is. We believe that there is another approach to theological knowledge which is adequate to its object, God, and which, moreover, is understandable. If we speak of a "way of knowing God," we do not mean a way created and decided by man himself; as a general principle taken from the world of

[2] For what follows see also "Der Einfluss der reformierten Theologie auf die Entwicklung der wissenschaftlichen Methode" by T. F. Torrence in *Theologische Zeitschrift* (Sept.-Oct., 1962), pp. 341 ff.

science and applied to theology. This is not the case. If we speak of a way of knowing God which is adequate to its object, this can only mean that this way is dictated by the object because this object is really always subject! The particular way of knowledge dictated by revelation and presented in the Christian faith is that which holds its object, God, as the subject of the knowledge of God and its conditions. It recognizes that the only objectivity which is available to theology is that in which God gives himself as the object of our knowledge in such a way as to require the submission of our traditions and culture to his disclosure of himself in Jesus Christ. Any other so-called objective approach is only and can be only the subjective transference of ourselves as objects into his place.

Is such an approach to the knowledge of God understandable? There is at least one tradition of philosophical, theological, and scientific thought which would indicate that it is. Tillich has often referred to the weakness of nominalism, especially as it was expressed by William of Ockham. Tillich finds this view inadequate to explain how knowledge is possible, and he therefore makes his choice for the classical and medieval ontological, "realistic," tradition. But there is another point at issue here which transcends the problem of particularism over against "realism" (which we would now call idealism), for it can be seen in Anselm, who is certainly as pure an idealist as one could wish, as well as in Ockham. The real issue concerns one's openness for the new, a realization, which in theology must be a confession, that God is not a "given" in the world, and can be the object of knowledge only as he gives himself to man. Such an openness we saw in Anselm's ontological and cosmological arguments which, regardless of their argumentative character, were nevertheless submitted to the a priori reality of God. Thus Anselm's proofs appear in the context of a prayer! For Anselm the object of theological knowledge was allowed to be itself, that is, one who is always subject and as such is always the subject of the knowledge of himself. This approach to knowledge was not brought to bear upon science and philosophy until the time of William of Ockham. Ockham denied the medieval thesis that

God has exhausted himself in creation, that the world is filled with final causes, and that one can perceive in creation the divine pattern as a "natural" revelation. Ockham denied the *aeternitas mundi* and argued for the possibility of the contingent. The immediate result, strangely enough, was not the emancipation of theology from its old thought-forms, but the freeing of science from the straitjacket in which it existed under the medieval doctrine of God. This new freedom expressed itself in a willingness to learn from nature, to receive the object of study as it presents itself without prejudice.

This emancipation did not take place in theology until the Reformation when the concept of *Deus sive natura* was abandoned in favor of a view of God as a living and active Creator and Redeemer of men. In the doctrine of accommodation, the Reformers presented God as giving himself to men as the object of their faith, and in the doctrine of election, God, who became a man among men, graciously elected man's humanity, including his subjectivity, for saving knowledge of himself. The doctrine of electing grace gave man the confidence that his intellect too was not outside the bounds of God's providence. In this situation even the empirical sciences flourished. Francis Bacon, for instance, held what was nearly a complete objectivity toward the truth and yet he himself described that objectivity in terms of faith. As one enters the Kingdom of Heaven in a "childlike" trust, said Bacon, so one enters analogously the kingdom of the natural sciences. In our own era this strict objectivity which is analogous to faith has been demonstrated by such men as Niels Bohr and Albert Einstein, who were not willing to remain encased in the gains of the past, but with great courage stood apart from "the given," the Kantian conceptions of space and time, and let the new break in upon them. Similarly, Sören Kierkegaard escaped the confines of both Hegelian and Lutheran orthodoxy and approached the object of theology in a radically new way. Kierkegaard spoke of "the leap of faith," by which he meant (among other things) simply that if we are to speak theologically we must approach the object of our inquiry in a manner appropriate to it. And because the truth with which we

have to do is the revelation of God in space and time, the entering of God into the history of man, and his saving of that history
in Jesus Christ, our only attitude can and must be one of openness and reception.

We are not suggesting that there is any substantive connection between the method of theology and that of natural science
—even less do we mean to imply that there is a way of moving
from one to the other. But we are suggesting that the proper
stance of both for their quite different aims can be described in
the same way. For both science and theology the relating of the
subject over against the object of inquiry involves "repentance"
(*metonoia*), a conversion of prior understanding based upon the
new reality which man encounters. This may be described as an
openness, a willingness to risk the place upon which we stand for
the sake of the object we approach. This similarity of approach
does not mean that theology can be based on any *philosophia
perennis*. The theologian will not nor can he learn to stand before
the object of his study by aping the movements of the scientists!
But if he will stand before the word of God and be open to it,
if he will let this object, who is always subject, *be* his object, and
require neither of this object nor of himself any "common
ground" or presuppositions, then he may discover that neither
his listening nor what he hears is irrelevant or unintelligible to
men in this age or any other. For men understand perhaps
better than we think that *"In ecclesia non valet: hoc ego dico,
hoc tu dicis, hoc ille dicit, sed: haec dicit Dominus!"*[3]

We have called attention to the parallel between the theological and scientific approach to knowledge only to demonstrate
that the absolute objectivity required of theology is a lucid and
explicable concept. We have put the matter in this way because
one of the main tenets of Tillich's theology is that if as object
God is approached in any way except through man's subjective
understanding of himself, revelation would come to man as something "strange" and heteronomous, and that its acceptance
would split man's rational center, destroying man himself. Thus
Tillich believes it is possible for man to understand the reality

[3] Augustine, quoted in Karl Barth, "Von der Paradoxie des 'positiven
Paradoxes,'" *op. cit.*, p. 296.

of God, not as that reality may present itself, but only in terms of man himself. " 'God' is the answer to the question implied in man's finitude; . . . This does not mean that first there is a being called God and then the demand that man should be ultimately concerned about him. It means that whatever concerns a man ultimately becomes god for him . . ."[4] Tillich has rightly seen that such a subjective projection of the self can only be a "god." But is he right in thinking that the understanding of this god, correlated with divine revelation, will render a true knowledge of God? Has God's revelation ever come in any other way except through the breaking of the idols men raise to their own subjectivity? Tillich argues that such destruction destroys man. But, to the contrary, does not this breaking into and through the time, space, self-consciousness, and self-understanding of man save man from the destructiveness of his own autonomy by electing him for knowledge and fellowship with God? The absolute necessity of the inviolate objectivity of God's revelation is required and determined by that revelation itself. That it means life rather than death is attested and demonstrated by the renewing and life-giving power of the Spirit in the church. Having said this, we can and must also say that when the theologian describes the determination of himself as subject by his object he is not, as Tillich maintains, speaking irrational nonsense, but is speaking in the most scientific and precise way of the one relationship which is adequate to his object.[5]

CONCLUSION

We cannot but feel that if Tillich had allowed the object of theology to be the object which as subject creates the conditions for its own reception, his intention to present both a kerygmatic and an apologetic theology would have been better served. If he

[4] *Systematic Theology*, Vol. I, p. 211.

[5] We do not mean to say more than this. Specifically, we resist the current attempt of Heinrich Ott to demonstrate a *useful* "correspondence" between the ontology of the later Heidegger and theological method and hermeneutics. (Cf. Heinrich Ott, "What Is Systematic Theology?" in *New Frontiers in Theology*, eds. James M. Robinson and John B. Cobb, New York: Harper and Row, 1963, pp. 77-115.) Does not theology involve itself in a contradiction when it looks either to natural science or to philosophy for an epistemology adequate for the special kind of knowledge (faith) peculiar to its own "Subject" (God)?

had allowed the Word of God to speak for itself and if he had
made the hearing of it the primary word of his system instead
of hiding it away in a theological a priori, then, even if he had
begun with man, it would have been the man addressed and
called by this Word. Man is who he has been determined to be in
the gracious decision of this Word; therefore his questions can
only be seen as expressions of an answer he has already been
given. If the saving Word of God which confronts us in Jesus
Christ had been allowed to confront us in all its objectivity and
truth as a reality which must in no case be adjusted to our experience, but one in terms of which all our experiences and presuppositions must be adjusted, and if this divine subject who
allows us to hold him as our object had been the systematic
starting place of Tillich's theology, then there would have been
no distortion of Christ's being, nor would there have been a shift-
ing of focus away from him, but he would have been seen as both
the author and finisher of our faith. If Tillich had begun with the
divine object of faith who is always subject rather than the
human subject who inevitably makes himself his own object,
there would be no tension between an "apologetic" and a
"kerygmatic" theology. They would not contradict each other,
for the one about whom we presume to ask is always the one who
has already answered us. If we ask about any other save the one
who has revealed himself as having already answered, we do not
ask about God.

> I was ready to be sought by those
>   who did not ask for me;
> I was ready to be found by those
>   who did not seek me.
> I said, "Here am I, here am I,"
>   to a nation that did not call on my name.[6]

There can be no thought of making here a final "evaluation"
of Paul Tillich's theology; his work has proven its own value in
the appreciation of many who have been led by it into a deeper
understanding of faith and who have heard in it an authentic

[6] Isaiah 65:1.

echo of the Word of God. Still less could these critical remarks be taken as an evaluation in themselves. We have tried to make clear that the corrections which we have suggested are not alien to Tillich's own thought, and that there is within his system a definite line which parallels the approach we have suggested. If, then, we are not able to agree with Christoph Rhein that Tillich's ontological principle, his interpretation of the *analogia entis*, and its accompanying method should be further developed and accepted by the church,[7] still less can we agree with William F. Albright that Tillich's theological system "resembles traditional Christianity only in superficial aspects."[8] No one who reads Tillich can fail to learn from him. His genius for analytical study will instruct theologians and ministers for generations to come in the depth and intricacies of human life. Nor will they fail to find here clear statements, faithful interpretations, and valuable insights concerning the Christian message. From another perspective we may even say that the apologetic approach and the method of correlation as used by Tillich do indeed show us the human situation, for the human situation is one in which men are always turning away from the answer they are given toward a question based upon an affirmation of themselves. Tillich has shown us, as perhaps no other theologian could do, the falseness and impossibility of this "human situation," and if it was not his intention to teach us in just this way, this does not in any way prejudice the value of the lesson we have learned.

But finally, the value of Paul Tillich's theology rests on the same foundation as every other theology. It rests on him in whose name it is written; and whether that name is spoken with clarity or ambiguity, in truth or in error, in strength or in weakness, he is able and has himself glorified it and "will glorify it again."[9] We would be poor students of Tillich indeed if we could not also say that, in whatever way, "Christ is proclaimed; and in that I rejoice."[10]

[7] Christoph Rhein, *Paul Tillich, Philosoph und Theologe* (Stuttgart: Evangelischer Verlag, 1957), p. 194.

[8] *Religion and Culture*, ed. Walter Leibrecht (New York: Harper & Brothers, Publishers, 1959), p. 125.

[9] John 12:28.

[10] Philippians 1:18.

Index

Abelard, Pierre, 171

Absolutism, 77, 78, 80, 89-91, 94

Adoption (adoptionism), 29, 166, 167-168, 180, 203

Aesthetics, 72, 77, 78, 91, 123, 135, 194

Agape, 135, 138, 193-194, 202, 206, 213

Albright, William, 269

Alexander of Hales, 51

Ambiguity, 39, 59, 69, 70, 74, 120, 163, 189, 191, 192-194, 195, 196, 197, 198, 205-215, 217, 221, 223, 230-236, 239, 240, 241, 242, 248-249, 251, 259, 260

America, 14, 18-19, 28

Anabaptists, 200-201

Analogia entis, 29, 33, 63, 67, 84, 93, 96, 97, 124, 139, 140, 186, 261, 269

Analogy, 33, 43, 63, 66, 84, 97, 126, 159

Anselm, 45, 117-118, 142, 161, 171, 264

Anshen, Ruth, 147

Anthropology, 20, 21, 22, 29, 31, 37, 38, 69, 70, 79, 96, 138, 168, 259

Anxiety, 115, 131, 133, 134, 147, 154, 155, 196, 209

Apologetics. *See* Theology, apologetic

Aquinas, Thomas, 32, 33, 191

Arianism, 163

Aristotle, 32, 62, 66, 73, 112, 146, 247

Asceticism, 156

Athanasius, 164

Atheism, 65, 123

Atonement, 171-172

Augustine, 32, 46, 51, 111, 130, 152, 232, 246, 266

Authority, 33, 60, 77, 78, 86, 90, 185, 212, 219

Autonomy, 33, 76, 77, 80, 89, 90, 94, 95, 267

Bacon, Francis, 265

Baptism, 178, 203, 207

Barth, Karl, 11-15, 19, 22, 24, 27-30, 32, 39, 41, 49, 88, 178, 181, 212, 266

Being, 12, 23, 27, 31, 41, 42, 43, 45, 47, 59, 61-67, 77, 103-118, 122, 128-143, 146, 149, 153, 173, 180, 191, 213, 244, 246, 247, 249, 256, 257, 258, 260, 262-263; elements of, 107-113, 125, 153, 257, 258; essential, 27, 33, 48, 59, 74, 112-113, 123, 128, 129, 131, 146, 148, 149, 150-151, 152, 154, 155, 156, 160, 165, 179, 197, 206, 217, 243, 244, 247, 259; estranged (*See* Estrangement); existential, 59, 112-113, 123, 146, 151, 154, 161; finite (*See* Finitude); ground of, 37, 38, 43, 45, 47, 52, 62, 63, 66, 67, 70, 76, 78, 80, 83, 85, 87, 90, 93, 100, 113, 118, 119, 122, 126, 129, 139, 145, 154, 189, 221, 222, 239, 246, 247, 249, 256, 257, 258, 259, 260 (*See also* God); of God, 103, 123, 128-136, 140, 154, 184, 257; of man, 12, 27, 41, 59, 65, 103-104, 123, 132, 137, 140, 154, 157, 249, 260;

271

Knowledge, of God); love of, 134-136, 138, 171-172, 257; judgment of (*See* Judgment); omnipotence of, 132, 133, 134, 136, 138, 257; omnipresence of, 134, 136, 138, 155, 257; omniscience of, 134, 138; proofs of, 117-118; view of, 27, 100. *See also* Being-itself

Gogarten, Friedrich, 19, 22, 181

Good, 112, 120, 146, 163, 194, 197, 218, 244

Gospel, 23, 61, 70, 99, 262

Grace, 29, 30, 32, 86, 95, 135-136, 138, 140, 154, 174, 176, 178, 185, 186, 208, 213, 215, 217, 218, 220, 251, 265

Greek (Greeks), 62, 87-88, 111, 120, 151, 163, 222, 223, 233, 238, 262

Ground of being. *See* Being; God

Guilt, 30, 145, 148, 149, 150, 151, 152, 154, 157, 163, 172, 234

Harnack, Adolf, 23, 87, 160, 163

Hartmann, Nicolai, 43

Hartshorne, Charles, 124

Hegel, Georg, 22, 40, 63-64, 65, 146-147, 222, 229, 265

Heidegger, Martin, 27, 46, 65, 250, 267

Herberg, Will, 65

Herrmann, Wilhelm, 19

Heteronomy, 24, 33, 76, 77, 78, 80, 89, 90, 94, 95, 212

Hick, John, 123

Hinduism, 121-122

History, 12, 13, 32, 44, 56, 59, 79, 83, 84, 93, 110, 138, 147, 149, 157-168, 172-173, 174, 180, 181-182, 203, 205, 221-253, 258, 259, 260-261, 266; church, 13, 49-50, 51, 54, 56, 60, 206, 237, 240, 255; divine, 28; human, 28, 225, 237,

246, 250-253, 262; natural, 22, 225; of religion and culture, 13, 49, 50-51, 54, 60, 87, 120, 122, 138, 196, 221, 237, 255; of revelation, 86, 89, 181; of salvation (saving, *Heilsgeschichte*), 26, 236-237, 240, 249-250, 251, 252, 253, 261, 262; philosophy of, 222, 223, 249, 253

Holy, the, 119, 120, 196, 197, 210, 239

Holy Spirit. *See* Spirit

Hopper, David, 37-38, 219

Hubris, 151-152, 153, 162

Humanism, 76, 86, 146, 175, 204

Humanity, 21, 180, 184, 186, 187, 195, 265

Hume, David, 77

Idealism, 21, 22, 23, 27, 32, 34, 63, 128, 234, 249, 264

Idolatry, 87, 94, 119, 133, 142, 234

Image of God (*imago Dei*), 96, 129, 130, 148, 151, 166, 186

Immortality, 154, 170, 245

Incarnation, 29, 31, 122, 164, 165, 166-168, 179

Infinitude, 20, 47, 63, 75, 96-97, 110-112, 123-124, 165, 245

Inspiration, 88

Islam, 204

Israel, 87, 121, 204, 236

James, William, 52

Jesus, 24, 25, 26, 30, 32, 85-86, 90, 94, 98-101, 154, 157-188, 199, 203, 208, 216, 238, 256, 257, 258, 259; as the Christ, 21, 23, 25, 38, 42, 45, 49, 53, 54, 55, 56, 59, 60, 69, 70, 71, 81, 85-87, 89-94, 98-101, 136, 145, 157-188, 189, 200, 201, 203, 204, 206, 214, 222, 231, 236, 237-238, 239, 240, 248, 252-253, 256, 258, 260;